D1748549

Towards a Knowledge-Based Society in Europe

SOFIA CONFERENCES ON SOCIAL AND ECONOMIC DEVELOPMENT IN EUROPE

Edited by
Prof. Dr. George Chobanov,
PD Dr. Jürgen Plöhn,
Prof. Dr. Horst Schellhaass

Volume 1

PETER LANG

Frankfurt am Main·Berlin·Bern·Bruxelles·New York·Oxford·Wien

George Chobanov
Jürgen Plöhn
Horst Schellhaass
(eds.)

Towards a Knowledge-Based Society in Europe

10th International Conference
on Policies of Economic and Social Development,
Sofia, October 5 to 7, 2007

PETER LANG
Internationaler Verlag der Wissenschaften

Bibliographic Information published by the Deutsche Nationalbibliothek
The Deutsche Nationalbibliothek lists this publication in the Deutsche Nationalbibliografie; detailed bibliographic data is available in the internet at <http://www.d-nb.de>.

Cover illustrations:
Printed with kindly permission of the Universities of Cologne and Sofia.

ISSN 1867-562X
ISBN 978-3-631-58859-8
© Peter Lang GmbH
Internationaler Verlag der Wissenschaften
Frankfurt am Main 2009
All rights reserved.

All parts of this publication are protected by copyright. Any utilisation outside the strict limits of the copyright law, without the permission of the publisher, is forbidden and liable to prosecution. This applies in particular to reproductions, translations, microfilming, and storage and processing in electronic retrieval systems.

Printed in Germany 1 2 3 4 5   7

www.peterlang.de

Contents

Jürgen Plöhn (D):
Introduction 7

TRANSFORMATION AND DEVELOPMENT IN EASTERN EUROPE

Georgy Ganev (BG):
Informal Institutions, Partial Enforcement, and Impersonal
Exchange: Observations from Bulgarian Streets 13

Anastasia Bankova / Todor Yalamov (BG):
Management, Knowledge, and Competitiveness of
Organizations. A Study of Bulgarian Enterprises 25

Desislava Yordanova (BG) / Maria-Antonia Tarrazon (E):
Determinants of Entrepreneurial Intentions Among Bulgarian
University Students: An Exploratory Investigation 39

Diana Boyadzhieva (BG):
Data Mining – Overview of the Technology and the Potential
for Adoption in the Bulgarian Banking Industry 59

EUROPEANIZATION AND ASPECTS OF EUROPEAN NATIONAL ECONOMIES

Anastasia Paris / Ioannis Patiniotis (GR):
The Evolution of the Gross Domestic Product
of all Sectors of Greek Economy since 1963 79

Ainhoa Herrarte / Felipe Sáez (E):
An Evaluation of Active Labour Market Policies:
the Case of Spain 103

Detelin S. Elenkov (USA):
Female Visionary-Transformational Leadership
and Innovation: The Moderating Role of
Multiple Intelligences and Ethical Leadership 129

Guergana Stanoeva (BG):
What Do Optimum Currency Area Criteria Tell Us
about the Readiness of Central and East European
Countries to Join the Eurozone? 141

Horst Schellhaass (D):
Superstars as Winners of the Common Market 153

GLOBAL AND GENERAL ASPECTS OF ECONOMIES

George Chobanov (BG):
The Dynamic Interaction of Two Markets 171
Jean-Pierre Gern (CH):
The Measurement of the Efficiency of Transaction Costs 187
Liana Badea / Nicolae Nedelco (RO):
E-Business – Perspectives and Challenges
in Global Competition 199

ATTACHMENTS

Abstracts 215
Editors and Contributers 218

INTRODUCTION
JÜRGEN PLÖHN
(MARTIN-LUTHER-UNIVERSITY HALLE-WITTENBERG, GERMANY)

1. The Faculty of Economics and Business Administration at Sofia University and its international conferences

The tenth anniversary of an institution amply demonstrates that it is solidly established. The annual international conference of the Faculty of Economics and Business Administration (FEB) at Sofia University "St. Kliment Ohridski" is such a well established institution. Though Economics was one of the first subjects taught at Sofia University, its present FEB has a "broken" history. Re-established in 1990 after the downfall of Communism in Europe, the faculty tried hard to catch up with the international discussion on its subjects. Even prior to the re-establishment, foreign economists, especially from Germany, tried to support the opening of Sofia University to Western knowledge (*Albeck* 2006: 191-192).

The efforts seemed to be worthwhile, for Sofia University, founded in 1888, is the oldest Bulgarian university. According to its own perception, it is also the first-rate school of higher education in Bulgaria.

At least with respect to the FEB, this claim has been recognized by international observers. After one decade, the faculty was very positively evaluated by a team of the World Bank (*Boris Plescovic* et al. 2000; *Jan Svejnar* 2000). In the following years, the international conferences became a major tool to attract scholars from various countries to visit Bulgaria and get into an exchange of ideas with one another as well as with Bulgarian scientists.

Up to now, the proceedings of these conferences have been published in the yearbook of the FEB. By this way of publication the international attention for the conferences remained unsatisfactory. In order to enhance to publicity of the lectures and debates, the organizing committee decided to establish a special series on the proceedings in an international publishing house. Now the editors can present the first volume of this series.

This new publication shall serve as a platform for the exchange of ideas with special reference to topics that are relevant for Southeast Europe. The establishment of the new series of books has become possible by a grant from the University of Cologne, a traditional partner of Sofia University. In 2007 the University of Cologne participated in the planning and realization of the conference.

The programme of the conference encompassed a total of 60 lectures, arranged in six sessions on the following topics:
- (A) Institutions for economic growth in Europe.
- (B) The efficiency of transaction costs.
- (C) Markets and educational systems in Europe.
- (D) The economics of a knowledge based society.
- (E) Economic and social problems of the EU enlargement.
- (F) Institutions, innovation, and productivity.

2. The contents of this volume

According to the recommendations of the experts, the editors selected twelve of those papers which had been handed in for review[1]. These contributions that are embodied in this volume.

The final outcome of the process of selecting and complementing the papers has been arranged in three chapters:
- I.   Transformation and Development in Eastern Europe.
- II. Europeanization and Aspects of European National Economies.
- III. Global and General Aspects of Economies.

In this arrangement, the differentiation between subjects of "Economy" and "Business Administration" could be dropped. Both disciplines contribute to the general theme of the present volume: knowledge based societies, their state and development in various nations, as well as problems which derive from a more or less advanced establishment of such societies.

Georgy Ganev has authored the first text of this volume. His starting point is an observation in the streets of Sofia in a longitudinal comparison. The nice piece of work provides valuable insights into the mentality of the Bulgarian business elite and their way to conduct transactions.

Additional insights are offered by *Anastassia Bankova* and *Todor Yalamov*. Their research is directed towards Bulgarian enterprises, especially towards the smaller ones. Based on interviews, the authors point to shortcomings of present-day business practices in Bulgaria.

In a different way, namely by analyzing the behaviour of Bulgarian students, *Desislava Yordanova* and *Maria-Antonia Tarrazon* address another aspect of the Bulgarian economic reality. Under the assumption

---

[1] The editors are grateful to the German and American reviewers for their opinions.

that today a prospering economy needs well-educated, dynamic entrepreneurs, they too identify deficiencies and restricting factors that hamper such a development.

Diana Boyadzhieva pleads in favour of broad analyses of data that exist in various enterprises. "Data mining" provides a tool for several strategies by which a company may try to optimize the pursue of its business. By its advices, the contents of the paper, *prima vista* addressed to businessmen rather than to scientists, reveals shortcomings of Bulgarian firms and shows potentials for their economic growth.

Taken together, these articles shed some light onto the Bulgarian economy, especially on the level of individual enterprises. Among others, potential foreign investors might be interested in these findings.

The scope of the second chapter is a broader one. In turn, the coverage of European national economies and trends of Europeanization has to concentrate on some individual aspects.

Anastasia Paris and *Ioannis Patiniotis* offer data on the long-term development of the Greek economy and its major sectors. Moreover, they dare to extrapolate the result into the future, offering a prognosis based on a time series analysis.

Ainhoa Herrarte and *Felipe Sáez* focus on another Mediterranean nation: Spain. They have pursued research on the evaluation of active labour market policies. Their assessment of the effectiveness of government programmes tries to identify relevant factors for success, because active labour market policies are expensive and success cannot be taken for granted.

The empirical research on leadership styles presented by *Detelin Elenkov*, still in a preliminary state, offers hypotheses and results of an international survey. Though this was not a representative one, the findings are relevant because of the breadth of the documented answers.

Guergana Stanoeva's contribution to this volume deals with the extension of the European Union towards Eastern Europe. Based on the seminal paper of Nobel Prize winner *Robert Mundell* on the optimal size of currency areas, *Stanoeva* estimates the achievements and chances of the newly admitted EU members to enter the European Monetary Union as well.

Horst Schellhaass presents some astonishing facts concerning the labour market of "superstars" in show business and sports. On first sight, there seems to be a contradiction to the factor price equalization theorem. Obviously, that small market has some amazing aspects.

Whereas *Schellhaass* describes and analyses his subject – *one* highly specialized market – in verbal phrases, *George Chobanov* uses mathematical expressions in order to describe the dynamic effects that can be derived from the interaction of *two* markets. We can get an impression of spillover effects that are of great economic relevance.

Jean-Pierre Gern points to the relevance of transaction costs. He demonstrates the variety of aspects that have to be considered under this category. *Gern* finds the theoretical base for his insights in the writings of the Physiocrats, but manages to construct a link from pre-classic economists to our time and its ecological problems.

Finally, *Liana Badea* and *Nicolae Nedelco* sum up what e-business is all about. Thus aspects of a globalized economy as well as aspects of future developments are marking the end of the proceeding's last chapter.

Abstracts of the articles and the list of the authors and editors serve as a round up of this volume. It cannot be a comprehensive one. But it may offer some important insights and inspiration for future research.

References

Albeck, Hermann 2006: Bulgarien auf dem Weg in die Europäische Union, in: Jürgen Plöhn (ed.): Sofioter Perspektiven auf Deutschland und Europa, Berlin: Lit-Verlag, pp. 191-208

Svejnar, Jan 2000: Economics Ph.D. Education in Central and Eastern Europe, in: Comparative Economic Studies, vol. 42 no. 2, pp. 37-50

Plescovic, Boris et al. 2000: State of the Art in Economics Education and Research in Transition Economies, in: Comparative Economic Studies, vol. 42 no. 2, pp. 65-108.

Chapter one:

TRANSFORMATION AND DEVELOPMENT IN
EASTERN EUROPE

INFORMAL INSTITUTIONS, PARTIAL ENFORCEMENT, AND IMPERSONAL EXCHANGE: OBSERVATIONS FROM BULGARIAN STREETS

GEORGY GANEV
(SOFIA UNIVERSITY "ST. KLIMENT OHRIDSKI", BULGARIA)

1. Slaveikov square, years ago

1.1. Slaveikov square, years ago: observation

Some years ago, the situation with a certain square at the center of Sofia, Bulgaria's capital, was becoming pretty interesting: There was a universal ban on parking anywhere on the square, yet it was easy to see how little by little cars started encroaching on this public space, protected by formal rules. Initially it was cars stopping for just several minutes and then quickly driving away before any reasonable enforcement could be expected. Then it was parking for longer periods. Then eventually major portions of the square turned into a *de facto* full-day parking, with the signs banning any form of parking still hanging around.

This *de facto* parking, however, had specific features. Not everyone had access to it – some cars could not use it as parking. Even if they came first in the morning and there was free space, the average car still ran an extremely high risk of being promptly tolled away with ensuing punishment. The cars which were able to utilize this limited and valuable space for parking purposes were not just any cars. Formally, they had various signs on them creating the impression of a formal permission to park: disability signs, special permits issued by the municipality for special purposes, or some other interesting papers hanging on the dashboard. But the most important specific feature of the cars which *de facto* used this *de facto* parking was their average price: nothing short of the latest BMW, or at least the more luxurious models of VW could be seen.

1.2. Slaveikov square, years ago: analysis

Quite obviously what was happening was a breach in the enforcement of legitimate impersonal formal rules. This observation from the streets of Sofia, as well as many other observations, does not simply show that rules are not well enforced. It shows something deeper. Imperfect enforcement in general would mean that the set of cars which manage to breach the rules would be an arbitrary set, while the observation clearly shows that this is not the case – for some cars the official rule is perfectly enforced, and it is non-existent for other cars. The result seems to be intentional.

In fact what is observed may be termed "partial" rather than "imperfect" enforcement. "Partial" here means both that it is not complete, and that it is the opposite of "impartial". It takes sides. It is an enforcement mechanism which almost officially announces that the rules do not apply for everyone equally. This very much looks like embezzling the public good of universal and impartial enforcement for private gain and can quickly fall under the title of corruption. Such a conclusion would naturally lead towards devising mechanisms for fighting the concrete corrupt practice.

While fighting corruption would be undeniably useful, from an analytical point of view, corruption as an explanation of the observation of the events on Slaveikov square does only one thing: lead to a new question. Why is corruption, rather some other mechanism of allocating scarce resources, used by the Bulgarian society in this case? From this perspective there emerges a layer of interpretation of this particular observation deeper than the usual anathema on corruption.

1.3. Slaveikov square and the choice of Bulgarian elites

This layer is revealed when one goes over the efforts necessary on the part of the BMWs and the luxurious VWs to obtain the partial enforcement. Corruption is not a free good. The owners of the expensive cars have to use complex social networking, maintain and use their social status and connections, trade favors, make explicit or implicit promises, to get the respective permits sanctioning the partial enforcement. Partial enforcement does not eliminate the need to get an answer to the question which car gets the scarce parking place, it just changes the mechanism for addressing the issue from relying on formal impartial rules towards relying on the informal rules embodied in specific social networks and the ways they work. Informal rules and social networks are costly.

So, if obtaining partial enforcement is costly, why not simply lobby to set up an official legitimate parking on a portion of the square or nearby, and then let the market determine the respective price of a parking place and pay it? After all, the market price mechanism is a pretty good tool for allocating scarce goods among people willing to pay. Given that the market is an incentive-compatible private-information revealing mechanism, and also the fact that it usually ensures that the scarce resource goes to the economic agents able and willing to pay the most for it, it can safely be assumed that under a market arrangement not only the parking spaces will be used by the same cars, but this will come cheaper to both, their owners and society as a whole. So why did Bulgarian elites of the early 1990s not choose the cheaper option?

Here, one answer is, naturally, the coordination and collective action problem in getting the rules changed. Formulating, promoting and obtaining a change in the formal institutional framework is both costly, and a one-time event. On both of these counts it is very difficult for a social group to organize itself and achieve the level of cooperation and commitment to be successful. This is a perfectly good hypothesis explaining the choice of the Bulgarian elites to not go to market in this case.

However, some recent studies of the Bulgarian economic history (Avramov 2001 and 2007), entrepreneurial culture (Chavdarova 2001b, Ganev 2004), and general public attitudes (Chavdarova 2001a, Ganev/ Koford 2003, Ganev 2005, Guenvo 2004) point towards another possible answer which can be added to the more traditional ones. This additional answer is that it is possible that Bulgarians, or at least some of them, intentionally seek partial enforcement and deliberately want to rely on informal rules, because in this manner they get the opportunity to personalize the exchange. In this frame, personalization is a deliberately sought outcome, and it is a strategic response to the uncertainties characterizing the present day Bulgarian environment.

2. Impersonal vs. personal exchange

It has been a longstanding staple of the new economic history that the present day economic development was made possible by the success of some human societies to transform the way in which societies organize economic interaction between agents. This is told as a tale of two transitions. One is the microeconomic transition from personal to impersonal exchange between individual economic agents (North 1981 and 1994). The other is the macroeconomic transition from societies based on limited access to economic opportunities towards societies based on open access (North/ Wallis/Weingast 2006).

In both tales the model, in large strokes, is based on Adam Smith's vision of wealth creation, namely that the extent of the market is correlated to specialization, productivity and wealth. The extent of the market is a function of the space of possible exchanges, where this space is defined by a number of dimensions: the space of economic agents, the space of possible transactions between them, the goods space, geographic space, time. Personalized exchange and limited access severely limit some of these dimensions – mainly the first two of them, and lead to a very limited space of possible exchanges, with the respective depressing effect on specialization, productivity and wealth. On the other hand, when issues of opportunistic behavior have been resolved to some acceptable extent, impersonal exchange and open access enormously expand the space of possible exchanges and increase the extent of the market, with all the beneficial results and incentives for improvement, higher productivity and growth.

Impersonal exchange, which is so necessary for present day economic development, relies on formal rules and their enforcement – either self-enforcement (Greif 2006, esp. chapters 3 and 4) or enforcement by a third impartial party (North 1981). The role of the nation state as such a third impartial enforcer of formal rule, and later as a major author of such rules as well, is a crucial part of the story of modern development.

However, as we know from numerous stories and experiences[1], economic development need not be the goal of any social, let alone personal decision-making process:

> "Institutions are not necessarily or even usually created to be socially efficient; rather they, or at least the formal rules, are created to serve the interests of those with the bargaining power to create new rules." (D. C. North 1994: 360).

Impersonal exchange and formal rules obtain only when a crucial set of social actors perceive the benefits for themselves from such an arrangement and become willing to pay the costs of putting the respective social mechanisms in place, including the costs of overcoming opposition. Many human societies may have never experienced such times.

Bulgaria is still one of them. Several recent studies (Avramov 2001 and 2007, Ganev 2003 and 2005) indicate that "modernization" attempts have been consistently unsuccessful over the last century and a half, that an impersonal exchange revolution is still pending in Bulgaria and is impeded by major aspects of culture, or mental models, which can be found in the attitudes of both, the general public and the entrepreneurs in particular.

This point will be illustrated by a summary of the findings of a project aiming at the study of encounters of Western with Eastern European entrepreneurial culture.[2] The observations are based on a series of in-depth semi-structured interviews with Bulgarian and Western entrepreneurs who have had extensive interactions with the "other" culture and way of doing things.

3. Dimensions of entrepreneurial cultural differences

The analysis of the in-depth interviews points towards several significant elements of the general way in which Bulgarian, as opposed to Western, entrepreneurs approach the world (Ganev 2004: 133-141). One such ele-

---

[1] North 1981 and 1990. For a particularly bright example see Eggertsson 1996.

[2] The studies resulting from the project are collected in Kabakchieva/Avramov (eds.) 2004. Specifically, the analysis here is based on the study of Ganev 2004.

ment of their culture is that they have a somewhat higher propensity to think that economic interaction is an inherently zero-sum exercise. It is very important to note, however, that according to the interviews this difference is actually diminishing with time and purely opportunistic behavior is not considered as competitive or acceptable. But there are several other dimensions of cultural differences between Bulgarian and Western entrepreneurs which are significant and telling.

3.1. Dimensions of entrepreneurial cultural differences: the nature of economic relations

A very fundamental difference between Western and Bulgarian entrepreneurs lies along a fundamental dimension – the very nature of economic interaction, and more specifically along the line personal vs. impersonal exchange. The language, the abstract attitudes, and the experience of the Western entrepreneurs point towards a conclusion that the Western way of doing business and making decisions is impersonal, and that the Bulgarian way is highly personalized. Bulgarian entrepreneurs consciously seek strongly personal, individualized relations. Interestingly, this is probably most clear in the statements of a Western entrepreneur, who mentions it as a major advantage of the Bulgarian way of doing things, attributing to the high level of personalization the qualities of "human warmth", while describing the Western attitudes as alienated and inhuman despite their efficiency.

Inasmuch as the Bulgarian economic life has never been modernized, it is to be expected that modes of behavior based on personalized exchange are prevalent. This is in fact the finding of the observation of the interviews. The Bulgarian entrepreneurs and managers tend to rely not on abstract cooperation strategies with agents outside the firm and on impersonal, efficiency-centered relationships within the firm, but on investing in personal loyalties and in relationships based not only on efficiency of performance, but on mutual favors, care, and emotions.

This dichotomy can be observed in two other characteristic observations surfacing in the interviews. The first is the different attitude towards risk. While the Western respondents try to avoid risk by learning its important aspects and then managing it, the Bulgarian respondents seem devoted to eliminating risks altogether, and willing to sacrifice efforts and efficiency to achieve this goal. Trying to eliminate risks, when applied to hazards inherent in the behavior of partners or employees, translates into investment in highly personalized loyalties, which are fostered through non-market exchanges such as favors, gestures of recognitions, explicit signs of belonging and of caring. Of course, this is done at the cost of foregoing the gains from impersonal efficiency.

The second characteristic of the personal-impersonal dichotomy concerns the internal ordering of interaction within the firms. It does not concern a difference between entrepreneurs so much as a difference in the corporate environments in the West and in Bulgaria. Different foreign respondents notice that their Bulgarian employees or managers are passive, and avoid taking initiative and making decisions. They may see a problem quite clearly, and may even have ideas about solving it, but prefer to wait for higher management or the owner to notice it and to devise a solution. It is realistic to assume that the situation is similar in most firms in Bulgaria, but that to Bulgarians this situation is not unusual. The fact remains that Bulgarian employees can be viewed as passive, with significant power distance and external locus of control, despite some of the Bulgarian managers noting a change in these attitudes over the recent years. Entrepreneurs have to take this feature of the business environment as given when devising their approaches to the internal organization of relationships within the enterprise.

3.2. Dimensions of entrepreneurial cultural differences: strategic horizons

Bulgarian and Western entrepreneurs have different strategic horizons. The first of these horizons is the time frame of the entrepreneurial strategy. Bulgarian respondents are inclined to think that, given the present day situation in Bulgaria, incorporating longer time horizons in the strategy and striving to incorporate longer term expectations and plans into present day decision-making is an unwarranted luxury. For Western entrepreneurs working in Bulgaria, incorporating such longer term elements, while recognized as a bit more expensive in Bulgaria than elsewhere, is still an unquestioned *sine qua non*.

Bulgarian entrepreneurs, due to their obsession with the present day and lack of a longer time horizon, tend to treat their business as a series of one-period optimization problems in which their task is to get the most out of the current situation, regardless of what this will mean for the conditions during the next period. Such a strategy is clearly subject to time inconsistency and can easily lead to dynamic sub-optimality, but this is still the case. Western entrepreneurs working in Bulgaria are playing an entirely different game in which the focus is on optimizing over a relatively long period of time, even if this means foregoing some short-run possible gains.

A second strategic horizon which differentiates the two groups of entrepreneurs is the choice not so much whom, but how to trust. Foreign entrepreneurs view trust as an investment in the long term capacity of the firm to achieve results. A consequence of this attitude is the fact that they choose very carefully whom to trust, but after they have chosen a partner, they are willing to reveal the whole information and to rely on the partner's cooperation and judgment. On the contrary, Bulgarians seem to trust in a more practical, and operational manner, as comes through from some of the comments by interviewees about their Bulgarian partners. The trust is for the specific interaction, for the concrete deal between the partners, and is not completely extended for the indefinite future. Partners are not given the full information, but only the information the entrepreneur deems necessary for the partner to perform his part of the deal, and control over the important resource of information and decision making is retained to the fullest possible extent till the last possible moment. Regardless of the recognition of the importance of trust, Bulgarian entrepreneurs seem unwilling to delegate responsibilities to partners.

A third difference in the strategic horizons of Western and Bulgarian entrepreneurs, concerns the ultimate objective of their business. For the westerners, this objective is undoubtedly the needs of the final client: the consumer of the product in whose creation they participate. They exhibit an almost merciless focus on this objective, and organize all the resources at their disposal to serve it. In contrast, Bulgarian entrepreneurs seem to hold other things in regard as well. They are concerned with the production process for itself, not only as a tool for serving the final consumer, and seem to think that a good production process and efficient practices will take care of themselves. They also pay specific attention to the personal lives of their employees, turning them into important stakeholders whose welfare is a valid objective of the firm besides the service to the needs of the final consumer (more on this below). In this strategic dimension, it seems that Western entrepreneurs are very strongly driven by a single objective, while their Bulgarian counterparts take into consideration various potential objectives of the existence of their firms and of their entrepreneurial decisions.

3.3. Dimensions of entrepreneurial cultural differences: attitude towards rules

Finally, a specific difference between Bulgarian and foreign entrepreneurs is the attitude towards rules, and laws in particular. For the average Westerner, not doing everything possible to comply with rules and laws is out of the question. As a matter of principle, they never cross the boundary of non-compliance, even when they are actively searching for the least costly way to comply.

This is not so for the average Bulgarian entrepreneur, for whom rules in general, and especially laws, often lack legitimacy and cutting corners is fair game. This difference emerges as a matter of principle, not just as a matter of personal moral discipline. It is a difference in the perceptions about the rule making mechanisms in the particular society. Coming from societies with traditions in markets and democracy, Westerners take the *a priori* view that rules are legitimate, can be changed by using the legitimate channels, and circumventing them is ultimately more costly than compliance. Coming from a long tradition of illegitimate government, especially in the sphere of business regulation, Bulgarian entrepreneurs feel that laws are devised to hurt their interests, and often feel justified in trying to avoid the grasp of illegitimate power. In the present situation in Bulgaria, both perceptions can find enough grounds to persist.

Another interesting aspect of the attitudes towards rules, is the different attitudes towards responsibility, which is also related to the differences in behavior towards risk. Westerners seem more concerned about having responsibilities clearly defined and personally attributed in the beginning, so that, if something undesirable happens, it is clear who is responsible and how. Once this is clear, they do not seem very keen about punishment. On the contrary, Bulgarians seem to care about identifying and punishing severely guilt only after the undesirable developments take place. "Punishing the guilty" vs. "identifying the responsible" seem to be very different approaches towards enforcing rules.

4. Two cultures and the environment

Clearly, two very different mental models about the world emerge. One of them is characterized by personal relationships, a strong desire to avoid risk altogether, short, but multi-directional strategic horizons. This could just be called "backwardness". But it could also constitute a rational response to the characteristics of the business environment, heritage from the past included.

This is a crucial observation. There is no present day empirical basis to conclude that one of the two entrepreneurial cultures defined by the study is wrong in the sense that it will exhibit poor survival traits given the environment. Both entrepreneurial modes can actually be more or less rational, i.e. they may be viewed as best responses to certain facets of the specific environment, to certain historical experiences (including those accumulated and inherited in the form of traditions and culture), to certain expectations based on the agents' models about the world and the economy.

If the presently existing modes of behavior of Bulgarian entrepreneurs are rational, this means that they are relatively competitive in comparison with the Western modes because they respond to objectively existing characteristics of the environment, to which the Westerners have not yet learned to respond. The entrepreneurial modes exhibited by Bulgarian respondents allow a focus on some of the elements of the Bulgarian environment, which may render these modes rational.

The Bulgarian economic development over the recent decades and even centuries can be characterized with unfinished modernization, with small and weak markets, with a complete lack of private initiative traditions and the ensuing legitimization of private entrepreneurial success, and with major and prolonged reversals, catastrophes and government oppression (Avramov 2007: throughout).

Bulgarian entrepreneurs have never had the opportunity to experience authentic market interaction in their own country and society. This means two things: First, there are no entrepreneurial traditions, no valuable, experience-based knowledge on how to do business in Bulgaria, and a corresponding lack of reasonable forecasts and expectations about the consequences of one or another decision or mode of behavior. Second, the Bulgarian environment can be characterized with fundamental uncertainty, or ambiguity, under which neither the domains, nor the probability distributions of possible future outcomes of present actions are known, and also with unfinished modernization under which personalized interaction and exchange remains dominant and universally adopted.

Personalized interaction, the very high level of risk aversion, the relatively short-term yet more dispersed strategic horizons may be a rational response to ambiguity. As already mentioned, personalized exchange, networks and relationships are an important form of flexible valuable asset. When an entrepreneur cannot see clearly ahead, when he does not know exactly what to expect, and even what is possible at all, and when many other players adopt similar modes of behavior, the long-term efficiency costs of locking himself in highly personalized links may be objectively outweighed by the accompanying tangible and relevant benefits of being able to flexibly and reliably respond when unforeseen and unforeseeable circumstances arise.

5. Conclusion

The story of a public square in Sofia which was gradually turned into a parking lot was used to demonstrate several potential deep insights about entrepreneurial modes in Bulgaria. First, the choice of the entrepreneurial elites was to achieve this result through partial enforcement rather than through market exchange. Second, this choice seems to be cultural, i.e. it seems to be the result of a specific entrepreneurial culture relying on a high level of personalization, informality, and loose compliance to rules.

This personalization of exchange is shown to be possibly deliberately sought as a rational equilibrium strategy on the part of Bulgarian entrepreneurs given the major features of the environment in Bulgaria and the existing general entrepreneurial culture leading to respective expectations.

Of course, the story with the parking on the square in Sofia is not the only story. The personalization of some exchanges is a process going on in parallel to the process of impersonalization, which is visible in other areas of the economy. It is very much related to big internationals, and due to many reasons such as the continuous and deepening integration of Bulgaria and Bulgarian firms into an economic space of highly developed impersonal exchange.

So the environment is changing, and so is the effectiveness of this type of entrepreneurial culture. However, this is a slow change. Until the relevant aspects of the business environment change "enough", one of the very rational responses to it can consist of deliberate personalization of relations, seeking of personal loyalties with the goal of eliminating risks in a situation of high uncertainty, short-term, diversified strategic horizons, maintenance of informal networks, and conscious preference for personal informal mechanisms rather than impersonal markets.

References

Avramov, R. 2001: Аврамов, Р., Стопанският XX век на България, Център за либерални стратегии, София (Avramov, R., The economic 20th century of Bulgaria, Centre for liberal strategies, Sofia)

Avramov, R. 2007: Аврамов, Р., Комуналният капитализъм. Из българското стопанско минало, Център за либерални стратегии, София (Avramov, R., Communal capitalism. Reflections on the Bulgarian economic past, Centre for liberal strategies, Sofia)

Chavdarova, T. 2001a: "Market Developments in Bulgaria: The Problem of Trust." In: Lang, R. (Hg.) Wirtschaftsethik in Mittel- und Osteuropa. Business Ethnics in Central and Eastern Europe, München und Merig: Reiner Hampp Verlag, pp. 177-196.

Chavdarova, T. 2001b: Чавдарова, Т., Неформалната икономика, ЛИК, София (Chavdarova, T., The informal economy, LIK, Sofia).

Eggertsson, T. 1996: No Experiments, Monumental Disasters. Why it Took a Thousand Years to Develop a Specialized Fishing Industry Iceland, in: Journal of Economic Behavior and Organization, vol. 30, No. 1, pp. 1-24

Ganev, G. 2004: Entrepreneurial attitudes and responses to EU accession in Bulgaria: two possible scenarios, in: Kabakchieva, P. and R. Avramov (eds.): "East"-"West" cultural encounters. Entrepreneurship, Governance, Economic Knowledge, Iztok Zapad, Sofia, pp. 131-150

Ganev, G. 2005: Where Has Marxism Gone? Gauging the Impact of Alternative Ideas in Transition Bulgaria, in: East European Politics and Societies, Vol. 19, No. 3, pp. 443-462

Ganev, G./K. Koford 2003: Society's attitudes toward the market economy in Bulgaria: personal values, social norms, institutions and implications for the economy, in: Le development durable dans les economies en transition: restaurer les flux economiques. Rapports de la conference international organisé par la Faculté d'Economie et de Gestion de l'Universite de Sofia «St Kliment Ohridski», Vol. II, Sofia 2003, pp. 71-78

Greif, A. 2006: Institutions and the Path to the Modern Economy. Lessons from Medieval Trade, Cambridge University Press

Guenov, J. 2004: Генов, Ю., „Защо толкова малко успяваме?", „Класика и стил", София (Guenov, J., "Why do we succeed so little?", "Classics and style" Publishing House, Sofia).

Kabakchieva, P. and R. Avramov (eds.) 2004: "East"-"West" cultural encounters. Entrepreneurship, Governance, Economic Knowledge", Iztok Zapad, Sofia,

North, D. C. 1981: Structure and Change in Economic History, Norton

North, D. C. 1990: Institutions, Institutional Change and Economic Performance, Cambridge University Press

North, D. C. 1994. "Economic Performance through Time", American Economic Review, American Economic Association, vol. 84 no. 3 (June), pp. 359-68

North, D. C./J. Wallis/B. Weingast 2006: A conceptual framework for interpreting recorded economic history, NBER Working Paper 12795

MANAGEMENT, KNOWLEDGE, AND COMPETITIVENESS OF ORGANIZATIONS. A STUDY OF BULGARIAN ENTERPRISES

ANASTASIA BANKOVA / TODOR YALAMOV
(SOFIA UNIVERSITY "ST. KLIMENT OHRIDSKI", BULGARIA)

1. Introduction

In all strategic documents of the EU and Bulgaria one can find the key words "competitiveness", "knowledge society", and "knowledge based economy". Although at least a nominal policy priority, on a firm level it is unclear how enterprises can integrate themselves in such a society, what kind of instruments they could use, what problems they have, etc. The paper tries to outline and discuss these issues in the context of the firms' transition to learning organizations.

A key question to explore is: What is making *knowledge* such an important resource nowadays? Several different trends, still evolving, are shaping the background:

- an intensive process of knowledge development, sharing, and utilizing;
- the infrastructure for facilitating knowledge creation, dissemination, preservation, and use;
- a globalized reallocation of knowledge, skills, and competences with different (some of them unpredictable) consequences for society. This is a process of intensive learning and knowledge dissemination, but also of forgetting and losing knowledge. – It seems that the latter is still under-researched (Boton et al. 2007: 47-55).
- The environmental agenda of any society requires knowledge and learning capabilities to cope with complexity (Heywood et al. 2007: 85-95).
- According to the phase of competitiveness: development of the country, region, branch, and organizations. They all need different – i.e.: appropriate – kinds of competences (Porter 1990) [1].
- Polarization of competences. The labour markets are still misbalanced: There are people with very high qualifications without a proper development of their careers and many people without any competence. In countries in transition, there are even people *without any* competence with very good careers, because their access to finances was guaranteed by belonging to certain political groups or

---

[1] Many organizations cannot comprehend this problem at all. A lot of problems exist before a cooperation between enterprises can be achieved, if they are in different phases of their development of competitiveness.

networks, not based on competence. Overcoming this trend is an important step for a society wth respect to its capability to work with knowledge.
- Fast dissemination of knowledge causes changes in the basis of competitiveness in the branches. The enterprises have to work an the creation of a new basis of competitiveness (Porter 1990).
- Organizations need knowledge not only about current markets, products and technologies (what usually is offered in management courses), but they also need knowledge and skills for the creation of the future: the creation of future markets and clients, which do not exist yet (Osterloh, 1999).
- The creation of knowledge is risky and expensive. Especially small organizations need partnerships, participation in networks, even with competitors. They need a specific managerial knowledge as well: how to create an effective network, how to cope with complexity, etc.

Observations in literature outline several reasons why knowledge is considered a specific resource and its use includes many contradicting aspects (Nonaka, 1995; Osterloh, 1999, North 2001):

- *Explicit knowledge* can be *bought*, it "goes" to the buyer without leaving the seller.
- *Implicit knowledge* is *personal*. – That is the reason why it could be bought only by "buying" the people and groups, the knowledge owners. The have to be given incentives to join the own organization.
- In both cases the buyer cannot implement the acquired knowledge immediately, without additional efforts. Desired results are not guarantied, for results of acquired knowledge are always in some way unique.
- Knowledge can be stolen: by observation and imitation; by attracting people and groups with knowledge; by spying.
- Once created somewhere, knowledge can be rediscovered or reinvented. This stimulates the searching process.

Many studies on the phases of competitiveness and innovativeness of organizations are based on fragmental and formal indicators. Sometimes they are inappropriate to give a real picture. For instance, the number of personal computers, the availability of internet connections, and the web-site of an enterprise are considered to be important factors for a firm in order to become a learning organization. However, it is not the mere *existence* of the tools for learning (a necessary condition), but the *quality of their use* that matters and has to be assessed. Furthermore, it is important to study whether enterprises are ready to cope with the threats coming from the transition to a knowledge economy, whether they are prepared for the use of all new opportunities and whether they actually do use them.

2. Methodological background - the approach, used in the study

Research on small and medium sized enterprises is very difficult – especially in some small countries in transition. There is a lack of reliable statistics. If you try to understand the state of the art, you have to consider some constructivistic approaches, because even a common language does not exist, or exists only formally. For example, many managers have no managerial education, and those who have, are influenced by different national schools, or they are coming themselves from various European countries, from USA or elsewhere. The basic economic and managerial terms used by the respective schools are different. That is why a formal, closed questionnaire is no appropriate tool in this case. Instead, it is necessary to have a clear concept, interviewers, who know it, and a conversation with the interviewed person to reach a mutual understanding. Reliable information can be obtained if the interviewer gets the impression that his or her counterpart is telling the truth and that he or she is legally entitled to speak about the topic (Kieser 2002). We can give some figures, but they only serve to give a very broad orientation. We have to discover some trends and problems in these trends. For this reason we organized the investigation in a certain way, described below. The approach is similar to an anthropological one.

The starting point for our analysis is the creation of a knowledge map about the organizations and their learning experience.

The documentation of the study consists of four parts. The first one is a passport of the interviewed person. The second is a passport of the organization; some additional facts are gathered and described. The third part includes some opinions (judgements) of the interviewed person about the organization based on closed questions. For instance, one such question is "Do you think the organization has problems with…?", and a checklist of domains are presented to the interviewee. The fourth part consists of open questions about the situation in the organization, its participation in networks und their effectiveness, about the strategic orientation of the organization, about its organizational learning and knowledge management. After completion of the interview and questionnaire, the interviewers have to summarize and analyse the outcomes, especially in a specific area.

The interviewers are master's students in different management programs. The students, being insiders, or working with an insider of the organization, who trusts them and wants to help them by the fulfilment of their project, we suppose, can provide more objective information. They are specialists in the field (they have already a bachelor degree and most of them have practical experiences of at least one year), they share a common conceptual framework about the studied contents and some of them are interested in a good performance of the study.

Since 2001 about 200 students per year have worked on such a project. Micro-enterprises have been excluded from the investigations. Due to various non-performances, about 30% of the interviews are not reliable documented. About 20% of the interviewers consider non-profit or public organizations which are irrelevant here. About 20% of the analyses have some problems: They are fragmental or the documented answers are close to the contents of the student's textbooks. Only about 30 % of the works can be used for further conclusions. About 5% consider rarely investigated branches and cannot be used for comparative purposes. So the analyses, which can be used, are usually dealing with one of the following branches: retail trade, marketing& advertising, ICT, logistics, tourism, food industries, the building and construction branch, and banks. The number of the remaining, reliably analyzed cases of small and medium sized enterprises and their respective branches are given in figure 1.

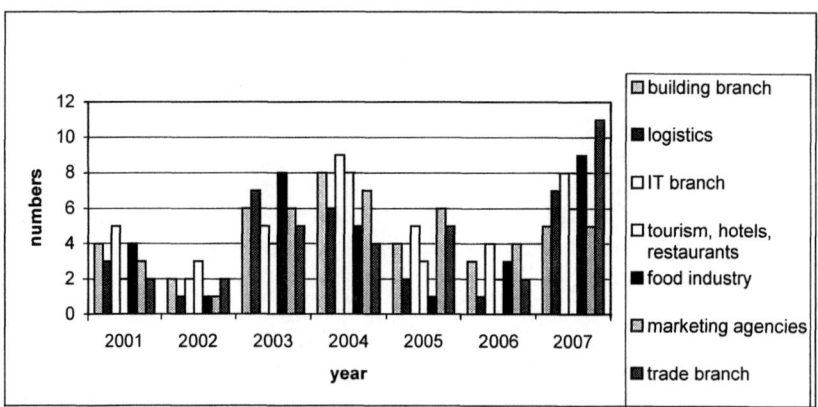

Figure 1: Number of investigated enterprises

As mentioned above, the final task of the interviewers is about choosing a topic from the knowledge map, determining the borders of interest (the closed connected topics and aspects, which the interviewers have to consider) using again the map and analysing the state of the arts in this area. So we have material for a case study and a content analysis. After presenting and defending the conclusions of their works, the student group has to summarize the results.

The *knowledge map* is based on the idea, that, when we try to define something, we can do it from different points of view:
(1) from the point of view of its sense of existence or purpose;
(2) from the point of view of its essence or substance – the very basic characteristic without which it is no more the given object; and
(3) from the point of view of the recognizable content – the arrangements, patterns, that we accept (see) and through which we recognize it as the investigated object and attribute the meaning to something (which we call with the given name) (Bankova, 2004, 38, Nikolov 1981, 15-25).

So we build a network of terms, which is helping us to define the important borders of the investigation

When we speak about *learning*, we usually consider the bahavioristic, cognitive and social approach (Luthans, 1995, 198-201). Many authors point out their connections. In some degree, these approaches correspond indeed to the definitions mentioned above. In our approach, we set as a prerequisite for clarifying the whole picture and for better understanding the acceptance of a given investigated object from different points of view. This is very important to the creation of the knowledge map. In order to understand the object of our considerations, we have to look at it from all mentioned points of view and to search for the connections between the different aspects.

For instance, when we investigate the goal-setting, we can include the problem "goals in the different strata" (Mesarovich, 1971) and harmonization and balance between them. The system of goals is considered on the level of the concepts (intuitive thinking and perceptions: vision, mission, purpose...); on the level of systems (system thinking – intuitive and rational: the strategies), and finally on the executive level – rational thinking and the percept practice (plans, budgets). Then the appropriate methods of their creation, the loops in which they appear, the subjects behind them, their roles and power should be considered. So we include the most important issues in the research design.

We have presented this approach in detail, because even the few existing studies in the country rest on pure anonymous and formal questionnaires. Thus their results depend on a proper understanding of the questions, which in turn depends on who is the interviewee. To our best knowledge no single analysis on innovation accounted for differences in perceptions and knowledge conditional on the type of the interviewee. Very often the misunderstanding is obviously, especially by questionnaires about the managerial methods used in the enterprise.

At last we mirror/benchmark, when possible, the conclusions by other studies and publications in Bulgaria and other documented experiences.

3. Problems of the Bulgarian enterprises (organizations) in the field "management – knowledge – competitiveness"

Our study has identified several problematic areas in the relation between public policy and management, knowledge, and competitiveness. Based on the findings and on the EU best practices, we can conclude that there is a *systemic disfunctionality and disequilibrium in the knowledge economy system* in Bulgaria on all levels – public policy, education system and private business.

The lack of focused strategies

In spite of existing numerous national strategies and programs in the field of competitiveness and knowledge economy, and of some infrastructure (research, intermediaries, etc.) – they are not effective enough, especially in their connection with business practice. The ineffectiveness of the strategies as policy instruments is rooted in the uncoordinated existence of strategies concerning substantively related issues, significant delays in the implementation of program budgeting at different ministries and short horizons of planning. There are about 80 public policy strategies[2], among them being the National Innovation Strategy, National Research Strategy, National Continuous Education Strategy, Information Society Development Strategy, e-Government strategy, ICT Competitiveness strategy and others, usually with different time-lines, centered around a specific ministry or an industry group with little if any coordination at program and implementation level. As a rule of thumb, at the time of adoption of a strategy there is no dedicated funding for its implementation. Subsequently, action plans for the strategies, required to be financially backed, usually include projects and activities with already secured funding from the state budget or EU projects. Effectiveness means (1) optimization of the utilization of resources and conditions (2) focusing on strengths, prioritized and sequenced actions, which is systematically missing in the whole process of strategy development and implementation.

---

[2] President Parvanov's speech at the launch of III annual report to the President "Strategy for accelerated development", June 15, 2007.

The lack of real recognition of the stage of competitiveness of Bulgarian business and enterprises and the lack of imagination what kind of knowledge it requires and how to get it

About 90% of the interrogated enterprises answer that the competitiveness has to do with cheap products and services with high quality (no other imagination about strategy and realization way exists), they have (resp. recognize) no problems with the quality and price, the interviewed persons think problems are (resp. come from) usually outside the enterprise. At the same time, SMEs have difficulties to identify their prime competitors or have limited knowledge about them (Stefanov and Petrov, 2008).

The need of networks (of working even with competitors) and the lack of competence for networking, i. e. how to establish successful networks, how to manage them

The existing forms of networks are manifestations of other interests, different from creation of learning opportunities, knowledge dissemination and use. Very seldom they could be described as good practice.

About 30% of the small enterprises mention that they use innovations. About 70% of them do it by themselves, without partners, only 10% have more than one partner. About 70-80% are financing these activities with money of the family or friends. No risk capital is used. The attitude to credits is changing according to the conditions of receiving: needed guarantees, rates, duration. These conditions are changing, but they are still not enough attractive for small enterprises. For that reason less than 50% are using credits.

Managerial innovations are rare. Decisive factors for innovativeness are (a) market orientation (towards the international or the European market), (b) cooperation agreements between the company and other partners, and (c) the planning horizon of the enterprises (Stefanov and Petrov, 2008).

The implemented forms of networks have problems with their performance and management. The majority of enterprises does not even recognize the networks in which they obviously participate. They have no imagination, how they could win from networks, what they have to do to create or look for effective networks.

Other investigations show the same picture:
In a study on producing enterprises (2006, more than 1400 enterprises)
30,12% of the micro-enterprises;
47,85% of the small enterprises;
58,02% of the medium sized enterprises
are involved in innovations – in average 33,29%.

Only 17,27% are working with a partner.
94,54% use their own financing for innovation,
37,55% receive money from relatives,
23,98% from friends,
48,34% use a bank credit (Stefanov and Petrov, 2008).

Feeling a lack of criteria for professionalism

People from many branches blame the newcomer (investor), that they are not professionals in the field and do not look for professional managers (for example in tourism, forestry and other branches). The new owners blame the universities for their lack of qualification, but nobody undertakes really systematic improving steps. Everyone is blaming the others, excluding himself from the group of not appropriate qualified people in the given field.

A more detailed study on a group of small enterprises, which we carried out in 2004[3], shows the following picture:

8% have changed the business and
32% did not have any previous experience in the branch.
62% of the entrepreneurs acquired the knowledge about their work from relatives and friends;
school was a source of knowledge for 33% of them.
Only 7% use sophisticated methods for personal selection, while the vast majority – 80% – rely on the opinion of friends and relatives.
Only 29% of the staff have an appropriate qualification.
About 50% have had some experience in the branch.
73% of the entrepreneurs think that experience is the best way of qualification for the personnel;
24% think qualification is an obligation of the staff itself.
Only 12% pay some part of the expenses for qualification of the staff.
3% try to make the knowledge of the staff explicit, to preserve the knowledge of the leaving personnel.
54% do not visit special events (exhibitions).
28% cannot use Internet.
For 63% the basic source of knowledge about markets and competitors are personal observations (Beshkova, 2004).

The fact that there is a systemic discrepancy between people's qualifications and their employment could be explained through several perspectives: a huge structural transformation of the economy, including long structural unemployment in 1990s (especially in machine building, electronics, etc.), vast brain-drain, tight social-networks of former people

---

[3] Distribution of respondents: 32% trade; 22% production; 6% services; 3% education; 14% health care; 11% transport; 6% restaurants, hotels; 6% others; from 100 enterprises.

with power which have acquired significant ownership over financial and industry sectors.

Expectations of help by foreign business in Bulgaria

Multinational companies help to improve the situation by the creation of the new managerial culture in Bulgaria. But even some of them have no interest in working on it. The quality and the interests of many others, especially middle sized and small foreign businesses in Bulgaria have little to do with the creation of a knowledge society. They work opportunistically and leave the country when their expectations (sometimes without argumentation) cannot be realized. Another reason is the quality of the foreign personal of these companies: The managers coming to Bulgaria are not the best or at least well qualified persons themselves. In-depth interviews with businessmen from some neighbouring countries suggested that even there was a trend in first half of the 1990s that people who had lost credibility in their home countries, came to Bulgaria as foreign investors, accessing the Bulgarian credit market, etc. Some studies also have shown that foreign investors or foreign trade partners of a country might limit the capacity of the recipient country to improve governance, transparency and accountability and in particular import corruption. After the accession to the EU, some positive developments are emerging, however the process of improving governance will take quite a long time.

Lack of connection between business and universities and scientific organizations

Business
- does not need additional knowledge. It is very optimistic about its future and cannot see its problems. Partially the reason why firms do not need knowledge and sophisticated technologies is that Bulgaria is specialized currently in low-tech, low-cost industries and lower sectors of high-tech. However, the competitive pressure for low-cost production coming from Asia would definitely lead to an increased demand for knowledge and technologies in the near future;
- is sometimes even cynic to the qualification of its personnel, exercises some cynic practices (tries to bind/enslave people with unacceptable training contracts);
- prefers to invest in qualification of family members of the owner's family (especially in small business);
- does not know how to discover, to use, and to preserve the knowledge of the personnel, of internees and part-time working students;
- is not ready or able to pay for knowledge.

- Information and communication technologies, although available in almost every enterprise[4], is quite often under-utilized or not effectively used. Estimates suggest that about 3-4% more computers are needed to meet all needs of firms. About 70% of computers in business are connected to the internet, however only a fourth of enterprises use e-business applications. About a third of the enterprises have web-pages, but just a marginal share provides opportunities for online ordering and payment (Yalamov 2006: 43-54; Stefanov and Petrov 2008).

Only 10-12% of the Bulgarian scientific staff is employed in enterprises. They pay less than 20% of the expenses for research and development in the country. Technologies and equipment in the enterprises are old – more than 5-10 years. Moreover, very often even newly bought equipment is old too (Stefanov and Petrov, 2007, 339-359). There were also a few privatization deals primarily motivated for acquisition of newly bought technology and replace the buyer's old technology in its home country.

The universities

The Bulgarian universities have many problems with their reforms. They need a discussion about the role and the specialization of their programs and their core business: Is it to create proactive people, competent to cope with all kinds of problems and shape the future? Or should they create reactive people, competent to solve a few very concrete contemporary problems of the enterprises? Bulgaria needs a differentiation of the universities offering business administration programs with different goals.

Bulgarian science

The output of Bulgarian science is low: only 300-400 inventions, patents, and licences a year[5]. The system is marked by a lack of facilities, underfinanced activities, and poor work with projects. Bulgaria is ranked 36th out of 49 countries (IMD, 2007) based on the averaged number of patents granted to residents in 2003-2005. Despite the relatively low level of patents, the researcher's productivity, measured as patents granted to residents per R&D personnel in business is relatively good, putting Bulgaria on the 15th place (IMD, 2007). This quite surprising result might be due to the different structure of patent holders in Bulgaria and other countries.

---

[4] Diffusion of computers in 2007 figures around 90% of enterprises; ¾ of all enterprises have equipped their workplaces with an optimal number of computers.
[5] In several categories, the quota per capita lies a 1000 citizens below that of other European countries.

For instance, after the changes in 1989 a lot of enterprises did not cover their interests to re-register the patents. Thus a lot of individuals registered patents, trade marks and rationalizations in their personal name. Further, a lot of researchers in public institutions (i.e. the Bulgarian Academy of Sciences and universities) does patent their results in their personal name and not for the institution they are employed at. This suggests some governance gaps in R&D sector. Private business is a marginal investor in the R&D sector.

Bulgaria is ranked 52nd out of 55 countries worldwide regarding the transfer of knowledge between companies and universities, followed only by Venezuela, the Slovak Republic and Croatia, the leader being Switzerland (IMD, 2007).

The learning style in Bulgaria is usually in a single loop learning

In a game, testing the learning style and abilities, from about 200 participants (students in a master's program for education management) – 30% of them were school directors, 40% teachers, 20% newly graduated teachers, and 10% others – no one and no one group has spontaneously chosen a double loop learning (Argyris, 1978, 1996).

Lack of skills and knowledge about how to cope with complexity

Managerial methods in practice are simple and formally used (the most frequently used method for business analysis is SWOT and PEST analysis, but even in this case the matrix with the strengths, weaknesses, threats and opportunities on the one hand, and the recognized problems and possible strategies on the other are not properly documented. The only exception for coping with internal complexity might be business process reengineering facilitated by modelling. However, even in this case, the leading motivation at the beginning was different: namely the preparation of the company for certification procedures.

Very poor or lack of risks evaluations (especially of strategically risks) and lack of competence how to cope with uncertainty

Many people have a diploma in business administration, but low levels of managerial competences. Among the reasons for this deplorable situation are
  - students work full-time,
  - enterprises are not able and ready to help with internships,
  - most of the universities make compromises in the choice of students (only to have students) if there are less candidates with poor quality;
  - just a few universities offer contemporary courses and
  - the generally poor infrastructural facilities in the educational system.

In the questionnaire more than 90% of the respondents think the portfolio method has nothing to do with risk evaluation, but about 70% use this method in practice. Only 1% of the participants use the scenario method, which is among the most commonly used methods to cope with uncertainty.

4. Conclusion

Bulgaria needs very urgent steps to improve its managerial and knowledge management practices: Large-scale public discussions in the country aimed at creating a common language are needed. Standards in the understanding the management approaches and practices should be set. Training support for small enterprises in an appropriate way is also a prerequisite for the successful building of and integration into a knowledge economy. Further needed is a restructuring of the existing supportive infrastructure and an increase in the level and the quality of the offered knowledge in theory and practice.

The Bulgarian society needs a rethinking of its strategies towards the creation of a knowledge society. It is necessary to formulate specific steps according to the real situation in the country.

For a small economy like Bulgaria it is impossible to have all priorities and action plans set by the European Commission, since we do not have the resources to work on each and every issue that the updated Lisbon strategy and related knowledge economy development plans provide as recommendations. Having *everything* as a priority is equivalent to saying: *nothing* has priority. Last but not least, another need is the intensification of studies in this field and communication of their results as a basis for the development of differentiated strategies – national and regional ones as well as strategies for branches and on the firm level.

References

Argyis, Ch./D.A. Schön 1978: Organizational Learning I (Theory, Method, and Practice), Reading, Mass. et al

Argyis, Ch./D.A. Schön 1996: Organizational Learning II (Theory of Action Perspective), Reading, Mass. et al

Бешкова Цв. 2003: "*Управление на знанието – основен инструмент за повишаване на конкурентноспособността на малките и микропредприятията в България*", дипломна работа, научен ръководител Анастасия Бънкова, Стопански факултет, Софийски университет

Boton, I.J.H./W. Campbell/M. Lindstrand 2007: Global Trends in Energy, in: The McKinsey Quaterly, No.1, p.47-55

Бънкова, А. 2004: Организационната теория и проектирането на организации, Изд. На ТУ, Пловдив

Heywood, S./ J. Spungin/P. Turnbull 2007: Cracking the complexity code, in The McKinsey Quaterly, No.2, p. 85-95
IMD 2007: IMD World Competitiveness Yearbook, June 2007, Lausanne, Switzerland
Kieser, Alfred (Hrsg.) 2002: Organisationstheorien, 5.Auflage, Kohlhammer
Luthans, F. 1995: Organizational Behavior, 7 ed., McGraw-Hill Inc., USA
МЕСАРОВИЧ, И. 1971: ТЕОРИЯ ЙЕРАРХИЧЕСКИХ СИСТЕМ, ИНОСТРАННАЯ ЛИТЕРАТУРА, М.
Николов, И. 1981:. Теория на социалните системи за управление, ИСУ, С.
Nonaka, I./H. Takeuchi 1995: The Knowledge-creating Company (How Japanese Companies Create the Dynamics of Innovation, Oxford University Press
North, Kl. 2001: Wissensorientierte Unternehmensführung. Wertschöpfung durch Wissen, 2. Auflage, Verlag Gabler, Wiesbaden
Osterloh, M./S. Wübker 1999: Wettbewerbsfähiger durch Prozess- und Wissensmanagement: mit Chancengelegenheit auf Erfolgskurs, Gabler Verlag, Wiesbaden
Porter, M. 1990: The competitive Advantage of Nations, Simon and Schuster, Inc., USA (Bulgarian translation, 2004)
Stefanov, R., M. Petrov (editors) 2008: Innovation, BG 2007 ARC Fund, Sofia.(in Bulgarian)
Stefanov, R., M. Petrov (editors) 2007: Innovation, BG 2007 ARC Fund, Sofia
Yalamov, T. 2006: e-Bulgaria 2006 ARC Fund, Sofia (in Bulgarian)

The study is financed by Sofia University "St. Kliment Ohridski".

DETERMINANTS OF ENTREPRENEURIAL INTENTIONS AMONG BULGARIAN UNIVERSITY STUDENTS: AN EXPLORATORY INVESTIGATION

DESISLAVA YORDANOVA / MARIA-ANTONIA TARRAZON
(SOFIA UNIVERSITY "ST. KLIMENT OHRIDSKI", BULGARIA -
AUTONOMOUS UNIVERSITY OF BARCELONA, SPAIN)

1. Introduction

During the last two decades, many developed countries experienced a shift away from a managed economy towards an entrepreneurial economy due to globalisation and new developments in the information and communication technologies (Audretsch and Thurik 2000:18, 2001:269). The growing importance of knowledge and ideas as a source of comparative advantages is associated with the emergence of different industrial structures, mainly dominated by new and small firms (Audretsch and Thurik 2000:24). Entrepreneurs play a key role in the knowledge-based economy as they create and implement new ideas (Audretsch and Thurik 2000:24). In Central and Eastern Europe, the transition period also led to the emergence of an entrepreneurial class and an SME sector, which are of great importance for the economies in this region (McMillan and Woodruff 2002:153). Today, both researchers and policy makers acknowledge the importance of entrepreneurship and the "small business" sector for economic growth, job creation, and innovation.

As entrepreneurship attracted academic interest, numerous theoretical frameworks have been advanced in an attempt to explain and predict entrepreneurial behaviour (Veciana 1999). However, many of them are deficient in various aspects (Robinson et al. 1991:14-17, Kolvereid 1996:48, Davidsson 1995:1). Cognitive approaches to new venture creation (Forbes 1999) include the strengths and overcome the deficiencies of other frameworks (Robinson et al. 1991:18). These approaches suggest that in circumstances associated with uncertainty and ambiguity as in the case of new venture formation, cognitive factors such as perceptions, intentions, attitudes, and beliefs are especially valuable for understanding human behaviour (Forbes 1999:416). Entrepreneurial behaviour is a planned behaviour, an intentional act, which requires planning how the perceived opportunity will be exploited (Bird 1988:442, Katz and Gartner 1988:431, Krueger et al. 2000:413-414, Krueger and Carsrud 1993:315-316, Krueger 1993:5-6). Therefore, understanding entrepreneurial intentions and their antecedents can help to better understand and predict entrepreneurial behaviour without witnessing it (Krueger et al. 2000:414, Tkachev and Kolvereid 1999:271, Krueger and Carsrud 1993:316).

The study of entrepreneurial intentions is seen as a promising field for a theory-based research in entrepreneurship (Bird 1988:442) for several reasons. First, intentions-based models contribute to understanding why individuals make certain decisions in the process of new venture creation by revealing what is inside the "black-box" of the entrepreneurial decision-making process (Krueger et al. 2000:426-427). Second, entrepreneurial intentions "offer a means to better explain – and predict – entrepreneurship" because they play a mediating role between potential exogenous antecedents – such as demographics, traits, perceived availability of critical resources, and situational role beliefs – and the act of new venture formation (Krueger et al. 2000:411). Third, in contrast to comparisons between entrepreneurs and non-entrepreneurs, the study of entrepreneurial intentions avoids the mistake of identifying individual characteristics as determinants of entrepreneurial behaviour, which have developed as a consequence of founding and running a business (Davidsson 1995:2). And finally, intentions and their underlying antecedents are perception-based and therefore could be changed (Ajzen 1991: 206, Krueger and Brazeal 1994:93). Thus, studying entrepreneurial intentions and their antecedents will help to formulate policy recommendations for enhancing entrepreneurial activities.

Despite the importance and the potential role of entrepreneurship and the SME sector for economies in Central and Eastern Europe (McMillan and Woodruff 2002:153, Smallbone et al. 2001:253-254), little attention has been devoted to identifying which factors contribute to the entrepreneurial activity in the region. The purpose of the present study is twofold. First, we explore what the antecedents of entrepreneurial intentions among Bulgarian university students in Economics and Business Administration are. The rationale for choosing university students as our object of research is that they are a significant share of potential entrepreneurs (Mueller and Thomas 2001:62) and are often seen as a promising source of entrepreneurs in the knowledge society (Veciana 1998 cited in Veciana et al. 2005:166, Gupta et al. 2005:3). In addition, business students in particular are more likely to be aware of entrepreneurship (Gupta et al. 2005:3). Second, as most research on entrepreneurial intentions has been conducted in Anglo-Saxon countries, we try to verify whether the Theory of Planned Behaviour (Ajzen 1991) is able to explain and accurately predict entrepreneurial intentions in a sample from South Eastern Europe.

2. Theoretical Framework: Theory of Planned Behaviour (TPB)[1]

In literature, various intention models have been proposed for understanding and predicting entrepreneurial intentions (Bird 1988, Boyd and Vozikis 1994, Shapero and Sokol 1982, Ajzen 1991, Katz 1992, Davidsson 1995 Krueger and Brazeal 1994, Busenitz and Lau 1996). However, Peterman and Kennedy (2003:130) highlight that the majority of these models "are largely homologous in that they all focus on the pre-entrepreneurial event and integrate attitude and behaviour theory (Ajzen, 1991), and self-efficacy and social learning theory (Bandura, 1986)".

The Theory of Planned Behaviour (Ajzen 1991) is the prevailing model for explaining behavioural intentions (Krueger and Brazeal 1994:93). It is an extension of the Theory of Reasoned Action (Aizen and Fishbein 1980), which assumes that people are rational beings that make a systematic use of the information they have and consider the implications of their actions before they decide to engage or not in certain behaviours (Ajzen and Fishbein 1980:5). The TPB postulates that the performance of behaviour is a function of intentions and perceived behavioural control (Ajzen 1991:182). Intentions reveal the motivation of the person to perform the behaviour and indicate what effort she or he is willing to exert in order to perform the behaviour. Intentions are positively associated with the likelihood of performing the behaviour (Ajzen 1991:181). The link between intentions and behaviour depends on the extent to which behaviour is under volitional control (Ajzen 1991:183). The performance of some behaviours is only partially under volitional control and depends on other factors such as the availability of resources and opportunities (Ajzen 1991:182). In that case, the performance of the behaviour depends not only on intentions but also on the person's control over the behaviour (Ajzen 1991:182).

Intentions are determined by three conceptually independent attitudinal constructs: attitude toward the behaviour, perceived subjective norms about the behaviour, and perceived behavioural control (Ajzen 1991:188). The more positive the attitudes and the perceived subjective norms, and the higher the perceived behavioural control, the stronger the person's intention to execute the behaviour (Ajzen 1991:188). The attitude toward the behaviour is defined as the individual's positive or negative evaluation or appraisal of the behaviour in question (Ajzen 1991:188). The perceived subjective norms reveal the perceptions of what people who are important for an individual think about performing the behaviour in question (Ajzen 1991: 188). The perceived behavioural control refers to the perceived ability to perform the behaviour under inves-

---

[1] The description of the Theory of Planned Behaviour is based on Ajzen (1991).

tigation (Ajzen 1991:188). The attitudinal constructs can be measured *directly* using scaling procedures or *indirectly* through the person's beliefs about the behaviour (behavioural beliefs, normative beliefs, and control beliefs) (Ajzen 1991:191-198). Personal factors and situational variables influence intentions and behaviour indirectly through affecting more directly the three attitudinal variables (Krueger and Carsrud 1993:326).

The TPB has received a substantial empirical support in various fields such as marketing research, health care, safety, entrepreneurship research, education, leisure, sport activities, voting behaviour, etc. (for a review, see Sutton 1998, Armitage and Conner 2001). Armitage and Conner's (2001:485-489) recent meta-analysis of the TPB shows that intentions and perceived behavioural control are able to predict significantly behaviour in various situations, while the three attitudinal constructs account for a considerable amount of variance in intentions.

3. Determinants of Entrepreneurial Intentions and Behaviour

3.1. Attitudinal Variables

Empirical research reveals that attitudes are important antecedents of entrepreneurial intentions. For example, attitudes toward entrepreneurship and autonomy (Schwarz et al. 2005:12, Lüthje and Franke 2003:142) and attitudes toward risk and independence (Douglas and Shepherd 2002:88) affect entrepreneurial intentions. The attitudinal variables proposed by the TPB are able to correctly predict and explain entrepreneurial intentions in different countries (Krueger et al. 2000:424, Kolvereid 1996:54, Tkachev and Kolvereid 1999:278, Tegtmeier 2006:11, Autio et al. 2001: 157).

3.2. Entrepreneurship Education

Education and training is considered as a socialization process into entrepreneurship and provides access to role models that make entrepreneurship an attractive career choice (Dyer 1994:9-11). Empirical research confirms that entrepreneurship education has a positive impact on entrepreneurial self-efficacy, intentions and behaviour (Kolvereid and Moen 1997: 157-158, Noel 2001, Fayolle et al. 2005:14, Varela and Jimenez 2001, Ehrlich et al. 2000). Entrepreneurship education has also been found to enhance the need for achievement and internal locus of control (Hansemark 2003:313-314).

3.3. Personality Factors

In entrepreneurship literature, risk-taking propensity, internal locus of control, and achievement motivation are considered as distinctive characteristics of entrepreneurs despite the fact that the empirical evidence is inconclusive (Veciana 1999). Entrepreneurs are characterized by a high need for achievement in a number of studies (Johnson 1990:43). Students with higher risk-taking propensity and an internal locus of control are more likely to have positive attitudes toward entrepreneurship (Lüthje and Franke 2003:142). Entrepreneurial intentions among students are significantly related to the students' tolerance for risk (Douglas and Shepherd 2002:88). Risk tolerance and internal locus of control are positively associated with self-employment preferences and actual self-employment (Verheul et al. 2006:13, Grilo and Irigoyen 2006:311).

3.4. Role Models

Entrepreneurship research offers consistent empirical evidence that individuals with close entrepreneurial role models are more likely to exhibit entrepreneurial intentions (Davidsson 1995:15, Crant 1996:46, Raijman 2001:405, Veciana et al. 2005:180, Kolvereid 1996:54). Several large-scale studies show that children of self-employed parents are more likely to enter entrepreneurship (Dunn and Holtz-Eakin 2000:288-289, Hout and Rosen 2000:686, Delmar and Davidsson 2000:16, Davidsson and Honig 2003:320). In addition to the presence of role models, the role model performance has a statistically significant effect on entrepreneurial intentions and their attitudinal antecedents (Scherer et al. 1989:64, Krueger 1993:17, Peterman and Kennedy 2003:138).

3.5. Perceptual variables

Entrepreneurial intentions, convictions and preferences are related to perceived entrepreneurship-related barriers and supporting factors (Autio et al. 1997:10, Lüthje and Franke 2003:142). Perceptual variables are also significantly associated with the creation of new firms (Arenius and Minniti 2005:239), self-employment preferences and actual self-employment (Verheul et al. 2006:14). Perceptions of the social status of entrepreneurship emerge as a good predictor of the interest in starting a business (Begley et al. 1997). The perceived image of entrepreneurship as a career alternative affects entrepreneurial conviction among university students (Autio et al. 1997:10).

3.6. Gender

Women have lower entrepreneurial intentions than men (Crant 1996:46, Kolvereid 1996:53, Veciana et al. 2005:177, Raijman 2001:404, Davidsson 1995:15, Routamaa et al. 2004:5). Several studies report that the gender effect is fully mediated by attitudes, subjective norms and perceived behavioural control (Kolvereid 1996:54), and risk disposition (Raijman 2001:405). A third group of studies finds that women continue to exhibit lower entrepreneurial intentions after controlling for other variables (Crant 1996:46, Davidsson 1995:15, Kolvereid and Moen 1997:159).

4. Conceptual Model and Hypotheses

The conceptual model of this study (Figure 1) is based on the TPB and the review of the literature presented in the previous section. It outlines potential antecedents of entrepreneurial intentions among university students. Following the TPB, the model suggests that entrepreneurial intentions are determined by:

(1) attitudes toward entrepreneurial behaviour,
(2) perceived social norms about entrepreneurial behaviour and
(3) perceived control for entrepreneurial behaviour.

The empirical research on determinants of entrepreneurial intentions suggests that education in entrepreneurship, role models, perceptions of entrepreneurship, perceptions of environment, and personality characteristics are associated with entrepreneurial intentions. We expect that an entrepreneurship education may influence positively entrepreneurial intentions. Previous empirical research shows that entrepreneurship education has a positive impact on entrepreneurial self-efficacy, intentions and behaviour (Kolvereid and Moen 1997: 157-158, Noel 2001, Fayolle et al. 2005:14, Varela and Jimenez 2001, Ehrlich et al. 2000). The TPB posits that exogenous factors including gender rarely influence intentions directly, but operate indirectly through attitudinal variables. This leads to the following hypotheses:

H1: *The more favourable the attitudes toward entrepreneurial behaviour, the stronger the individual's intention to become an entrepreneur.*

H2: *The more favourable the subjective norms about entrepreneurial behaviour, the stronger the individual's intention to become an entrepreneur.*

H3: *The higher the perceived behavioural control, the stronger the individual's intention to become an entrepreneur.*

H4: *Women are more likely to have lower entrepreneurial intentions than men.*

H5: *Students with education in entrepreneurship are more likely to exhibit stronger entrepreneurial intentions.*

H6: *The presence of role models increases the likelihood of reporting stronger entrepreneurial intentions.*

H7: *The more positive the perception of the image of entrepreneurs in society, the stronger the individual's entrepreneurial intentions.*

H8: *The more positive the perception of the prestige of entrepreneurship as an occupation, the stronger the individual's entrepreneurial intentions.*

Figure 1: Conceptual model of determinants of entrepreneurial intentions among university students.

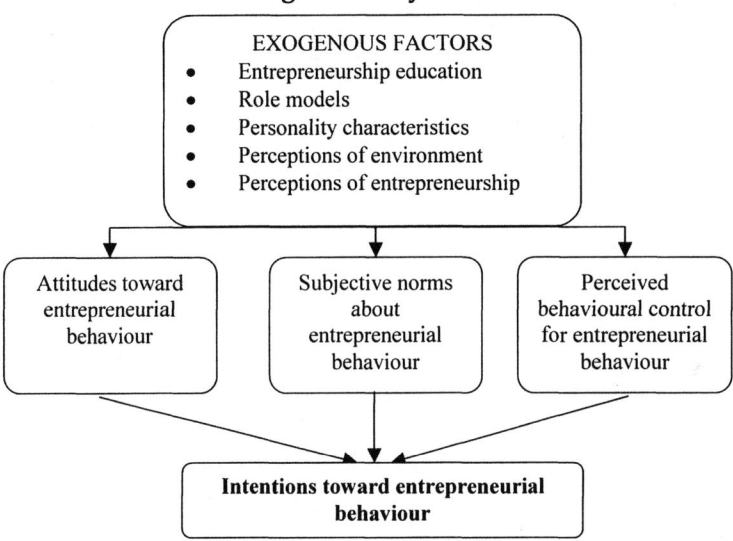

```
┌─────────────────────────────────────┐
│         EXOGENOUS FACTORS           │
│  • Entrepreneurship education       │
│  • Role models                      │
│  • Personality characteristics      │
│  • Perceptions of environment       │
│  • Perceptions of entrepreneurship  │
└─────────────────────────────────────┘
              │
    ┌─────────┼─────────┐
    ▼         ▼         ▼
┌────────┐ ┌────────┐ ┌────────┐
│Attitudes│ │Subjective│ │Perceived│
│ toward │ │  norms  │ │behavioural│
│entrepre-│ │  about  │ │ control │
│neurial │ │entrepre-│ │for entre-│
│behaviour│ │ neurial │ │preneurial│
│        │ │behaviour│ │behaviour│
└────────┘ └────────┘ └────────┘
     │         │         │
     └─────────┼─────────┘
               ▼
     ┌──────────────────────┐
     │ Intentions toward    │
     │ entrepreneurial      │
     │ behaviour            │
     └──────────────────────┘
```

Source: Own elaboration based on the literature review and the TPB (Ajzen 1991).

H9: The more positive the perceptions about the influence of economic reforms on entrepreneurship, the stronger the individual's entrepreneurial intentions.

H10: The higher the achievement motivation, the stronger the individual's entrepreneurial intentions.

H11: The higher the willingness to take risks, the stronger the individual's entrepreneurial intentions.

H12: The more internal the locus of control, the stronger the individual's entrepreneurial intentions.

H13: The effect of exogenous factors on entrepreneurial intentions is fully mediated by the attitudinal variables.

5. Research Methodology

5.1. Sample and Data Collection

This study uses a cross-sectional survey among university students in Business Administration and Economics in two leading Bulgarian public universities conducted in 2006. The use of students is quite convenient in entrepreneurship research (Mueller and Thomas 2001:63). This approach allows identifying the antecedents of entrepreneurial intentions in a prospective manner. The questionnaire used in the study was distributed during class sessions. The participation was anonymous and voluntary. A pilot study was conducted among 12 students (6 men and 6 women) in order to pre-test the initial version of the questionnaire.

Table 1: Characteristics of the sample

Characteristics	Number	%
Gender		
Female	184	50.3%
Male	182	49.7%
Age		
Less than 21	146	39.9%
Between 21 and 25	191	52.2%
More than 25	29	7.9%
University		
Sofia University "St. Kliment Ohridski"	255	69.7%
University of National & World Economics (Sofia)	111	30.3%
Role models		
Yes	257	70.2%
No	109	29.8%
Education in entrepreneurship		
Yes	129	35.2%
No	237	64.8%
Location		
Village	5	1.4%
Small town	159	43.7%
Big city	201	54.9%

The sample selection was hampered because universities avoid providing information about their alumnae. Therefore, the sample is not random and includes 366 students in Economics and Business Administration. Table 1 shows the characteristics of the sample. It is roughly composed of a similar number of male and female students (184 women and 182 men). The proportion of women in our sample is similar to the proportion of female students in Bulgarian public universities, which according to NSI (2006) is around 51% for the academic year 2004/2005. About one third of the respondents have taken either elective or compulsory university courses in entrepreneurship or small business management. The majority of respondents are between 21 and 25 years old. Only less than one third of the students do not have entrepreneurs among their relatives and close friends.

5.2. Definition of Variables

The dependent variable in this study is *entrepreneurial intentions* (ENT_INT). In the previous entrepreneurship research, entrepreneurial intentions have been measured in different ways mainly focusing either on a time dimension or on the preferences for an entrepreneurship career (Schwarz et al. 2006:9). Following Kolvereid (1996:50-51), we assume that students must choose between two alternatives: running their own business or working for someone else. Therefore, we measure students' intentions with the index proposed by Kolvereid (1996:50-51). The Cronbach's alpha of this index is 0.624.

A *belief-based measure of attitudes* (ATTITUDES) is adopted in the present study, which is computed as the sum of outcome attractiveness scores multiplied by outcome likelihood scores and averaged by the number of outcomes associated with entrepreneurial behaviour (Ajzen 1991:191). The outcomes related to entrepreneurship included in the final version of the questionnaire are: autonomy, good financial performance, stress, good quality of life, and personal sacrifices (lack of leisure time, etc.). They were identified through the literature review and the pilot study. *Perceived subjective norms* (SUB_NORMS) are measured through the sum of normative belief scores for 3 referents (closest family, closest friends, and other important people) multiplied by the scores representing the respondent's desire to comply with these beliefs and averaged by 3 (Kolvereid 1996:51). The index used to measure the factor *perceived behavioural control* (BEH_CONTROL) is adopted from Kolvereid (1996:51) (the Cronbach's alpha is 0.688).

The *presence of entrepreneurs* among friends and relatives is coded 1 and the absence 0 (ROLE_MODEL). ENTR_EDU takes the value 1 if a respondent has taken *academic courses in entrepreneurship* and value the 0 if not. GENDER is a dummy variable (1=male, 0=female). In this study, we employ self-perception measures of personality characteristics. In order to measure the *locus of control* (LOCUS_CONTROL), respondents were asked: "To what extent solving the problems in your life depends on you?" (1=nothing depends on me, 7=everything depends on me). *Achievement motivation* (ACH_MOT) is measured by asking students to what extent they strive for high achievements in their personal and professional life (1=to a very low extent, 7=to a very high extent). RISK represents respondents' *willingness to take risks* (1=very low, 7=very high). Students' perceptions of the *image of entrepreneurs in society* (IMAGE) and the *prestige of entrepreneurship* as an occupation (PRESTIGE) are both measured on a 7-point Likert scale (1=very low, 7=very high). Respondents' perceptions of the *influence of economic reforms on entrepreneurship* (EC_REFORMS) are measured as follows: 1=negative influence; 2=no influence; and 3=positive influence. As control variables we include two variables. LN_AGE is the natural logarithm of the respondents' *age* in years. LOCATION indicates *where the respondent has lived* most of his or her life (1=village, 2=small town, 3=big city).

5.3. Data analysis

Data are analysed with both, correlation analysis and multivariate statistics. Correlations between independent variables are measured using Pearson correlation and Spearman's rho coefficients. The determinants of entrepreneurial intentions are explored using an ordered logit model (Davidson and MacKinnon 1993:529-531) because this variable is categorical taking values between 3 and 21. A Logit model is a more robust method than OLS regression, mainly because it is not dependent on assumptions of normality of distributions, linear relationship between dependent and independent variables, homoscedasticity of the dependent variable for each level of the independent variable(s); and the use of interval or unbounded independent variables (Hair et al. 1998:239-325, Maddala 1983:22-26). The use of the maximum likelihood approach is recommended when a sample selection bias is possible (Nawata 1994: 40). In order to test for possible mediating effects of attitudinal constructs on the relationship between exogenous factors and entrepreneurial intentions, we follow the procedure outlined by Baron and Kenny (1986: 1177).

6. Empirical Results

6.1. Correlation Analysis

We observe significant correlations between the three attitudinal variables and some of the exogenous factors (Table 2). They can be explained by the TPB and are consistent with previous empirical research. Students, who are willing to take risks, have entrepreneurship education, perceive entrepreneurship as a prestigious occupation, are male, and have more positive attitudes toward entrepreneurship than the rest of the sample. The presence of role models, the willingness to take risk, perceptions of entrepreneurship and entrepreneurs, and gender are correlated with perceived subjective norms. Perceived behavioural control is significantly associated with the locus of control, the willingness to take risks, perceptions of entrepreneurship and entrepreneurs, and gender. Since the correlations among independent variables are relatively modest (not exceeding 0.39), we exclude multicollinearity problems.

Table 2: Correlations between independent variables [1]

	1	2	3	4	5	6	7	8	9	10	11	12	13
1. ATTITUDES	1												
2. SUB_NORMS	.26**	1											
3. BEH_CONTROL	.30**	.23**	1										
4. ROLE_MODEL	.05	.12*	.10	1									
5. ENTR_EDU	.11*	.02	.09	.03	1								
6. LN_AGE	.03	-.08	.04	.03	.24**	1							
7. IMAGE	.04	.11*	.17**	.05	-.03	-.07	1						
8. PRESTIGE	.16**	.27**	.23**	.05	.07	-.04	.39**	1					
9. LOCATION	-.01	.01	-.00	.03	.06	-.03	-.02	-.05	1				
10. LOCUS_CONTROL	.07	.09	.24**	.02	.01	-.09	.17**	.17**	-.06	1			
11. RISK	.15**	.25**	.26**	.07	.06	.03	.07	.18**	-.02	.23**	1		
12. ACH_MOT	.08	.07	.09	.00	.03	-.13*	.09	.13*	-.03	.26**	.19**	1	
13. EC_REFORMS	-.02	.02	-.02	-.01	-.17**	-.12*	.02	-.05	-.01	.12*	-.02	.02	1
14. GENDER	.15**	.14**	.27**	-.02	-.00	.04	.08	.06	.03	.03	.21**	-.08	-.03

[1] Correlations between categorical variables are measured with Spearman's Rho coefficients. –
** Correlation is significant at the 0.01 level (2-tailed). – * Correlation is significant at the 0.05 level (2-tailed).

6.2. Regression Analysis

Table 3 presents the result of ordered logistic regression with entrepreneurial intentions ENT_INT as a dependent variable. We estimate three regression models. Model 1 in table 2 includes only personality, demographic, perceptual, and educational variables, while model 2 contains only the three attitudinal variables. In model 3 attitudinal variables are entered in a regression analysis along with exogenous factors. The models show a good fit to the data as indicated by likelihood ratio chi-square statistics (LR statistics) (p< 0.001) and pseudo R^2.

Table 3: Ordered logistic regression with ENT_INT as a dependent variable

	Model 1 Coefficient	Model 2 Coefficient	Model 3 Coefficient
ATTITUDES		0.063286**	0.052703**
SUB_NORMS		0.133587***	0.116608***
BEH_CONTROL		0.799271***	0.594684***
ROLE_MODEL	0.830397***		0.712997***
ENTR_EDU	0.747667***		0.668311**
GENDER	0.585038**		0.200695
LN_AGE	-0.965920		-0.845272
IMAGE	-0.037559		-0.025932
PRESTIGE	0.276825***		0.128661
LOCATION	-0.095716		-0.122743
LOCUS_CONTROL	0.207630**		0.144241
RISK	0.374120***		0.274783**
ACH_MOT	0.083993		0.057872
EC_REFORMS	-0.207547**		-0.265874**
LR index (Pseudo-R^2)	0.054928	0.062956	0.089657
Log likelihood	-936.2907	-928.3372	-901.8843
LR statistics	108.8345***	124.7415***	177.6473***
Number of cases	366	366	366

***p < 0.001, **p<= 0.05, *p<= 0.1

According to model 1, the coefficients of the variables ROLE_MODEL, ENTR_EDU, PRESTIGE, LOCUS_CONTROL, RISK, and GENDER are statistically significant as indicated by Wald statistics and have the expected signs. Thus, H5, H6, H8, H11, and H12 are supported. Contrary to what was hypothesized, the coefficients of the variables IMAGE and ACH_MOT are not significant. Therefore, H7 and H10 are not supported. The variable EC_REFORM influences the dependent variable in the opposite direction compared to what was suggested in H9. The control variables LOCATION and LN_AGE have no impact on the dependent variable.

In model 2, we test the hypotheses derived from the TPB. The coefficients of the variables ATTITUDES, SUB_NORMS, and BEH_CONTROL are significant and positive. These variables are found to contribute significantly to the likelihood of reporting strong entrepreneurial intentions. The TPB receives strong support. Hypotheses H1, H2, H3 are supported.

In order to test H13, we add exogenous factors to attitudinal variables in model 3. ATTITUDES, SUB_NORMS, and BEH_CONTROL have significant effects on the likelihood of having strong entrepreneurial intentions even after controlling for exogenous factors. The coefficients of the variables GENDER, PRESTIGE, and LOCUS_CONTROL are significant in model 1, while in model 3 none of them is significant. Following Baron and Kenny (1986:1177) we can conclude that the three attitudinal variables fully mediate the effect of GENDER, PRESTIGE, and LOCUS_ CONTROL on entrepreneurial intentions. The variables ROLE_MODEL, ENTR_EDU, EC_REFORMS, and RISK have direct effects on the likelihood of reporting strong entrepreneurial intentions after holding the three attitudinal constructs constant. Hypothesis H13 is partially supported.

7. Discussion

The TPB seems to be able to explain and predict accurately entrepreneurial intentions in our sample of Bulgarian university students. As in Krueger et al. (2000:424), Kolvereid (1996:54), Tkachev and Kolvereid (1999:278), Tegtmeier (2006:11), and Autio et al. (2001:157), *attitudes, subjective norms*, and *perceived behavioural control* determine entrepreneurial intentions. In addition, a number of *individual characteristics* influence the probability of reporting strong entrepreneurial intentions. We find some support for the psychological approach to entrepreneurship. While achievement motivation does not impact entrepreneurial intentions, a *strong willingness to take risks* and an *internal locus of control* lead to a preference for an entrepreneurial career. In addition, our results grant support to the social learning theory. Students with *entrepreneurial role models* and an *entrepreneurship education* are more likely to exhibit strong entrepreneurial intentions. Women are less likely to choose running their own business than men. Students' perceptions of the image of entrepreneurs in society do not impact their entrepreneurial intentions, while perceptions of *entrepreneurship as a prestigious occupation* do. These results are good news for the new market economies in Eastern Europe, where entrepreneurs not always possess a good image in society. Contrary to our expectations, students, who believe that *economic reforms* have a *negative* influence on entrepreneurship in the country, are *more likely* to exhibit strong intentions to enter entrepreneurship.

Gender, locus of control, and perceptions about the prestige of entrepreneurship as an occupation influence entrepreneurial intentions only *indirectly* through their effect on attitudes, subjective norms, and perceived behavioural control. However, the attitudinal constructs are not able to mediate the effect of some exogenous factors such as the presence of role models, willingness to take risks, perceptions of economic reforms, and entrepreneurship education on entrepreneurial intentions.

The present research has several limitations; therefore our findings should be accepted with caution. First, the cross-sectional design decreases the explanatory power of the study. Second, the sample used here is not random and includes only students in Economics and Business Administration. And finally, this study investigates only the antecedents of entrepreneurial intentions and cannot determine who will actually select an entrepreneurial career. Future research on a larger randomly drawn sample of students is needed to test the hypotheses outlined here. Future research should also examine to what extent the findings of this study can be generalized to students from other fields and from other countries in the region. Additionally, a longitudinal analysis should complement the findings of this research in order to confirm causal relationships.

This study illustrates that entrepreneurial intentions among Bulgarian university students are determined by factors that are possible to change, which has important implications for policy makers. Our findings suggest that entrepreneurship can be encouraged in various ways. The TPB provides guidelines for designing behavioural interventions aimed at altering behavioural, normative, and control beliefs about entrepreneurial behaviour (Ajzen 2005:136-139). According to the TPB, changes in these beliefs will be reflected in attitudes, social norms, and behavioural control toward entrepreneurship, entrepreneurial intentions and entrepreneurial behaviour.

Behavioural interventions can use a number of different strategies: e.g. persuasion and information, increasing skills, goal setting, and rehearsal of skills (Hardeman et al. 2002:139-151). Such interventions are especially desirable for Bulgarian female university students, who exhibit lower entrepreneurial intentions than male university students. As social norms appear to have a direct impact on entrepreneurial intentions, influences directed at attitudes toward entrepreneurship among the general population may also have a positive impact on entrepreneurial intentions and behaviour. In addition, it is necessary to strengthen the link between entrepreneurial intentions and behaviour, for example, by establishing and enhancing implementation intentions (Gollwitzer 1999: 493-503) through specific plans that describe when, where, and how the start-up will be carried out. Encouraging students to formulate such plans will make it easier for them to become involved in entrepreneurship.

Greater emphasis should be placed on entrepreneurship education in Bulgarian universities. Entrepreneurship courses, which now are offered mainly as electives, need to be adopted as compulsory for both bachelor and master students in Economics and Business Administration. In addition, following Davidsson (1995:23-24), we recommend that an entrepreneurial perspective is introduced in all business courses. Thus, students will become acquainted with different aspects of pre-founding and founding stages and with young and small firms' management, which in turn will affect positively entrepreneurial intentions and their antecedents (Davidsson 1995:23-24).

As students without entrepreneurial role models are underrepresented among those intending to start their own business, it is necessary to make positive entrepreneurial role models more visible through information and educational measures (Davidsson 1995:23) in order to break this pattern. In new market economies in Central and Eastern Europe, making positive entrepreneurial role models more visible may also influence attitudes toward entrepreneurship and entrepreneurial intentions as well as a respective behaviour in the whole population.

8. Conclusions

This study extends the literature on determinants of entrepreneurial intentions presenting evidence from Eastern Europe. We demonstrate that the Theory of Planned Behaviour is able to explain and accurately predict entrepreneurial intentions in this context. The results of this study suggest that entrepreneurial intentions among Bulgarian university students are determined by perception-based factors and therefore are possible to change. Despite the limitations of the sample analyzed, composed solely of students in Economics and Business Administration, we draw upon our findings and suggest a wide range of policy measures for enhancing entrepreneurial intentions and behaviour in the new market economies in Central and Eastern Europe.

References

Ajzen, I., (1991): "Theory of planned behaviour". *Organizational Behaviour and Human Decision Processes*, 50, pp. 179 – 211

Ajzen, I. (2005): *Attitudes, personality, and behaviour*. 2nd edition. Chicago, IL: Open Univ. Press

Ajzen, I., & Fishbein, M. (1980): *Understanding attitudes and predicting social behavior*. Englewood Cliffs, NJ: Prentice.Hall

Arenius, P., and Minniti, M. (2005): "Perceptual variables and nascent entrepreneurship". *Small Business Economics*, 24, pp.233-247

Armitage, C. and Conner, M. (2001): "Efficacy of the Theory of Planned Behavior: A meta-analytic review". *British Journal of Social Psychology*, 40, pp. 471-499

Audretsch, D. and Thurik, R. (2000): "Capitalism and democracy in the 21st century: from the managed to the entrepreneurial economy". *Journal of Evolutionary Economics*, 10, pp. 17-34

Audretsch, D. and Thurik, R. (2001): "Sources of growth: the entrepreneurial versus the managed economy". *Industrial and Corporate Change*, 10, pp. 267-315

Autio, E., Keeley, R.H., Klofsten, M., Parker, G., and Hay, M. (2001): "Entrepreneurial intent among students in Scandinavia and in the USA". *Enterprise and Innovation Management Studies*, 2(2), pp. 145-160

Autio, E., Keeley, R.H., Klofsten, M., and Ulfstedt, T. (1997): "Entrepreneurial intent among students: testing an intent model in Asia, Scandinavia and USA". *Frontiers of Entrepreneurship Research, Babson Conference Proceedings*, www.babson.edu/entrep/fer

Bandura, A. (1986): *The Social Foundations of Thought and Action*. Englewood Cliffs, NJ: Prentice Hall

Baron, R. and Kenny, D. (1986): "The moderator-mediator variable distinction in social psychological research: conceptual, strategic, and statistical considerations". *Journal of Personality and Social Psychology*, 51 (6), pp. 1173-1182

Begley, T., Tan, W., Larasati, A., Rab, A., Zamora, E., and Nanayakkara, G. (1997): "The relationship between socio-cultural dimensions and interest in starting a business: a multi-country study". *Frontiers of Entrepreneurship Research, Babson Conference Proceedings*, www.babson.edu/entrep/fer

Bird, B. (1988): "Implementing entrepreneurial ideas: The case for intention". *Academy of Management Review*, 13(3), pp. 442-453

Boyd, N. and Vozikis, G. (1994): "The influence of self-efficacy on the development of entrepreneurial intentions and actions". *Entrepreneurship Theory and Practice*, 18 (4), pp. 63-77

Busenitz, L. and Lau, C. (1996): "A cross-cultural cognitive model of new venture creation". *Entrepreneurship Theory and Practice*, 20(4), pp. 25-39

Crant, M. (1996): "The proactive personality scale as a predictor of entrepreneurial intentions". *Journal of Small Business Management*, 34(3), pp. 42-49

Davidsson, P. (1995): "Determinants of entrepreneurial intentions". Paper presented at the RENT IX Conference, Piacenza, Italy, November

Davidsson, P. and Honig B. (2003): "The role of social and human capital among nascent entrepreneurs". *Journal of Business Venturing* 18, pp. 301-331

Delmar, F. and Davidsson, P. (2000): "Where do they come from? Prevalence and characteristics of nascent entrepreneurs". *Entrepreneurship and Regional Development*, 12, pp. 1-23

Douglas E. and Shephard D. (2002): "Self-employment as a career choice: attitudes, entrepreneurial intentions, and utility maximization". *Entrepreneurship Theory and Practice*, 26(3), pp. 81-90

Dunn, T. and D. Holtz-Eakin, (2000): "Financial capital, human capital, and the transition to self-employment: evidence from intergenerational links". *Journal of Labour Economics* 18 (2), pp. 282-305
Dyer, W. G. (1994): "Toward a theory of entrepreneurial careers". *Entrepreneurship Theory and Practice*, 19(2), pp. 7-21
Ehrlich, S.B., de Noble, A.F., Jung, D. and Pearson D. (2000): "The impact of entrepreneurship training programs on an individual's entrepreneurial self-efficacy". *Frontiers of Entrepreneurship Research, Babson Conference Proceedings*, www.babson.edu/entrep/fer
Fayolle, A., Gailly, B., and Lassas-Clerc, N. (2005): "The long-term effect of entrepreneurship teaching programmes on entrepreneurial intention". *Proceedings from RENT XIX Conference*, Naples, Italy, November 17-18, 2005
Forbes, D. (1999): "Cognitive approaches to new venture creation". *International Journal of Management Reviews*, 1(4), pp. 415–439
Gollwitzer, P. M. (1999): "Implementation intentions: strong effects of simple plans". *American Psychologist*, 54, pp. 493-503
Grilo I. and Irigoyen J. (2006): "Entrepreneurship in the EU: to wish and not to be". *Small Business Economics*, 26, pp. 305–318
Gupta, V., Turban, D., Wasti, S., and Sikdar, A. (2005): "Entrepreneurship and stereotypes: are entrepreneurs from Mars or from Venus?". *Academy of Management Proceedings*, pp. C1-C6
Hair F. J., Anderson E. R., Tathan L. R., Black C. (1998) *"Multivariate Data Analysis"*. Fifth Edition. New Jersey: Prentice Hall
Hansemark, O.C. (2003): "Need for achievement, locus of control and the prediction of business start-ups: a longitudinal study". *Journal of Economic Psychology* 24, pp. 301-319
Hardeman, W., Johnston, M., Johnston, D., Bonetti, D., Wareham, N., and Kinmonth, A. (2002): "Application of the Theory of Planned Behavior in behavior change interventions: A systematic review". *Psychology and Health*, 17 (2), pp. 123-158
Hout, M. and Rosen, H. (2000): "Self-employment, family background, and race". *The Journal of Human Resources* 35 (4), pp. 670-692
Johnson, B. R. (1990): "Toward a multidimensional model of entrepreneurship: The case of achievement motivation and the entrepreneur". *Entrepreneurship Theory and Practice*, 14(3), pp. 39–54
Katz, J. (1992): "A psychological cognitive model of employment status choice". *Entrepreneurship Theory and Practice*, 17(1), pp. 29-37
Katz, J. and Gartner, W. (1988): "Properties of emerging organizations". *Academy of Management Review*, 13(3), pp. 429-441
Kolvereid, L., (1996): "Prediction of employment status choice intentions". *Entrepreneurship Theory and Practice*, 21 (1), pp. 47-57
Kolvereid. L. and Moen, O. (1997): "Entrepreneurship among business graduates: does a major in entrepreneurship make a difference?". *Journal of European Industrial Training*, 21(4), pp. 154-160
Krueger N. (1993): "Impact of prior entrepreneurial exposure on perceptions of new venture feasibility". *Entrepreneurship Theory and Practice*, 18 (1), pp. 5-21
Krueger N. and Brazeal D. (1994): "Entrepreneurial potential and potential entrepreneurs". *Entrepreneurship Theory and Practice*, 18 (3), pp. 91–104

Krueger N. and Carsrud A. (1993): "Entrepreneurial intentions: applying the theory of planned behaviour". *Entrepreneurship and Regional Development*, 5, pp. 315-330

Krueger, N., Reilly, M., and Carsrud, A. (2000): "Competing models of entrepreneurial intentions". *Journal of business venturing*, 15, pp. 411-432

Lüthje, C. and Franke, N. (2003): "The making of an entrepreneur: testing a model of entrepreneurial intent among engineering students at MIT". *R&D Management*, 33(2), pp. 135-147

Maddala, G. (1983): "*Limited Dependent and Qualitative Variables in Econometrics*". New York, Cambridge University Press

McMillan, J. and Woodruff, C. (2002): "The central role of entrepreneurs in transition economies". *Journal of Economic Perspectives*, 16(3), pp. 153-170

Mueller, S. L. and Thomas, A. S. (2001): Culture and entrepreneurial potential: a nine country study of locus of control and innovativeness. *Journal of Business Venturing*, 16(1), pp. 51-75

Nawata K. (1994): "Estimation of sample selection bias models by the maximum likelihood estimator and Heckman's two-step estimator". *Economic Letters*, 45, pp. 33-40

Noel, T.W. (2001): "Effects of entrepreneurial education on intent to open a business". *Frontiers of Entrepreneurship Research, Babson Conference Proceedings*, www.babson.edu/entrep/fer

NSI (2006) "*Education in the Republic of Bulgaria 2006*". Sofia

Parker, S.C., 1996. "A time-series model of self-employment under uncertainty". *Economica,* 63 (3), pp. 459-475

Peterman, N. and Kennedy, J. (2003): "Enterprise education: Influencing students' perceptions of entrepreneurship". *Entrepreneurship Theory and Practice*, 28(2), pp. 129-144

Raijman, R. (2001): "Determinants of entrepreneurial intentions: Mexican immigrants in Chicago". *Journal of Socio-Economics*, 30, pp. 393-411

Robinson, P., Stimpson, P., Huefner, J., and Hunt, H. (1991): "An attitude approach to the prediction of entrepreneurship". *Entrepreneurship Theory and Practice,* 16(4), pp. 13-31

Routamaa, V., Hautala, T., and Rissanen, A. (2004): "Hunting for female entrepreneurs: Entrepreneurial capacity and gender". *Proceedings from 2004 ICSB World Conference*

Scherer, R., Adams, J., Carley, S., and Wiebe, F. (1989): "Role model performance effects on development of entrepreneurial career preference". *Entrepreneurship Theory and Practice,* 13(3), pp. 53-71

Shapero, A. and Sokol, L. (1982): "The social dimensions of entrepreneurship". In C. Kent, D. Sexton, and K. Vesper (eds.): *Encyclopaedia of Entrepreneurship*, 72-90. Englewood Cliffs, NJ: Prentice Hall

Schwarz, E., Almer-Jarz, D., and Wdowiak M. (2005): "A structural model of entrepreneurial intent among students: findings from Austria". *Proceedings from RENT XIX Conference,* Naples, Italy, November

Smallbone, D., Welter, F., Isakova, N., and Slonimski, A. (2001): "The Contribution of Small and Medium Enterprises to Economic Development in Ukraine and Belarus: Some Policy Perspectives". *MOCT-MOST*, 11, pp. 253-273

Sutton, S. (1998): "Explaining and predicting intentions and behavior: How well are we doing?". *Journal of Applied Social Psychology, 28*, pp. 1318-1339

Tegtmeier, S. (2006): "Entrepreneurship and the „Theory of Planned Behavior" - empirical Implications for promoting students' entrepreneurial activity". *Proceedings from RENT XX Conference, Brussels (Belgium), November, 2006*

Tkachev A. and Kolvereid L., (1999): "Self-employment intentions among Russian students", *Entrepreneurship and Regional Development*, 11, pp. 269 - 280

Varela, R. and Jimenez, J.E. (2001): "The effect of entrepreneurship education in the universities of Cali". *Frontiers of Entrepreneurship Research, Babson Conference Proceedings*, www.babson.edu/entrep/fer

Veciana, J. (1998): "Teoria y Politica de la Creacion de Empresas". Paper presented at *"Jornada dels Economistes"*, Barcelona

Veciana, J. (1999): "Creacion de empresas como programa de investigacion cientifica". *Revista Europea de Direcciron y Economia de la Empresa*, 8(3), pp. 11–36

Veciana, J. M., Aponte, M. and Urbano, D., (2005): "University students' attitudes towards entrepreneurship: a two countries comparison". *International Entrepreneurship and Management Journal*, 1, pp. 165-182

Verheul, I., Thurik, R. and Grilo, I. (2006): "Determinants of self-employment preference and realization of women and men in Europe and the United States". *RENT XX*, Brussels (Belgium), November, 2006

Data Mining –
Overview of the Technology and the Potential for Adoption in the Bulgarian Banking Industry

Diana Boyadzhieva
(Sofia University "St. Kliment Ohridski", Bulgaria)

1. Introduction

During the last decade, the Bulgarian banking industry has undergone enormous changes in the political and social life of the country, in the regulatory and financial system, in the enabling technology and communication media that led to tremendous changes in the way the business is conducted. The intensity of the business in the new global economy and the increase of the number of sources of information are responsible for the huge amount of data that should be monitored. Furthermore, during recent years image and other types of data with complex structures were added to the usual types of numerical, textual and time-stamped data. The advances in the hardware and software technology made possible the collection and storage of all data potentially interesting for an organization, in particular for banks. However, the volume of these data usually grows at such speed that it is beyond the capability of the human brain or of the traditional computerized analytical tools to analyze these raw data. The volume of the data by its own has little value if they were not transformed into information and then into useful knowledge for the bank. The ability to quickly and effectively convert data into comprehensible information has become the main determinant of competitive success (John et al, 2001:1). Thus the organizations that seek to improve their decision-making, image, operation or quality of service should develop a holistic information technology infrastructure and a comprehensive Business Intelligence (BI) system.

BI systems are referred to as systems that provide consolidated and organized data for better business decisions as well as help to uncover and leverage those business advantages that will lead the company to the competitive edge (Reinschmidt et al., 2000:4).

Enterprises that decide to organize themselves around the need to develop BI skills could equip parts or – preferably – all aspects of their business with the tools to perform BI. The adoption of BI tools could be realized in series of steps that will drive the organization to progress through the different levels of BI maturity. A schematic presentation of these maturity levels and the associated BI-related organizational goals and the BI-delivered output was developed by the autor and is shown in figure 1.

Figure 1: BI Maturity Levels

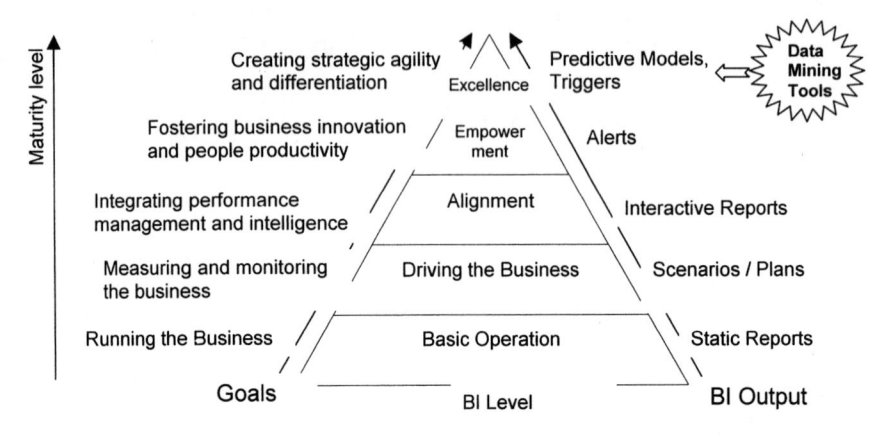

Goals	BI Level	BI Output
Creating strategic agility and differentiation	Excellence	Predictive Models, Triggers — Data Mining Tools
Fostering business innovation and people productivity	Empowerment	Alerts
Integrating performance management and intelligence	Alignment	Interactive Reports
Measuring and monitoring the business	Driving the Business	Scenarios / Plans
Running the Business	Basic Operation	Static Reports

(Maturity level increases from bottom to top)

As the focus of this paper is on the Bulgarian banking industry, we have to note that the necessity for adoption of BI tools is already recognized by most of the banks (D. Boyadzhieva 2006:10). Although the state of adoption is different, all the banks work towards the implementation of their BI projects.

During the last years the role and importance of data mining (DM) as a strategic business tool for BI has increased a lot. However, as DM is the most sophisticated BI tool, often it is not provided in the BI platforms and enterprise BI suites but in separate data-mining workbenches (Buytendijk et al., 2005:18). That is the reason why, when an organization seeks to adopt DM, it should not expect to obtain it as another BI tool of the BI suite but devote targeted resources and a separate project. Banks are usually among the early adopters of the DM technology and it is interesting to investigate the aptitude towards its implementation in the Bulgarian banking industry.

As in Bulgaria the usage of DM in a business context is just emerging, the technology is still unknown to most of the business practitioners or is known just on an inceptive level. Thus, first in the paper a short introduction into the subject is presented, providing an overview of the core concepts and techniques. Then a few of the diverse examples for usage of DM in the banking industry follow. In the last part of the paper a SWOT analysis of the current environment in the Bulgarian banks is presented. The goal is to assess the prevailing aptitude towards the adoption of data mining and the appropriateness of the moment.

2. The technology within scope

2.1. Definitions

DM is a relatively new discipline, but a lot of research in the area is done and it continues to attract scientists from different fields and practitioners from different industries. As a result a lot of definitions are available in literature and only a few are provided below:
- Statistics at scale and speed (Pregibon, 2005:1).
- Data mining is the process of exploration and analysis by automatic or semiautomatic means, of large quantities of data in order to discover meaningful patterns and rules (Berry et al., 2000:7).
- Data mining involves the analysis of data to discover previously unknown relationships that provide useful information (Chan et al., 2002:56).
- Data mining is the process of discovering meaningful new correlations, patterns and trends by sifting through large amounts of data stored in repositories, using pattern recognition technologies as well as statistical and mathematical techniques (Gartner Group, on-line glossary).

2.2. The DM Environment

DM tasks could be executed on any large data set but the results most probably will not be sound and trustworthy. As the data are the main resource, required for the DM, the questions
- where the data come from,
- how they look like, and
- whether they should be preprocessed somehow,

have to be considered first.

The data for the DM could come from everywhere – from the myriad information systems throughout the organization, they could be purchased from external data providers, shared in cooperation with partners, shared within the respective industry or may be publicly available. These are different heterogeneous sources and the data are potentially in different formats and quality. On the other hand, the volume of these data usually grows at tremendous speed. The size of the world's data is estimated to be doubling every 20 months (Frawley et al., 1992:57). The storage and maintenance of these constantly increasing data in an enterprise could be in a database or a data warehouse. The importance of the data warehouse as a basis for the DM tasks is already recognized (John et al., 2001:2). To clarify this importance we could refer to a definition that is directly related to the concept of diverse data discussed in this paragraph: A data warehouse is a single, complete and consistent store of data, obtained from a variety of sources and made available to end users

in a way that they can understand and use the data in a business context (Ma et al., 2000:125). Main principles of the data warehousing are the data cleaning and data transformation which could be viewed as an important preprocessing step for the DM. Furthermore, the data warehouse is usually equipped with tools for on-line analytical processing (OLAP). These tools provide interactive analysis of multidimensional data and facilitate effective data mining (J. Han et al., 2001:39). It is generally believed that there is a symbiotic relationship between the activity of DM and the data warehouse, and DM is one of the major applications of a data warehouse (Brachman et al. 1996:47). However, even the construction of a first version of an active data warehouse is a task that requires a lot of time, financial and work-force resources. Typically, the longer a data warehouse is in use, the more it evolves, as well as the employed tools for analysis. In this context, the tools could be categorized into (J. Han et al., 2001:93):
- access and retrieval tools;
- database reporting tools;
- data analysis tools;
- data mining tools.

The data mining package is the most powerful of these tools and is usually adopted at a later stage of maturity of a data warehouse. In general, the banking industry has been the leader in the use of data warehouses (Gupta, 1997:1), and therefore, considering the competion, for a bank it is reasonable to be among the first ones to adopt DM as well. But the initial expectation is that most of the Bulgarian banks do not use DM at the moment. Nevertheless, most of the Bulgarian banks have recently elaborated and started their DW projects (Boyadzhieva D., 2006:5) and it is interesting to explore the maturity of their environment for adoption of the DM technology. However, the data warehousing phase may consume 50% to 80% of the total data mining effort (A. C. John et al., 2001:2).

2.3. The DM Process

As with the definition of the DM, there are differences in the literature about the suggested steps within the data mining process. Actually, the tasks in the process are similar, but the authors present them in different steps. To keep the exposition shorter but informative, I have developed the presentation of the steps in the DM process as a flow chart which is shown in figure 2. The flow chart is composed on the basis of the framework for a DM process suggested by Berry and Linoff (2000:39-58).

Figure 2: The DM Process

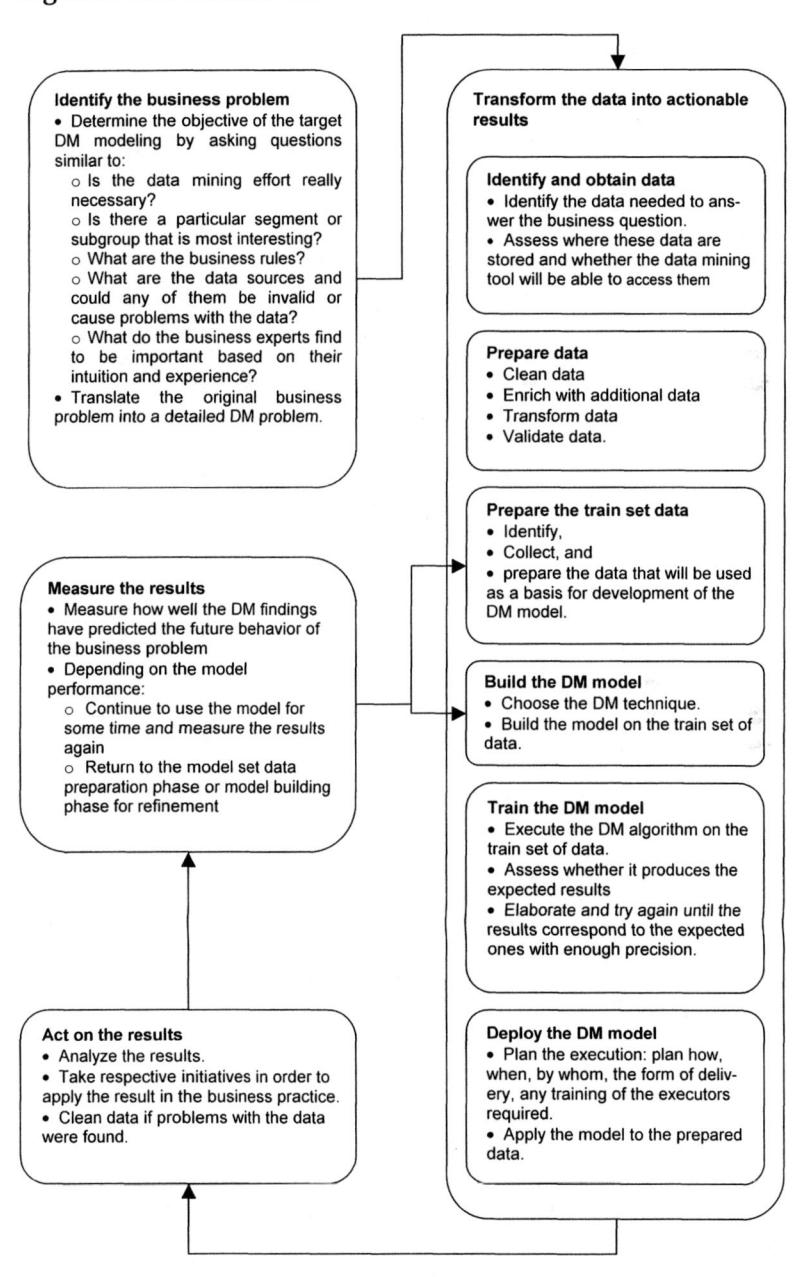

Identify the business problem
- Determine the objective of the target DM modeling by asking questions similar to:
  - Is the data mining effort really necessary?
  - Is there a particular segment or subgroup that is most interesting?
  - What are the business rules?
  - What are the data sources and could any of them be invalid or cause problems with the data?
  - What do the business experts find to be important based on their intuition and experience?
- Translate the original business problem into a detailed DM problem.

Transform the data into actionable results

Identify and obtain data
- Identify the data needed to answer the business question.
- Assess where these data are stored and whether the data mining tool will be able to access them

Prepare data
- Clean data
- Enrich with additional data
- Transform data
- Validate data.

Prepare the train set data
- Identify,
- Collect, and
- prepare the data that will be used as a basis for development of the DM model.

Measure the results
- Measure how well the DM findings have predicted the future behavior of the business problem
- Depending on the model performance:
  - Continue to use the model for some time and measure the results again
  - Return to the model set data preparation phase or model building phase for refinement

Build the DM model
- Choose the DM technique.
- Build the model on the train set of data.

Train the DM model
- Execute the DM algorithm on the train set of data.
- Assess whether it produces the expected results
- Elaborate and try again until the results correspond to the expected ones with enough precision.

Act on the results
- Analyze the results.
- Take respective initiatives in order to apply the result in the business practice.
- Clean data if problems with the data were found.

Deploy the DM model
- Plan the execution: plan how, when, by whom, the form of delivery, any training of the executors required.
- Apply the model to the prepared data.

All the steps in the process will be executed more effectively if the DM task is managed as a project. We will not focus on the project management practices but will note that the success of the task depends considerably on the way the execution of the process steps is managed. As the DM project is a cross-departmental and cross-disciplinary one, it is crucial to clearly determine in advance the roles and responsibilities of the project leader, business experts, DM experts and IT experts that will take part in the project.

It is important to emphasize that the steps of a DM process are not necessarily executed in a sequential order. The process is adaptive, i.e.: the next step in the sequence often depends on the outcomes associated with the preceding step. The process is also iterative, which means that the results obtained in one step might cause a return to one or more of the previous steps. Therefore the arrows on figure 2 show just a simple case of a sequential execution of the phases. Furthermore, the model performance usually degrades over time, because the models perform less well the further they get from the set of data used to create the model (Berry et al., 2000: 58-59).

2.4. The DM Tasks and Techniques

The origins of the DM techniques come from the fields of statistics, machine learning and database theory. As this is an introductory overview, only a short presentation of the DM techniques is given here. Moreover, the target audience of this paper is rather composed of business practitioners, who could not be interested in the details of the algorithms. However, in order to be able to decide when a given technique is to be chosen, at least a basic understanding of the different data mining tasks, as well as of the most important data mining algorithms is necessary.

First we have to make clearer the difference between the concepts "task" and "technique".

- The task comes from the respective business sphere where the DM is applied. The task is the formulation of the business problem that is to be addressed with DM.
- The technique is the algorithm that is used to build the DM model.

The DM could be classified according to the task or the technique. The overview which is presented here follows a popular categorization according to the different tasks given by Berry et al. (2000: 8):

  o **Classification.** Classification consists of examining the features of a newly presented object and assigning it to one of a predefined set of classes (Berry et al., 2004:9). This is the most common mining task (John et al, 2001:3). It is a task of finding the function to map the records from the mined data to one of several discrete classes.

- **Estimation.** The result of classification is a discrete value, mapped to one of a finite number of preliminary defined classes, like, for instance, a loan could be mapped to one of the following classes: consumer loan, mortgage loan, loan with deposit guaranty, loan with guarantee, etc. The estimation deals with continuously valued outcomes. Based on the input data, the estimation comes up with a value for some unknown continuous variable such as income, height, or credit card balance (Berry et al., 2004:9).
- **Prediction.** Another term for this type of tasks is forecasting. In a prediction task, the past and current values of the studied variable are known. The task is to build a DM model that finds patterns of the available values and is able to use these patterns in order to predict future values of the target variable or to classify the records according to the predicted future behavior. For instance, it might be useful to predict which customers are likely to respond to a marketing campaign.
- **Affinity Grouping.** An alternative name of this type of tasks is "association rule mining". The task of affinity grouping is to determine which things "go together" (Berry et al., 2000:10). Association rule analysis finds interesting association or correlation relationships among a large set of data items (Han et al., 2001:225). The associations discovered are in the form "attribute – value". The information supplied is which of these associations occur frequently in the studied data set and thus form an affinity group. The proverbial example is the one with the market basket analysis – the task of determining what things go together in a shopping cart at the supermarket.
- **Clustering.** Clustering is the task of segmenting a heterogeneous population into a number of more homogeneous subgroups or clusters (Berry et al., 2000:11). According to Han et al. (2001:25), clusters of objects are formed so that objects within a cluster have high similarity in comparison to one another, but are very dissimilar to objects in other clusters. The difference between clustering and classification is that in clustering there are no predefined classes and no example values. The objects are grouped together based on self-similarity (Berry et al., 2000:11). The clusters are formed dynamically based on the principle to maximize intracluster similarity and to minimize intercluster similarity. The typical task for clustering is to find the best groupings of customers for a target marketing campaign.
- **Description and profiling.** Up to now the tasks that were discussed required some form of prediction to produce the result. For

this reason they are called *predictive* DM tasks. The *descriptive* DM implies tasks to describe the data set in a concise and generalized manner and to present interesting properties of the data (Han et al., 2001:179). According to Berry et al. (2000:11), the purpose of this type of DM is to describe simply what is going on in a complicated database in a way that increases our understanding of the people, products or processes that produced the data in the first place. Descriptive DM techniques enable the creation of clear and understandable interpretation of the knowledge mined from data in the form of graphs, formulas, rules and tables.

Since the focus of this paper is not on DM techniques, an overview of the different algorithms is missed out. A concise overview of the main DM techniques is given by Lee and Siau (2001:41-46). Actually, it is not compulsory to know how a given technique works exactly in order to use it. A basic understanding of the different algorithms gives the knowledge that a business practitioner needs to take the decision which technique is suitable for a respective DM task. The contemporary DM toolsets all provide a friendly graphical user interface that eases the creation of the models. So, the actual building of the model is the least time-consuming part of the DM because it is nowadays as simple as point and click (Berry et al., 2000: 54). Table 1 is shown as a help for the decision which algorithm could be chosen in order to perform a given task (adapted from Lachev T., 2005:227).

Table 1: DM tasks and respective techniques (adapted from T. Lachev (2005)).

Task \ Technique	Decision Trees	Clustering	Association	Naïve Bayes	Newral Network	Time Series
Classification	✔	✔		✔	✔	
Segmentation		✔			✔	
Association	✔		✔			
Regression	✔	✔				
Forecasting						✔

3. Applications of Data Mining in the banking industry

Data are the organizational challenge of the new millennium (John et al, 2001:4). Most organizations are piled up with data, but only a few extract efficiently, effectively, accurately and thoroughly information from these data. This "information gap" is addressed by a lot of contemporary techniques for analysis but in many cases only the data mining could sift out the enormous amount of data and deliver informative insight. DM has proved the value of its practical applications by significantly adding to the bottom line of many companies – for a pity, most of them out of Bulgaria. DM could improve existing models of business problems by finding additional information and patterns that were unknown before or were discovered by some other form of analysis.

The banks which successfully adopt DM could utilize effectively this technology by applying it to areas like marketing, risk management, fraud detection, customer acquisition and retention. Exemplar applications in each of these areas would expand the text of the paper a lot and thus the following examples highlight just some of the most widespread usages in the Customer Relationship Management (CRM).

The banking industry collects customer data through all the possible contact points and beyond doubt it has one of the riches and largest databases of customer related information covering demographical data, transactional data, credit card usage patterns, and so on. As banking is a service industry, the conduction of strong and effective CRM is a critical success factor. Although the promises of how CRM can improve the performance of business are many, the practical guidelines on how to design and implement CRM successfully are few, and practitioners have been struggling because of that (A. Lindgreen et al., 2005:136-137).

For a better understanding of their existing and prospective customers, banks need to invest their resources to fulfill some key factors for success of the CRM initiative. SAS points out six business imperatives that any financial institution seeking to adopt a customer relationship model should consider (SAS, 2001:5-7):

- Create a customer-focused organization and Infrastructure.
- Gain an accurate picture of your customer categories.
- Accurately assess the lifetime value of your customers.
- Maximize the profitability of each customer relationship.
- Understand how to attract and keep your best customers.
- Maximize the rate of return on marketing campaigns.

Data mining is a technology that could support the fulfillment of each of these requirements. Some of the DM applications relevant to CRM in the banking industry are: targeted marketing, attrition prediction/churn analysis, fraud detection, market segmentation, cross sales improvement.

3.1. Targeted marketing

The business problem here is that usually the list of prospects for direct marketing campaigns consists of too many persons and the costs of mailing all of them will be too high. Some of the questions that could be posed are: Who has the highest propensity to become a client? Which customer characteristic is the strongest indicator for the most profitable customers?

Data mining could be used to identify the most promising respondents combining demographic and geographic data with data on past transactions of former customers or externally provided data on purchasing behavior in the past. Marketing professionals could utilize pre-established DM models. They could select from a list of such models and apply the model to selected target customers identified by using the campaign management system. Then the scoring is executed within the DM product, and the scored file is returned to the marketing specialist, providing enough information for further refinement of the target-marketing campaign. Moreover, additional DM work could be performed to identify the best time of the day, the best season, and the best media for marketing to the targeted group. The benefit will be not only a decrease in the campaign costs, but also a better customer response rate.

3.2. Cross-Selling and Up-Selling

Cross-selling or up-selling involves selling products to existing customers by taking into consideration their previous purchases to analyze what kind of products should be offered and in which time, in order to have the highest customer propensity to buy. The marketing specialists in the banking industry could put DM into harness by applying prebuilt models to reveal the different product affinities. As a result of the data mining, associations between the selection of one banking product and of another may be discovered: whether they are sold at the same time or separately, the chronology of the sales, etc. Then profiles of customers with a similar behavior could be derived and the respective group would be identified as most probable buyers of the associated products.

For example, banks could apply DM to the segment of customers who hold numerous accounts or lines of credit, in order to identify the path they went from simple checking and savings accounts to loans and home mortgages. Then the discovered characteristics and associations could be applied to other customers in order to determine who are most likely to follow the same path – they will be good candidates for cross-selling and up-selling.

4. Methodology of the survey

For my own empirical research, a questionnaire and a project description were sent by e-mail to half of the Bulgarian banks with an invitation to participate in the survey. The survey consists of two parts. During the first part of the survey unstructured interviews were held with the upper management of the IT departments of five banks, which were interested to participate in the survey. The paper in hand is the pilot paper, based on the data gathered during these interviews. The method of unstructured interview was selected as it was appropriate for conveyance during the initial presentation of the project goals to the IT managers. The interviewee had to be on the middle or upper level of management in order to be able to give relevant replies to questions concerning the current state of the business intelligence activities in the bank as well as to questions related to the strategic initiatives and goals.

The second part of the survey is conducted through a structured questionnaire, handed in to the upper IT management of the banks. Some of these questionnaires are still due to be returned to the researcher and will be analyzed in a future paper. For the second part of the survey, the questionnaire method was chosen, as it is an appropriate method to present the variety of questions and possible answers that highlight most thoroughly the existing status of bank data warehousing and business intelligence environment.

The survey covers 20% of the commercial banks in Bulgaria with an international banking license registered at the Bulgarian National Bank (BNB). There are banks from the first group of banks (composed of the five biggest banks, ranked on the basis of their total assets) and banks from the second group (composed of the rest of Bulgarian banks), according to the classification of the BNB (BNB, 2007). The third group of banks which includes foreign banks that have only branches in Bulgaria is not covered. The investigated group of banks forms a considerable part of all commercial banks in Bulgaria and thus the assumption might be justified that the results of the survey could be valid for the whole banking industry. The exact names are not mentioned due to request from some of the banks. The interviews were conducted during October 2007.

5. SWOT Analysis

The following SWOT analysis contains a study of the major internal and external factors that are assessed as strengths or weaknesses and respectively as opportunities or threats for the strategic option that the Bulgarian banks face – to implement data mining as a BI tool or to postpone the initiative. The analysis could be used as a benchmark by a bank to evaluate its own environment and to develop impression to what extent the respective moment in time is appropriate for the adoption of DM technology.

Strengths	Weaknesses
• The existing infrastructure - most of the banks have an integrated data environment and a data warehouse that is in development phase or in exploitation. • A large set of data, collected through different sources and touch points. • Awareness of the benefits of using the DM technology. • Strong know-how and experience in the areas where business problems could be addressed by DM. • CRM is a core business strategy for banks and it will serve as a driver for the adoption of DM. • Change management is another core management practice that is used in the Bulgarian banks and it will serve as a driver for adoption of DM. • Organizational culture – the employees have a positive attitude to the new technologies and usually they are ready to broaden their knowledge and skills. • Recent experience in the management of related projects (the data warehouse project).	• Lack of strong supporters - the necessity of DM is often unrecognized by the top-level management. • Not all the banks have a data warehouse that is brought into exploitation. • Unwillingness to start a new project could exist due to numerous current IT projects and related timescales, deadlines and pressures that should be met. • Lack of tools for data quality/metadata management. • Most IT professionals are not familiar with the DM issues. • Most of the business users are not familiar with the benefits of DM analysis and could not act as advocates of an initiative for adoption of the technology. • Often there is absence of good project management capabilities and/or practices.
Opportunities	**Threats**
• Dramatic drop in costs of storage hardware that makes the maintenance of huge databases affordable. • Drop in costs of DM software and availability of cheap but powerful packages. • Maturity of the DM technology and continuing research and development. • Availability of multiple vendors of DM workbenches. • Availability of applications focused on the financial industry DM. • Best practices available. • Increase in number and type of the customer touch-points – it leads not only to increase in quantity of the collected data but also to an increase of the informative value. • The presence of strong competition in the Bulgarian banking sector will serve as a driver for adoption of the DM technology. • The necessity to detect fraudulent attempts also will serve as a driver for adoption. • The constantly changing environment also will be a driver for adoption. • The stability in the Bulgarian banking sector is a favorable economic environment which usually leads to an increase of investments not only in operational infrastructure but also in systems that will give qualitative supplements.	• Too small numbers of external DM consultants with experience in Bulgarian DM projects. • Too small numbers of references from Bulgarian companies to consultants that have adopted DM successfully– this could harden the choice of a consultant. • There are no established external providers of DM services in Bulgaria whose DM analyses could be used as a benchmark for the internal DM capabilities of a bank. • The relatively high prices of the DM work-benches and the pricing structure.

5.1 Strengths

The existing infrastructure is regarded as a strength of the Bulgarian banks as most of them have integrated their data environment or have on-going projects for integration of the different systems. Most of the banks have also initiated data warehouse development projects. Some of these projects have already reached the phase of exploitation. As a data warehouse is the best source of information for a DM task, those banks that have it in place (now or soon) have the priority to deal with more reliable data and will prepare data sets for the DM task faster and easier.

The data that are collected through the different sources and touch points (bank-branches, Internet-banking, POS terminals, ATMs, etc.) are of an enormous amount. They could be used to form very large sets of data for DM tasks. A large data set usually increases the accuracy of DM, so this is a strong condition.

Although in most of the banks the IT staff is not familiar with DM as a technology, it is aware of the benefits of using the DM technology and could present those benefits to the management and to beneficiary departments. An adequate presentation of the benefits to the upper management, coupled with the assessment of the organizational readiness to adopt the technology is required as it will determine the green or red light for the project initiation.

Beneficiary departments of the DM results will be the marketing, financial, planning departments, etc. They have a strong know-how and experience in their own functional area where different business problems could be addressed by DM. This proficiency is a key factor for the development of good DM models as well as for the maximization of the knowledge gained during the model development step.

Customer relationship development is a core business strategy for the Bulgarian banks and it will serve as a driver for adoption of DM. A number of CRM systems exist and are being implemented in Bulgarian banks (N. Krysteva 2007). But only those banks that have integrated DM tools also will perform the most powerful analytics and will utilize the CRM systems to their full advantage.

Change management is another core management practice in the Bulgarian banks. It will also serve as a driver for the adoption of DM as this technology is one of the best that could be utilized to achieve real time analytics even in ad-hoc situations.

The organizational culture is regarded as a strength because the employees' readiness to use new technologies and to broaden their skills is considerable, no matter whether a result of internal or external motivation. Furthermore, most of the employees in the banks are young people that have grown up around constantly changing technologies and are accustomed to learning how to use a new technology.

Due to the current work on the data warehouse project[1], the staff has gained managerial and technical experience that will be favorable for a DM project. The IT managers are aware of the preliminary requirements and the potential threats so the implementation of a DM project will be done more efficiently and more effectively.

5.2. Weaknesses

The interviews revealed that in most of the surveyed banks a lack of strong top-management support for a DM initiative can be observed. The necessity of DM is not yet recognized by the top-level management, which explains the fact that no resources are yet allocated for a DM project. If some initiatives exist, they are rather fruits of individual interests in the area.

Some of the banks have a data warehouse that is already brought into exploitation, but most of them are still in some earlier phase of development or are even in the beginning of a data warehouse project. This means that in the recent future many of the banks will concentrate their resources on a data warehouse development and the DM adoption will be postponed.

The technical/data infrastructure that is in place in the banks is one that can boggle the average mind. Its on-going maintenance and improvement could absorb all resources, including those dedicated to the development of a BI environment – even in banks with big financial power and numerous skillful IT employees. Unwillingness to start a new project is possible due to numerous current IT projects and timescales, deadlines and pressures related to them.

Most of the banks lack comprehensive tools as well as an explicit strategy for metadata and data quality management. This fact will harden the execution of tasks during each step of a DM process. If metadata and data quality management are brought to a more mature state, each DM project will require less efforts, will deliver better results more rapidly and will boost its worth in the business and senior management's eyes by increasing its ROI (Return on Investment).

Most IT professionals in the Bulgarian banks are unfamiliar with the DM issues yet. There are some initiatives for acquisition of DM related knowledge but not as a focused goal of a clearly determined group of specialists designated as the "Data Mining Group".

Most of the business users are not familiar with the benefits of DM analysis and could not act as advocates of an initiative for the adoption

---

[1] One data warehouse project is regarded as a current one, because even though it is already in the exploitation phase for a long time, it cannot be considered as finalized. The project continues with on-going maintenance and next drafts.

of the technology. If the IT group presents the benefits of DM to the business analysts, they could act together for a justification of the necessity of a DM initiative in the bank and assure the top-management their support.

The recent experience of the banks in the management of their data warehouse project (which is closely related to a DM project) was considered earlier in this analysis as a plus but often there is an absence of good project management capabilities and/or practices which is definitely a weakness. DM is a project that requires strengths of several departments and often of an external consultant as well, so the strong project management know-how is a key requirement for success of the project.

5.3. Opportunities

During the last years the price of data storage media has dropped significantly and in the same time the possible capacity of a single hard disk device has increased tremendously. As a result, the maintenance of huge databases became cheaper and easier. Even if an organization does not have a data warehouse but possesses a comprehensive set of data, it could still organize it for use in DM tasks.

The tendency for a decrease of prices is also present in the DM software industry. Fortunately, it is coupled with an increase of the functionalities of the software packages, with improvement of the user interface, as well as of the compatibility with other applications and heterogeneous sources.

Another important opportunity that would favor the adoption of DM is the continuing research in the area and the significant maturity of the DM market. The technology is on the slope of enlightenment according to the Hype Cycle for Business Intelligence and Data Warehousing prepared by Gartner (Buytendijk F. et al., 2005). New vendors continuously emerge and offer comprehensive DM work-benches, so a variety of choices are available for the companies that plan to deploy DM.

The competition among the DM vendors led to the emergence of DM applications focused to different specific tasks or industries, including the financial industry. Most of the vendors now are niche players (Herschel G., 2007:7) which means they work not only on the technology side of their software but also on the development of industry-specific functionalities as well as capabilities to make the results of the analysis easily available to the respective beneficiaries, such as senior executives, functional managers, sales agents, etc.

Best practices are available and could be used as a benchmark and guide during the adoption of the DM technology. Up to the moment of survey, however, there are no case studies for Bulgarian companies describing the local adoption challenges.

The variety of customer touch-points (POS terminals, mobile devices, Internet), the automatic data capturing of the transactions in many of these touch-points and the increase in the frequency of the transactions lead to an increasing rate of data volume expansion. However, the data collected often increase not only in quantity but also in their informative value. The new touch-points often provide additional information for the transaction that could be mined.

The presence of strong competition in the Bulgarian banking sector will serve as a driver for the adoption of the DM technology. In order to achieve a competitive advantage, in general the banks try to catch every opportunity. Those that appraise the benefits of DM usage and adopt it first will manage to reach the competitive edge.

The necessity to detect fraudulent attempts as well as the constantly changing external environment will also serve as drivers for adoption. Provision of secure transactions and in the same time of maximum flexibility is a goal for every bank which could be strongly supported by the adoption of DM.

The growth of the Bulgarian economy and the expectations for further stabilization and growth of the Bulgarian banking industry form a favorable environment for investments not only in the operational infrastructure but also in systems that will give qualitative suplements. Moreover, in a relatively stable economy the prediction results of the DM tasks are more accurate.

5.4. Threats

Currently the number of external DM consultants with experience in Bulgarian DM projects is too small. During the elaboration of a DM project a serious analysis of the local environment where the models are built is necessary. When a consultant company does not have experience in local projects, it should rely on analysis developed by the organization implementing the DM. If the consultant is a Bulgarian firm, most probably it will not have extensive experience in DM projects. In both cases the early state of spread of the DM technology among Bulgarian companies could cause potential threats for a DM project. The small number of references to consultants from Bulgarian companies that have already adopted DM successfully could harden the choice of a consultant and is also considered as a hampering factor.

Currently, there are no established external providers of DM services in Bulgaria, which could sell DM project assessments or custom DM analyses to be used as a benchmark for the internal DM capabilities of a company. Such externally provided DM services would be beneficial not only as a source of comparison but also as an alternative during the development of internal DM capabilities.

The relatively high prices of DM work-benches and rather, the pricing structure could be a threatening factor. Some of the vendors offer unpredictable pricing schemes and moreover, there could be a lack of alignment between the pricing and the value a company has received. The assessment of software, its pricing schemes and the possibility for acquisition of a DM vendor by some other company should be evaluated carefully.

6. Conclusion

The development of the banking sector in Bulgaria gone through significant changes during the last years, due to the restructuring of the industry, changes of ownership, consolidations and regulatory changes. The accession to the European Union has stimulated the economic growth of Bulgaria and was another factor for the establishment of sustainable stabilization in the banking industry. The expectations are for further continual growth of the sector that will exceed the growth rate of the GDP of the country. However, these positive trends are coupled with the expectation of an increase of the competition among the banks. To attain a competitive advantage, the banks must improve every aspect of their business functioning: their management practices, customer relationships, infrastructure, and organizational culture.

The short overview of the data mining (DM) as a technology for analysis presented in this paper, as well as the few examples for applications were given in order to enhance a clear comprehension for the wide scope and benefits that are associated with DM. The omnipresent opinion in literature is that DM should be a core BI tool for the banking industry. So it is not a question of "whether" it should be but rather of "when" it will be adopted in Bulgarian banks too. The SWOT analysis of the current internal and external environment factors that are related to the DM adoption shows significant prevalence of the positive ones. The current IT-related attempts of the banks do not include DM and are concentrated mainly on the integration and data warehousing projects, but in fact these efforts will overcome a lot of the negative factors described in the SWOT analysis. As a conclusion we could state that the use of DM in the Bulgarian banking industry could be pervasive. The technology represents a fundamental shift from the conventional information systems and those that manage to apply it first will attain significant advantage over their competitors.

References

Berry M., Linoff G., (2000): "Mastering Data Mining – The Art and Science of Customer Relationship Management", John Wiley and Son Inc.

M., Linoff G., (2004): "Data Mining Techniques for Marketing, Sales, and Customer Relationship Management", Wiley Publishing, Inc.

BNB, October, 2007
http://www.bnb.bg/bnb/home.nsf/fsWebIndexBul?OpenFrameset

Boyadzhieva D., (2006): Data Warehousing and Business Intelligence in the Spotlight – the Case for the Bulgarian Banks, Annual of the St. Kliment Ohridski University, Faculty of Economics and Business Administration (under print)

Brachman, R. J., T. Khabaza, Kloesgen W., Piatetsky-Shapiro G., Simoudis E., (1996): Mining Business Databases, Communications of the ACM, vol. 39, no. 11, pp. 42-48

Buytendijk F., Friedman T., Hostmann B., et al. (2005): Hype Cycle for Business Intelligence and Data Warehousing, Gartner Research, ID Number: G00127569

Chan C., Lewis B., (2002): IT and the organisation. A basic primer on data mining. Information Systems Management, Volume 19, Issue 4, pp. 56 – 61.

Pregibon D. (2005): Institute for Operations Research and the Management Sciences, Roundtable, http://roundtable.informs.org/public-access/min051a.htm

Frawley, W., Piatetsky-Shapiro G., Matheus C., (1992): Knowledge discovery in databases: An overview, AI Magasine, AAAI Press, pp. 57-70.

Gupta, V. R., (2002): An Introduction to Data Warehousing, http://systemservices.com/dwintro.asp

Han J., Kamber M., (2001): "Data Mining: Concepts and Techniques", Morgan Kaufman Publishers, 39

Herschel G.,(2007), Magic Quadrant for Customer Data Mining, Gartner Inc., RAS Core Research Note G00145685

John, A.C., Robert, W., Omar, E.M.K., Mehnaz, A. (2001): "*Mind Your Business by Mining Your Data*", Sam Advance Management Journal, pp. 1-4

Krysteva N, (2007): "The Bulgarian market of business software – the quantity accumulations are followed by quality changes", CIO Magazine, issue 11, 2007, http://www.cio.bg/?call=USE~home;&page=paper&n=1672, (in Bulgarian)

Lachev T., (2005): "Applied Microsoft Analysis Services 2005 and Microsoft Business Intelligence Platform, Prologika Press

Lee S., Siau K., (2001): "A review of data mining systems", Industrial Management & Data Systems, 101/1, MCB University Press, pp. 41-46

Lindgreen A., Antioco M., (2005): Customer relationship management: the case of a European bank, Marketing Intelligence & Planning, Vol. 23 No. 2, pp. 136-154.

Ma C., Chou D., Yen D., (2000): Data warehousing technology assessment and management. Industrial Management and Data Systems. Volume 100, Issue 3/4, MCB University Press, pp. 125 – 135.

Reinschmidt, J., Francoise, A. (2000): Business intelligence certification quide. IBM, International Technical Support Organization, http://www.redbooks.ibm.com

SAS, (2001): Customer Relationship Management in Banking – Key Challenges Facing Banking Executives, A SAS White Paper, SAS Institute Inc, pp. 5-7.

Chapter two:

EUROPEANIZATION AND ASPECTS OF
EUROPEAN NATIONAL ECONOMIES

THE EVOLUTION OF THE GROSS DOMESTIC PRODUCT OF ALL SECTORS OF THE GREEK ECONOMY SINCE 1963

ANASTASIA PARIS / IOANNIS PATINIOTIS
(EUROPEAN UNIVERSITY ATHENS, GREECE)

1. Introduction

Economic growth is calculated in terms of an increase in the size of a nation's economy. A broad estimate of an economy's size is its output. The best known measure of economic output is the Gross Domestic Product (GDP).

The GDP of a country is defined as the market value of all final goods and services produced within the geographic boundaries of this country – regardless of the producer's nationality – in a given period of time. Furthermore, it is considered the sum of value added at every stage of production of all final goods and services produced within a country in a given period of time (NZIER 2007).

Firstly, this article will look at the contribution of six sectors of activity to Greece's GDP across the period 1963-2005. These sectors are: (1) Agriculture, Forestry, Fishing; (2) Mining, Quarrying; (3) Manufacturing; (4) Electricity, Gas, Water; (5) Construction; (6) Services. Then the annual percent change of each sector will be studied across the entire period of time. Furthermore, all six sectors' average percent change will be considered for the periods 1963-1973, 1974-1983, 1984-1994, 1995-2005 and 1963-2005. The forecast of GDP of Greece by sector will be analyzed for the years 2006-2010.

Then, the emphasis is placed on Greece's eighteen manufacturing industries that are: (1) food and beverage industries; (2) tobacco manufactures; (3) textiles; (4) manufacture of footwear, other wearing apparel and made-up textile goods; (5) manufacture of wood and cork, except manufacture of furniture; (6) manufacture of paper and paper products; (7) printing and publishing industries; (8) manufacture of leather as well as leather and fur products, except footwear and other wearing apparel; (9) manufacture of rubber and plastic products; (10) manufacture of chemicals and chemical products; (11) manufacture of products of petroleum and coal; (12) manufacture of non-metallic mineral products, except products of petroleum and coal; (13) basic metal industries; (14) manufacture of metal products, except machinery and transport equipment; (15) manufacture of machinery, except electrical machinery; (16) manufacture of electrical machinery, apparatus, appliances and supplies; (17) manufacture of transport equipment; and (18) miscellaneous manufacturing industries that include the manufacture of furniture.

The contribution of each of the above eighteen sectors to GDP in total manufacturing is analyzed across a period of 43 years starting in 1963. The annual percent change of the GDP of each of the eighteen manufacturing industries will be studied across the entire period of time. In addition, average percent changes will be considered across the periods 1963-1973, 1974-1983, 1984-1994, 1995-2005 and 1963-2005. Then, the forecast of Greek GDP in manufacturing for all eighteen sectors is looked at for the years 2006-2010.

The purpose of the present study is threefold. It shall demonstrate:
- First, the development of the GDP of all six sectors of the Greek economy and the factors that influenced its conduct across the period 1963-2005.
- Second, the performance and factors that caused the achievement of the GDP of eighteen Greek manufacturing industries over the above period of time.
- Thirdly, the estimation of forecast of the GDP of all six sectors of the Greek economy as well as eighteen manufacturing industries over the period 2006-2010.

The outline of this paper is as follows:
- Section 2 highlights the meaning and measurement of GDP.
- Section 3 explains the research methods and findings concerning the GDP of the entire Greek economy.
- Section 4 indicates the research methods and results concerning the GDP of eighteen Greek manufacturing industries.
- Section 5 underlines the conclusions.

2. Review of meaning and measurement of GDP

2.1 Measurement of GDP in Greece

The National Accounts is an integrated and organized quantitative description of the economic occurrences, taking place in an economy during a specific period of time. The starting point of the National Accounts Systems in Greece was in 1953. Later, the 1958 OECD system was followed as a pattern. According to the European Union (EU) Council Regulation no. 2223/96 of June 25, 1996 on the EU system of National and Regional Community Accounts, since April 1999 all member states of the EU are required to adapt to the New European System of Accounts (ESA 1995) with 1995 as a reference year (Statistical Yearbook of Greece 2003: 564-567).

The methods used in Greece for the calculation of GDP on the basis of the ESA are (QuickMBA 2007):

- the production method[1];
- the expenditure method[2];
- the income method[3].

Utilizing the input-output techniques and the accounts of the system, these three methods are used simultaneously in the framework of a synthetic procedure. Through the new system, the National Statistical Service of Greece (NSSG) pursues the adoption of the ESA rules and therefore, the harmonization and amelioration of the GDP comparability, the reliability of estimates thereof and the progress in the completion of data on the Greek economy.

It becomes obvious, therefore, that the national accounts as a system establish the framework within which the current operations of the economic activity are recorded. Through the classifications applied by the system of national accounts, the massive number of flows taking place in an economy is depicted in figures. For this reason, national accounts are internationally used as the most suitable framework for the analysis and study of an economy, being an information system yielding all data indispensable for the adaptation of rational short-term and long-term economic policy.

3. Research methods and findings concerning the GDP of the entire Greek economy

The source of information of Greek GDP has been the NSSG. The data refer to factor cost in the period 1963-1987 and Gross Value Added (GVA) in basic prices in the following years. The figures covering the span of time from 2000 to 2005 were revised in 2006.

The price index was calculated for all six sectors of the Greek economy. The data on GDP were taken from the NSSG in constant prices as well as in current prices in drachmas. Then the following formula was used:

$$\frac{\text{Nominal GDP}}{\text{Real GDP}} \times 100 = \text{Price Deflator}$$

Then the deflators derived from the above formula were used in order to get GDP in constant 2000 prices in drachmas. As soon as real GDP in

---

[1] The production method calculates the market value of goods and services produced.
[2] According to the expenditure method, a country's GDP is given by the equation: GDP = Consumption + Investment + Government Purchases + Net Exports, whereas consumption and investment are the expenditures on final goods and service, net exports in an economy are defined as gross exports minus gross imports.
[3] The income method sums the income received by all producers in the country.

2000 prices in drachmas was calculated, it was converted into euro prices. The findings can be seen in Table 3 (attached to this article).

3.1 GDP of Greece by sector of activity

The GDP of all six sectors of the Greek economy as well as total GDP in 2000 constant prices in million € can be viewed in Table 3.

Agriculture, Forestry and Fishing was increasing more or less on a constant basis until 1973. The first oil crisis affected its performance and there was a constant fall between 1973 and 1977. The conduct of this sector improved between 1977 and 1978 but the second oil crisis influenced negatively its position. Since 1980 there has been a continuous more or less drop of the GDP of Agriculture, Forestry and Fishing. It must be said that in 2005 the level of GDP of this economic activity was less than in 1963 mainly due to contraction of agriculture and stockbreeding while fishing has kept its contribution to the total GDP stable.

Mining and Quarrying is mainly represented by excavation of anthrax, lignite, oil, natural gas and various metals. It is a sector that contributes very little to total GDP. The GDP of Manufacturing increased between 1963 and 1991, then its growth decelerated only to start improving its position again since 1997. More or less, there has been a continuous increase of the GDP of Electricity, Gas and Water over the entire period examined.

The GDP of the sector of Construction grew between 1963 and 1973. Both oil crises influenced this economic activity negatively. Its performance has been stable over the period from 1988 to 1991. There has been a fall during the period from 1992 to 1995 and an increase since then, due to the 2004 Olympic Games in Athens. Characteristically, there was a drop in 2005.

Services represent the largest sector of the Greek economy. More or less, there has been a constant growth of this economic activity during the entire period examined. Shipping and tourism are the greatest contributors to Services.

To sum up: The Greek GDP has grown more or less continuously between 1963 and 2005. This development has been influenced mainly by Services.

3.2 Contribution of each sector of activity to Greece's GDP

Table 4 exhibits the contribution of all six sectors of economic activity to Greece's GDP. In 1963 Agriculture, Forestry and Fishing represented 19% of total GDP. Since then, the sector's share in the total has been declining, reaching only 4% in 2005. This is due to contraction of agriculture and stockbreeding while fishing has kept its position stable. This diminution was mainly caused because of urbanization and the Common Agricultural Policy (CAP) of the EU.

Mining and Quarrying contributes less than 1% to Greece's GDP across the entire span of time.

Manufacturing represented 6-8% of GDP in the period 1963-1969. Since then, the sector increased its share between 9-12%. There has been a fall in 2003-2004 but Manufacturing improved its position in 2005.

Electricity, Gas and Water's contribution to the total GDP was less than 1% in the period 1963-1976. Then, between 1977 and 2005, it grew slightly into the region of 1-2.3%.

Construction symbolized 10-14% of the entire GDP in the period 1963-1979 and 8-9% since 1980.

Services have always been the largest economic sector of Greece. It delivered 62-69% of the whole GDP during the 1963 to 1986 period and 70-76% since 1987. The greatest contributors have been shipping and tourism. The Greek shipping community has a leading world presence (K. Karamanlis 2007: 6-7). It must be highlighted that, though Greece is a shipping superpower in the world, only one out of four boats is found under Greek flag. In 2005 shipping contributed 13,871 billion € to Greek economy (N. Efthimiou 2006: 52-60). At present the Greek government is offering high incentives to ship owners so that more Greek ships may return under the Greek flag.

3.3 Annual change of GDP by sector in Greece

Table 5 shows the annual change of GDP in percent by economic activity over the entire period examined. Furthermore, it highlights the average percentage of changes of all economic sectors during the periods 1963-1973, 1974-1983, 1984-1994, and 1995-2005 as well as 1963-2005.

In the 1963-1973 period, the average total GDP experienced the highest growth in relation to the other periods examined. Considering the individual economic activities, Electricity, Gas and Water realized the fastest increase, leaving Manufacturing on the second place and Agriculture, Forestry and Fishing on the last.

From 1974 to 1983 the average increase of total GDP was only 2%, while the sectors Mining and Quarrying as well as Electricity, Gas and Water realized a 7% growth. On the other hand, Agriculture, Forestry and Fishing as well as Construction experienced a 2% downfall of their GDP.

During the span of time from 1984 to 1994, the total GDP realized an average rise of 1%. The sectors Services, Mining and Quarrying and Manufacturing succeeded in growing by 2%, while Agriculture, Forestry and Fishing experienced a drop of 2%.

Between 1995 and 2005 the average growth of GDP was 3%. Services as well as Electricity, Gas and Water achieved a 4% increase, while Construction developed an average rate of 3%. Once again, Agriculture, Forestry and Fishing decreased by 1%.

In general, Greece enjoyed relatively high rates of growth since the end of the Second World War until 1973. The medium rhythm of increase of GDP amounted to roughly 7% in the years 1954-1973. This percentage was higher than that of all the other OECD countries except Japan. Furthermore, this rate of growth was around 50% higher in relation to the mean of the EU nations. The high propensity for saving, the intense surge of foreign direct investments, as well as the abundant and relatively cheap workforce, could be reported as some of the factors that led to this rapid growth of the Greek economy. The connection of the country with the then called EEC constituted also an important factor of progress for the Greek economy. Exports to the EEC were realized and for a relatively long period of time, the Greek domestic production was protected, because of the progressive adaptation of the Greek tariffs to the common exterior tariff of the EEC (Th. Georgakopoulos 2002: 96-102).

Since the first oil crisis the development of the Greek economy changed radically. The rhythms of growth were decreased, but up to 1978 economic growth remained higher than the corresponding progress of most OECD countries and 35% above the average of the European Union. The greatest fault in economic policy during the period 1974-1978, which harmed severely the Greek economy and society, was the nationalization of a series of private units such as Commercial Bank, Ioniki Bank and their affiliated companies as well as Olympic Airways, the Organisation of Urban Transport etc. The situation worsened after the second oil crisis.

Over the period 1979-1995 the average progress of the Greek economy was only 1% against 2% of the EU. The Greek economy suffered due to the increases of oil prices. There were two main reasons for the bad economic position of Greece between 1979 and 1985: Firstly, the enormous costs of adaptation of the economy to the new competitive environment of the free single market of the EU. Secondly, the expansive instead of restrictive economic policy that the country followed. In this period the size of the public sector increased to 20 percentage points of the GDP, the annual deficits amounted to roughly 10% of the GDP and the public debt exceeded 110% of the national GDP. The drachma lost 85% of its value against the ECU (Th. Georgakopoulos 2007: 146-150)

The amelioration of the Greek economy that began in 1994 continued. The rhythm of growth of the Greek economy exceeded by 35% the medium pace of growth of countries of the EU over the period 1995-2000. In 2001 Greece became the 12th member of European Monetary Union

(EMU), though not all Maastricht criteria had been met, especially the public debt of 104% of the annual GDP remained far beyond the 60% threshold (Axt 2002: 141). Since 2002 the euro has replaced the drachma. Greece continued expanding over the years 1996-2005. It must be added that in the years 1995-2005 the contribution of the structural funds had greater importance for the economic promotion of the country.

To sum up, the entrance of Greece into the EU in 1981 had important favourable repercussions in the prosperity of society and ensured important consuming resources from the EU. Moreover, it led to important reductions of prices of products after the suppression of the exceptionally high protection that domestic production had enjoyed before.

However, the costs of rationalisation of the Greek economy because of the integration into the EU have not been paid yet and they will have to be paid progressively in the future. The relatively high inflationist pressure is considered a matter of concern. The complete integration of Greece into the EU led to an important deterioration of the exterior balance of trade that has had negative repercussions on the domestic production and employment.

3.4 Forecast of the GDP of Greece by sector

Forecasting is the procedure of estimation in unknown situations. Forecasting is often used in discussions of time-series data. The categories of forecasting methods include:
- Time series methods
- Causal / Econometric methods
- Judgmental methods
- Other methods.

One of the most frequently used forecasting methods is time-series analysis or the analysis of time-series data (D. Salvatore 2007: 190-199). Time series methods utilize historical data as the basis for calculating future outcomes. It must be said that time series analysis deals with a variable that is altered with time and which can be said to rely only upon the current time and the previous values that it took (i.e. not dependent on any other variables or external factors). Hence if Y_t is the value of the variable at time t then the equation for Y_t is:

$$Y_t = f(Y_{t-1}, Y_{t-2}, ..., Y_0, t),$$

i.e. the value of the variable at time t is entirely expressed as some function of its previous values and time, no other variables/factors are of relevance. The objective of time series analysis is to find out the nature of the function f and hence allow us to forecast values for Y_t.

Some forecasting methods such as Causal/econometric methods exercise the assumption that it is possible to distinguish the underlying factors that might influence the variable that is being forecast. Judgmental forecasting methods embody intuitive judgments, opinions and probability evaluations. Furthermore, there are also other methods of forecasting such as Simulation, Prediction market, Probabilistic forecasting and Ensemble forecasting as well as Reference class forecasting.

The analysis of forecast in this article is based on time series analysis.

Table 1: Forecast of GDP of Greece by sector, ESA, 2000 constant prices [million €]

Year	Agricult., Forestry, Fishing	Mining and Quarrying	Manufacturing	Electricity, Gas and Water	Construction	Services	Gross Domestic Product
2006	7114	626	17019	4000	13678	136087	178524
2007	7144	658	17896	4322	14105	141844	185969
2008	7174	691	18819	4671	14546	147845	193745
2009	7204	727	19789	5047	15000	154099	201866
2010	7234	764	20809	5454	15468	160619	210348

GDP: Gross Domestic Product and Gross Value Added since 1988 – ESA: European System of Accounts – Source: Calculations based on Table 3 and Table 5.

Graph 1

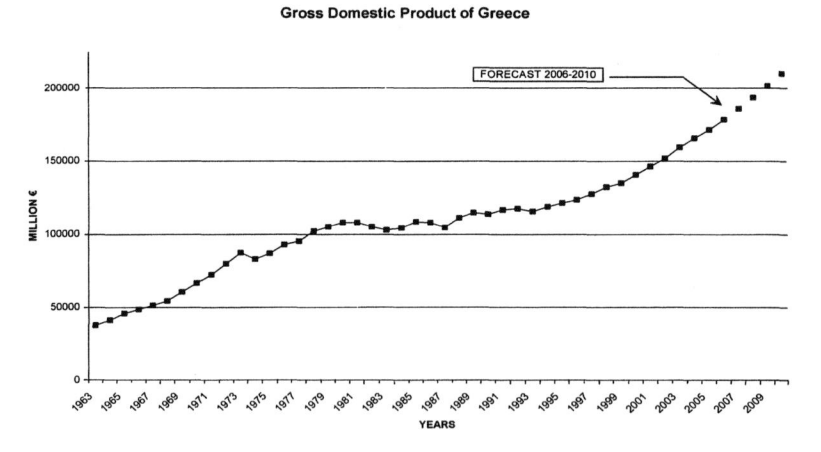

Gross Domestic Product of Greece

Source: Table 3 and Table 5.

Table 1 shows the forecast of GDP of Greece by economic activity for the period 2006-2010 and was calculated using time series analysis. The average annual percent change of the span of time 1963-2005 was utilized for each sector of the Greek economy. In addition, Graph 1 exhibits the evolution of total GDP for the entire period examined as well as its forecast for the length of time 2006-2010.

3.5 Present Developments

In 2006 Greek shipping exchange inflows exceeded 14.3 billion euros (M. Kafalogiannis 2007: 24-27).

It must be added that from the beginning of 2007 the Ministry of Mercantile Marine put the new regulations of support of Greek commercial shipping in application in order to enhance the competitiveness of Greek vessels.

For each vessel that raises the Greek flag, the government will issue a special agreement, following the provisions of article 13 ND 2687/53. According to these new terms, there is a readjustment of the requirements which ensure a minimal Greek component of the crew: Depending on the size of the ship (measured in GRT), under the new provisions no more than 4 to 6 Greek seamen are necessary (3.000-30.000 GRT 4 Greeks, 30.000-80.000 GRT 5 Greeks and above 80.000 GRT 6 Greeks). In all cases, only the captain should be Greek. The old system obliged the ship-owner to pay contributions for all seamen positions (possibly 9 to 11) whether the positions were filled by Greek or foreign seamen – or not at all. Due to the new regulations, the ship owner has achieved a 20% decrease of crew costs that amounts to a 8-10% decrease of the total daily operating costs.

In addition, the Greek government subsidizes the social security contributions of Greek seamen in ocean-going shipping. There is a reduction of tax rates on the salaries of merchant vessel crews from 6% to 3% with respect to officers, and from 3% to 1% with respect to other crew members.

At present, the American coast guard considers the Greek flag as a "white" (powerful, law enforcing) flag. This means that Greek dry and wet vessels do not need continuous controls from American authorities. In this way, Greek ship-owners save money and Greek shipping becomes more competitive.

The developments mentioned above tremendously influenced Greek shipping. According to the "Greek Shipping Directory 2007 and Shipping-Finance Newspaper", today one out of three Greek vessels is under the Greek flag, whereas it used to be only 1 out 4 before.

Important initiatives and reforms have been established (G. Alogoskoufis 2007b: 8-9). Among these measures are to be mentioned:
- cuts in the rate of corporation taxes from 35% to 25% as well as considerable reductions in personal income taxes;

- a new investment law for promoting the country's comparative advantages;
- a new framework for Public Private Partnerships;
- an efficient use of the European Union's structural funds;
- the continuation of privatizations;
- a new policy for the promotion of exports;
- the incorporation of modern IT technologies in the public sector;
- a reduction of bureaucratic procedures.

Hence, shipping, investments and exports are expected to keep supporting the high rhythms of growth of Greek GDP over the period 2006 and 2010. Private investments have been increasingly supported by the favourable prospects of enterprising profitability. The tax alleviations, the investment motives and the cooperation of the public and private sector have improved the investment environment. The positive prospects are also strengthened by the relatively favourable international economic situation (P. Sakellaris 2007: 72-73).

4. Research methods and findings concerning the GDP of eighteen Greek manufacturing industries

This section is looking at eighteen Greek manufacturing industries that are highlighted at the introduction of this paper. The origin of the data of GDP of these eighteen Greek manufacturing industries has been the NSSG. The datasets represent GDP in factor cost over the period 1963-1987 and GVA in basic prices since 1988. The figures covering the period of time 2000-2005 were revised in 2006.

4.1 Contribution of each sector to GDP in manufacturing

Table 6 shows the share of eighteen industries to GDP in manufacturing over the entire period examined 1963-2005.

Food and Beverages is the industry with the highest share in the total manufacturing GDP over the entire period examined. Textiles was the sector that kept the second best performance in the period 1963-1994. Since then its position has deteriorated due to powerful competitive pressure, mainly in terms of price, from countries of low costs such as China. The Footwear and Wearing sector which contributes largely to the total manufacturing GDP, has also been negatively affected, due to an infiltration of Chinese products.

Non Metallic Minerals manufacturing has always been one of the most vital fields of the Greek manufacturing industry. The products which this industry produces, constitute raw materials for other sectors. The rise of building activities, in combination with the growth of individual sectors of industry, has given an important impulse of growth in that sector.

The Basic Metals industry is an important area of Greek manufacturing that leads a constant course of growth with auspicious prospects, strengthened by the maintenance of building activities at high levels as well as the undertaking of infrastructure projects.

The prospects and developments of the Metal Products industry are connected to the course of the Basic Metals field. Metal Products manufacturing has had a more or less stable course of growth that is owed to the improved records of exports.

The Printing and Publishing industry has steadily increased its contribution to total manufacturing GDP.

Tobacco industry has reduced its contribution to the total manufacturing GDP, due to unfavourable international arrangements of prohibitions and regulations against smoking.

4.2 Change of Greek GDP in manufacturing by sector

Table 7 exhibits the annual percentage of change for eighteen manufacturing industries that were highlighted in the introduction of this paper over the entire period examined. In addition, the average percentage of change is shown for all eighteen sectors, covering the periods 1963-1973, 1974-1983, 1984-1994, 1995-2005, and 1963-2005.

During the entire period examined, the sectors that realized the highest percentage of average annual changes from 1963 to 1973 were the following: Food and Beverages; Textiles; Footwear and Wearing; Wood and Cork; Paper and Paper Products; Rubber and Plastics; Chemicals; Petrol and Products; Non Metallic Minerals; Basic Metals; Metal Products; Electrical; and Transport Equipment.

For the Tobacco manufacturing industry the peak of its average annual growth rates was reached in 1974-1983. The sectors that achieved their highest average annual growth in 1995-2005 were: Printing and Publishing; Leather; Machinery and Miscellaneous.

The sectors with the highest average annual rise during 1963-2005 were: Miscellaneous; Leather; Petrol and Products; and Basic Metals. In the same period of time Textiles succeeded in no more than an 0.1% average annual growth.

The strong expansion observed in most manufacturing sectors over the decade from 1963 to 1973 was largely affected by increased investment expenditures, due to expanded loans and advances to the manufacturing sector (A. Paris 1990: 87-90).

In the summer of 1974 the dictatorship that previously controlled Greece was replaced by democracy. In the period 1974-1978 the manufacturing output grew, but at a slower rate than before the first oil crisis. The deterioration of manufacturing production over 1978-1983 was largely due to the second oil crisis and to the increase of labour costs per unit of output as well as to strict administrative controls. Furthermore, the fall in the share of credit allocated to manufacturing and the increase of the costs of borrowing added to the burden of industrial costs. The Federation of Greek Industries pointed out that the temporary stoppage of production in some industries in 1983, due to high industrial costs, was restored in 1984, mainly as a consequence of the rise of credit to manufacturing (Federation of Greek Industries 2004: 85-120).

The crisis of manufacturing in the 1980s was the result of the combined effect of many factors: From one side, there was insufficient home demand. From the other side, the macroeconomic policy that was practised resulted in the fall of profits, the investment stagnation, and the interruption of operation of many units as well as the proliferation of problematic and indebted manufacturing enterprises. These factors contributed to the shrinkage of productive potential of Greek industry with the natural consequence of a reduction of the volume of production.

There has been a fall of manufacturing GDP in the period 1991-1993 but an improvement since then. Greek manufacturing has been progressively experiencing the creation of dynamic enterprises with intense export orientation. Furthermore, there has been an effort of improvement of productive possibilities via the import of technologies of production, but also through a more effective use of existing ones. It must be said that the Olympic Games and infrastructure works gave impulses to Greek economy and manufacturing.

Manufacturing GDP expanded greatly between 1999 and 2003 as a result of improved productivity, an increase of investments and a reduction of unit costs. There was a fall in 2004, influenced by the international climate and fluctuations of oil prices, and growth again in 2005. Nevertheless, the contribution of manufacturing to the total GDP was reduced in 2004 as well as in 2005 (Federation of Greek Industries 2005: 87-127).

In the last decade manufacturing investments were greatly increased and Greek industries have been going through a process of expansion and modernisation in order to be more competitive in the international and mainly in the European environment.

4.3 Forecast of GDP in manufacturing by sector of Greece

Table 2 demonstrates the forecast of eighteen manufacturing industries over the period 2006-2010. The forecast was calculated for each sector using time series analysis and the average annual percentage of changes during the span of time from 1963 to 2005.

The rhythms of growth that were achieved during the last years constitute the vaulting horse for further improvement of Greek manufacturing. The GDP of the eighteen manufacturing industries is expected to keep expanding in the frame of a climate of general improvement of the Greek economy. The Athens Olympic Games of 2004 and infrastructure works gave an impulse to Greek economy and manufacturing. The proper management of those infrastructure works as well as the exploitation of the financial gains derived from the successful organization of Athens Olympic Games will to a large extent influence the further development of the Greek economy as well as Greek manufacturing (G. Alogoskoufis 2007a: 68-70).

Table 2: Forecast of GDP in manufacturing by sector of Greece, 2000 prices [million €]

	2006	2007	2008	2009	2010
Food - Beverages	3163	3331	3509	3696	3893
Tobacco	187	191	196	200	205
Textiles	238	239	239	239	239
Footwear - Wearing	1025	1081	1141	1204	1270
Wood - Cork	381	401	422	444	467
Paper - Products	114	118	121	125	129
Printing - Publishing	1476	1606	1748	1901	2069
Leather	159	180	205	232	263
Rubber - Plastics	333	362	393	428	465
Chemicals	772	818	866	918	973
Petrol - Products	999	1111	1236	1375	1529
Non Metallic Minerals	1697	1809	1928	2055	2190
Basic Metals	1061	1179	1311	1457	1620
Metal Products	2081	2242	2416	2603	2805
Machinery	653	709	771	838	911
Electrical	1186	1277	1376	1482	1596
Transport Equipment	626	659	695	732	772
Miscellaneous	1272	1450	1653	1884	2148

Since 2005 the investment law 3299/2004 is applied that gives incentives and provides subsidies which reach up to 60% of the investments. In recent years the Greek government has been reducing taxation. In December 2006 the second phase of a tax reform was voted. The reduction of taxation for all citizens, progressively in the three-year period 2007-2009, is henceforth national law. Furthermore, in 2007 the first phase of the tax reform will be completed, concerning a reduction of tax rates for all enterprises. In addition to that, the Greek government is after a better use of European funds as well as the continuation of privatization of state companies (G. Alogoskoufis 2007a: 68-70).

The further enlargement of the EU will be of benefit formany industries and boost their export activities since they are given the chance to infiltrate those new markets. The presence of many Greek enterprises in the Balkans, of which the activity is characterized satisfactory, constitutes a proper environment for favourable future developments since those enterprises are given possibilities of exploitation of important investment activities in the wider region.

The amelioration of competitiveness of Greek manufacturing does not allow fragmentary solutions but demands a stable economic environment, combating bureaucracy, and the excessive number of laws.

5. Conclusions

The positive records of the Greek economy over the last three-year period and the auspicious prospects for the future are not coincidental. They resulted from a well drawn programme and a mixture of economic policies, which were supported by the budgetary revitalization and the promotion of a bold reforming programme.

Investments and exports will support the high rhythms of growth over the next years. The private investments are expected to increase supported by the positive prospects of enterprising profitability. The tax alleviations, the investment motives and the cooperation of the public and private sector will improve the investment environment. The positive expectations are also strengthened by the relatively favourable international environment since the extraversion is rewarded in periods where the world economy prospects.

The Greek government should accelerate the structural changes in the economy and get rid of the big number of public enterprises that are ineffective. In addition it must pursue the further reduction of the size of the public sector. The unnecessary interventions of the public sector in the economy must be stopped. In order to reach balanced or even surplus budgets by 2010 or at the latest 2012, Greece should continue the effort of budgetary adaptation with the required pace.

References

Alogoskoufis G. 2006: Nea Epochi Antagonistikotitas kai Exostrefias gia tin Ellada in: Taseis-Ediki Etisia Ekthosi, Allmedia A.E (eds.), Athens, pp. 70-72

Alogoskoufis G. 2007a: Me Stocho Megaliteri Anaptixi kai Kinoniki Sinochi in: Taseis-Ediki Etisia Ekthosi, Allmedia A.E (eds.), Athens, pp.68-70

Alogoskoufis G. 2007b: The New Economic Policy, from Reforms to Results in: Trade with Greece, Annual Business Economic and Political Review, issue 38, The Athens Chamber of Commerce and Industry (ed.), Athens, pp. 8-9

Axt, Heinz-Jürgen 2002: Griechenland, in: Europa-Handbuch, Werner Weidenfeld (ed.), Bonn, pp. 136-143
Efthimiou N. 2006: Enosi Ellinon Efopliston Etisia Ekthesi 2005-2006 in: Deltion Dioikisis Epichiriseon, May-June 2006, year 44th, issue 358, G. Papamichalaki (ed.), Athens, pp. 52-60
Federation of Greek Industries 2004: The State of Greek industry, Athens, pp. 85-120
Federation of Greek Industries 2005: The State of Greek industry, Athens, pp. 87-127
Federation of Greek Industries: The State of Greek industry, editions 1963 until 2007, Athens
Georgakopoulos Th. 2002: Macroeconomikes Exelixis tis Ellinikis Economias in: Taseis-Ediki Etisia Ekthosi, Allmedia A.E (eds.), Athens, pp. 96-102
Georgakopoulos Th. 2007: E Ellada stin EE: Axiologisi tis Protis 25etias in: Taseis-Ediki Etisia Ekthosi, Allmedia A.E (eds.), Athens, pp. 146-150
Investorwords 2007: Gross Domestic Product
<http://www.investorwords.com/2240/Gross_Domestic_Product.html>
Karamanlis K. Prime Minister 2007: The Greek Economy, Robust Growth, Visible Progress in: Trade with Greece, Annual Business Economic and Political Review, issue 38, The Athens Chamber of Commerce and Industry (ed.), Athens, pp. 6-7
Kefalogiannis M. Minister of Mercantile Marine 2007: The Prospects of Greek Shipping in Trade with Greece, Annual Business Economic and Political Review, issue 38, The Athens Chamber of Commerce and Industry (ed.), Athens, pp. 24-27
NZIER 2007: Definition of GDP, Gross Domestic Product
<http://www.nzier.org.nz/Site/economics_explained/GDP.aspx>
Paris A. 1990: Comparative Performance between Greek and UK Manufacturing Industries 1963-1984, PhD thesis submitted at the University of Bath, UK, pp. 87-90
QuickMBA 2007: Gross Domestic Product
<http://www.quickmba.com/econ/macro/gdp/>
Sakellaris P. 2007: Dimisionomiki Exigiansi kai Metarithmiseis Apodidoun Karpous in: Taseis-Ediki Etisia Ekthosi, Allmedia A.E (eds.), Athens, pp. 72-73
Salvatore D. 2007: Managerial Economics in a Global Environment, Oxford University Press (ed.), pp. 190-199
Statistical Yearbook of Greece 2003, National Statistical Service of Greece (ed.), Athens, pp. 564-567
Taseis & Provlimata tis Ellinikis Economias in: Taseis-Eidiki Etisia Ekthosi 2002, Allmedia A.E (eds.), Athens, pp. 68-190
Taseis & Provlimata tis Ellinikis Economias in: Taseis-Eidiki Etisia Ekthosi 2005, Allmedia A.E (eds.), Athens, pp. 66-168
Taseis & Provlimata tis Economias in: Taseis-Eidiki Etisia Ekthosi 2006, Allmedia A.E (eds.), Athens, pp. 70-150
Taseis & Provlimata tis Economias in: Taseis-Eidiki Etisia Ekthosi 2007, Allmedia A.E (eds.), Athens, pp. 68-176
The Greek Economy in Figures, editions 1997-2007, Allmedia A.E (eds.), Athens
Wikipedia, The Free Encyclopedia 2007: Gross Domestic Product
http://en.wikipedia.org/wiki/Gross_domestic_product

Attachment: Additional tables

Abbreviations in the following attachment:
  GDP: Gross Domestic Product and Gross Value Added since 1988.
  ESA: European System of Accounts.
Source of the tables:
  Calculations based on information taken from the National Statistical Service of Greece.

Greek GDP since 1963　　95

Table 3: GDP of Greece by sector of activity, ESA, 2000 constant prices [million €]

Year	Agriculture Forestry, Fishing	Mining & Quarrying	Manufact- uring	Electric., Gas & Water	Con- struction	Services	GDP
1963	7327	92	2163	156	4507	23373	37617
1964	7468	98	2532	188	5583	25261	41130
1965	8222	118	2769	210	6074	28251	45643
1966	8501	130	3222	258	6055	30214	48380
1967	9158	119	3572	281	6012	32020	51162
1968	9033	153	3881	299	7277	33589	54232
1969	9944	191	4606	365	8502	36722	60329
1970	11818	203	5645	415	8065	40233	66379
1971	12057	224	6210	482	9199	43903	72075
1972	12982	261	6784	612	11096	47923	79658
1973	13946	280	8360	685	11491	52442	87205
1974	12925	250	8459	634	8014	52598	82881
1975	12764	284	9152	728	8617	55121	86666
1976	12365	318	10059	817	9063	60115	92737
1977	11744	350	10462	924	10302	61201	94982
1978	13813	343	11371	1057	10718	64792	102093
1979	12058	396	12263	1136	11519	67697	105069
1980	14582	391	12372	1185	9958	69337	107825
1981	14534	401	12169	1231	9207	70384	107926
1982	13269	466	11269	1228	8287	70522	105042
1983	10494	522	11034	1282	8589	71039	102960
1984	9506	618	11711	1407	8632	72431	104306
1985	9162	636	12966	1515	9004	75136	108418
1986	8874	540	12796	1535	9222	74896	107864
1987	6270	599	12543	1605	8764	74763	104545
1988	7167	678	13181	1755	10130	78410	111321
1989	7446	655	13405	1917	10171	81178	114772
1990	6448	623	13137	1964	10252	81314	113739
1991	7409	603	13623	2029	10488	82544	116696
1992	7409	605	13146	2194	10026	84249	117630
1993	7387	612	12738	2110	10297	82485	115630
1994	7823	614	12993	2313	9360	85765	118868
1995	8152	607	13006	2385	9345	87936	121432
1996	7883	589	13514	2328	9439	89865	123617
1997	7915	569	13014	2393	9674	94132	127697
1998	8097	643	13703	2556	10700	96595	132294
1999	8380	528	13881	2901	10946	98436	135072
2000	8070	650	14520	3040	11570	102760	140610
2001	7844	647	15870	3280	12831	105902	146375
2002	7452	717	16299	3349	12934	111186	151937
2003	6953	677	16462	3600	14719	116972	159382
2004	7265	676	15112	3654	14954	124096	165757
2005	7084	595	16185	3702	13264	130563	171393

Table 4: Contribution of each sector of activity to Greece's GDP, ESA, percentages

Year	Agricult., Forestry, Fishing	Mining & Quarrying	Manufac-turing	Electric., Gas & Water	Construc-tion	Services	GDP
1963	19	0,2	6	0,4	12	62	100
1964	18	0,2	6	0,5	14	61	100
1965	18	0,3	6	0,5	13	62	100
1966	18	0,3	7	0,5	13	62	100
1967	18	0,2	7	0,5	12	63	100
1968	17	0,3	7	0,6	13	62	100
1969	16	0,3	8	0,6	14	61	100
1970	18	0,3	9	0,6	12	61	100
1971	17	0,3	9	0,7	13	61	100
1972	16	0,3	9	0,8	14	60	100
1973	16	0,3	10	0,8	13	60	100
1974	16	0,3	10	0,8	10	63	100
1975	15	0,3	11	0,8	10	64	100
1976	13	0,3	11	0,9	10	65	100
1977	12	0,4	11	1,0	11	64	100
1978	14	0,3	11	1,0	10	63	100
1979	11	0,4	12	1,1	11	64	100
1980	14	0,4	11	1,1	9	64	100
1981	13	0,4	11	1,1	9	65	100
1982	13	0,4	11	1,2	8	67	100
1983	10	0,5	11	1,2	8	69	100
1984	9	0,6	11	1,3	8	69	100
1985	8	0,6	12	1,4	8	69	100
1986	8	0,5	12	1,4	9	69	100
1987	6	0,6	12	1,5	8	72	100
1988	6	0,6	12	1,6	9	70	100
1989	6	0,6	12	1,7	9	71	100
1990	6	0,5	12	1,7	9	71	100
1991	6	0,5	12	1,7	9	71	100
1992	6	0,5	11	1,9	9	72	100
1993	6	0,5	11	1,8	9	71	100
1994	7	0,5	11	1,9	8	72	100
1995	7	0,5	11	2,0	8	72	100
1996	6	0,5	11	1,9	8	73	100
1997	6	0,4	10	1,9	8	74	100
1998	6	0,5	10	1,9	8	73	100
1999	6	0,4	10	2,1	8	73	100
2000	6	0,5	10	2,2	8	73	100
2001	5	0,4	11	2,2	9	72	100
2002	5	0,5	11	2,2	9	73	100
2003	4	0,4	10	2,3	9	73	100
2004	4	0,4	9	2,2	9	75	100
2005	4	0,3	9	2,2	8	76	100

Greek GDP since 1963

Table 5: Annual percent change of GDP by sector of Greece, ESA, 2000
[constant prices]

Year	Agric., For., Fishing	Mining & Quarrying	Manu-facturing	El., Gas & Water	Con-struction	Services	GDP
1963-64	2	7	17	20	24	8	9
1964-65	10	20	9	12	9	12	11
1965-66	3	10	16	23	-0,3	7	6
1966-67	8	-8	11	9	-1	6	6
1967-68	-1	28	9	6	21	5	6
1968-69	10	25	19	22	17	9	11
1069-70	19	6	23	14	-5	10	10
1970-71	2	11	10	16	14	9	9
1971-72	8	16	9	27	21	9	11
1972-73	7	7	23	12	4	9	9
1963-73	**7**	**12**	**15**	**16**	**10**	**8**	**9**
1973-74	-7	-11	1	-8	-30	0,3	-5
1974-75	-1	13	8	15	8	5	5
1975-76	-3	12	10	12	5	9	7
1976-77	-5	10	4	13	14	2	2
1977-78	18	-2	9	14	4	6	7
1978-79	-13	15	8	8	7	4	3
1979-80	21	-1	1	4	-14	2	3
1980-81	-0,3	3	-2	4	-8	2	0,1
1981-82	-9	16	-7	-0,2	-10	0,2	-3
1982-83	-21	12	-2	4	4	1	-2
1974-83	**-2**	**7**	**3**	**7**	**-2**	**3**	**2**
1983-84	-9	18	6	10	1	2	1
1984-85	-4	3	11	8	4	4	4
1985-86	-3	-15	-1	1	2	-0,3	-1
1986-87	-29	11	-2	5	-5	-0,2	-3
1987-88	14	13	5	9	16	5	6
1988-89	4	-3	2	9	0,4	4	3
1989-90	-13	-5	-2	3	1	0,2	-1
1990-91	15	-3	4	3	2	2	3
1991-92	0	0,4	-4	8	-4	2	1
1992-93	-0,3	1	-3	-4	3	-2	-2
1993-94	6	0,2	2	10	-9	4	3
1984-94	**-2**	**2**	**2**	**6**	**1**	**2**	**1**
1994-95	4	-1	0,1	3	-0,2	3	2
1995-96	-3	-3	4	-2	1	2	2
1996-97	0,4	-3	-4	3	3	5	3
1997-98	2	13	5	7	11	3	4
1998-99	4	-18	1	14	2	2	2
1999-00	-4	23	5	5	6	4	4
2000-01	-3	-0,4	9	8	11	3	4
2001-02	-5	11	3	2	1	5	4
2002-03	-7	-6	1	8	14	5	5
2003-04	5	-0,2	-8	1	2	6	4
2004-05	-2	-12	7	1	-11	5	3
1995-05	**-1**	**0,3**	**2**	**4**	**3**	**4**	**3**
1963-05	**0,4**	**5**	**5**	**8**	**3**	**4**	**4**

Table 6: Contribution of each sector to GDP in manufacturing, 2000 constant prices, percentages

Industries	'63	'64	'65	'66	'67	'68	'69	'70	'71	'72	'73	'74	'75	'76	'77	'78	'79	'80	'81	'82	'83	'84
Food – Bev.	19	18	18	18	17	18	17	17	16	16	15	15	16	15	17	18	17	17	18	18	18	19
Tobacco	5	5	5	5	4	3	3	2	2	2	2	2	2	2	2	2	2	1	1	2	2	1
Textiles	15	15	16	15	15	16	15	14	15	16	16	17	17	20	18	18	18	17	17	16	16	17
Footw. Wear.	12	12	11	11	12	10	10	9	9	10	9	9	9	9	9	9	9	9	7	8	7	7
Wood–Cork	3	3	4	3	4	3	3	3	3	3	4	3	4	3	3	3	4	4	3	3	3	3
Paper-Prod.	2	2	2	2	2	3	2	2	2	2	2	2	2	2	2	2	2	2	2	2	3	3
Print. Publ.	3	2	2	2	2	2	2	3	3	3	2	2	3	2	2	2	3	3	3	3	3	3
Leather	2	1	1	1	2	2	2	2	2	2	2	2	1	1	1	1	1	1	1	1	1	1
Rub. Plastics	2	1	1	1	2	2	3	3	3	3	3	3	3	3	3	3	3	3	3	3	3	3
Chemicals	4	5	7	7	5	5	6	6	6	7	6	6	7	6	6	6	6	6	6	6	6	7
Petrol-Prod.	3	2	2	2	3	3	2	2	2	1	3	3	3	2	2	2	3	3	2	2	3	3
Non Met. Min	7	7	8	7	7	7	7	8	7	7	6	7	7	7	8	8	8	9	9	9	8	8
Basic Metals	2	2	1	3	3	4	6	7	6	5	7	7	6	6	5	5	5	6	5	5	6	6
Metal Prod.	6	6	6	6	6	6	6	6	6	6	6	6	5	5	5	5	5	5	5	6	6	6
Machinery	3	3	3	3	3	3	3	2	3	3	2	3	3	3	3	2	2	2	2	2	2	2
Electrical	4	4	4	4	5	5	5	5	5	6	5	5	4	4	4	4	3	4	4	4	4	3
Transport Eq	5	5	5	5	4	4	4	5	6	6	6	6	6	6	6	6	6	7	7	8	7	7
Miscellan.	3	4	4	4	4	4	5	4	4	4	4	4	4	4	4	4	3	3	3	3	3	3
TOTAL	100	100	100	100	100	100	100	100	100	100	100	100	100	100	100	100	100	100	100	100	100	100

GDP: Gross Domestic Product and Gross Value Added since 1988 – ESA: European System of Accounts – Source: Calculations based on information taken from the National Statistical Service of Greece.

Greek GDP since 1963

Table 6 (continued): Contribution of each sector to GDP in manufacturing, 2000 constant prices, percentages

Industries	'85	'86	'87	'88	'89	'90	'91	'92	'93	'94	'95	'96	'97	'98	'99	'00	'01	'02	'03	'04	'05
Food - Bev.	20	19	19	19	20	20	22	24	30	31	21	21	22	22	22	19	21	19	19	19	19
Tobacco	1	1	1	1	1	1	1	1	1	2	2	2	2	2	2	2	1	1	1	1	1
Textiles	17	17	18	16	15	15	13	12	11	11	7	6	6	6	6	5	3	2	2	2	1
Footw. Wear.	7	7	7	7	7	7	7	7	7	6	13	13	12	12	12	10	10	11	11	10	6
Wood – Cork	2	2	2	2	2	2	3	2	2	2	3	3	3	3	3	3	2	2	3	3	2
Paper – Prod.	3	3	4	4	4	4	4	5	5	5	2	2	2	2	2	2	1	1	1	1	1
Print. Publ.	3	3	3	3	3	3	3	3	3	3	4	5	5	5	5	5	5	7	7	7	8
Leather	1	1	1	1	1	1	1	1	1	1	3	3	3	2	2	2	2	2	1	1	1
Rub. Plastics	3	3	3	4	4	4	4	3	3	3	3	3	3	2	2	3	3	2	2	2	2
Chemicals	7	7	6	7	7	7	7	6	6	7	6	6	6	6	6	5	5	4	5	4	4
Petrol – Prod.	3	3	3	3	3	4	4	4	4	5	4	3	4	4	5	9	3	4	3	4	6
Non Met. Min.	7	8	8	8	8	8	8	7	7	7	5	6	7	8	8	7	10	11	12	11	10
Basic Metals	6	5	4	6	6	5	5	4	4	4	5	4	4	4	4	5	5	5	5	4	6
Metal Prod.	5	5	5	5	5	4	4	4	4	4	4	5	4	4	5	5	8	8	10	12	12
Machinery	2	2	1	1	2	2	2	2	1	1	3	4	4	4	3	3	5	4	4	4	4
Electrical	4	4	3	3	3	3	3	3	3	3	2	2	2	3	3	3	5	4	4	6	7
Transport Eq.	6	6	7	7	7	9	9	9	6	5	4	4	5	5	4	4	4	6	4	4	4
Miscellan.	3	3	3	2	2	2	3	2	2	2	7	7	7	7	7	7	6	5	6	5	7
TOTAL	100	100	100	100	100	100	100	100	100	100	100	100	100	100	100	100	100	100	100	100	100

Table 7: Percent change of GDP in manufacturing by sector of Greece, 2000 prices

Growth	Food, Bever.	Tobacco	Textiles	Footwear, Wearing	Wood, Cork	Paper-Prod.
1963-64	6	15	11	16	14	16
1964-65	9	9	17	-1	14	9
1965-66	18	9	5	12	12	18
1966-67	5	-13	14	24	15	8
1967-68	12	-2	15	-5	-3	17
1968-69	9	-4	10	5	6	10
1069-70	22	1	14	20	41	-14
1970-71	7	2	17	9	12	1
1971-72	7	-5	13	10	8	15
1972-73	12	-2	25	12	33	35
1963-73	**11**	**1**	**14**	**10**	**15**	**12**
1973-74	5	10	5	1	-14	30
1974-75	9	16	10	9	28	-13
1975-76	10	26	26	12	-3	-4
1976-77	9	-6	-5	3	3	-2
1977-78	15	-1	3	8	3	19
1978-79	2	2	7	7	24	20
1979-80	2	-10	-4	-4	4	4
1980-81	5	-10	-1	-15	-14	8
1981-82	-0,4	15	-8	5	-8	-3
1982-83	-6	-2	-1	-11	-10	8
1974-83	**5**	**4**	**3**	**2**	**1**	**7**
1983-84	6	-12	7	2	-12	15
1984-85	15	5	7	7	-7	16
1985-86	-2	-2	5	2	8	11
1986-87	-6	-17	2	-1	6	27
1987-88	7	1	-7	3	-13	-6
1988-89	5	-19	-10	-10	5	2
1989-90	-7	6	-5	-6	2	-8
1990-91	10	-1	-14	3	8	10
1991-92	5	6	-12	-6	-11	2
1992-93	25	45	-6	2	-3	1
1993-94	8	8	4	-6	-7	6
1984-94	**6**	**2**	**-3**	**-1**	**-2**	**7**
1994-95	-19	50	-22	170	91	-42
1995-96	8	0,3	-1	1	4	-6
1996-97	-2	17	-9	-10	-10	-11
1997-98	5	-5	6	4	-2	9
1998-99	1	-18	-3	-2	6	-2
1999-00	-16	-15	-16	-18	-12	-6
2000-01	33	-1	-32	25	-1	-6
2001-02	-7	5	-20	8	15	-27
2002-03	1	6	-8	2	6	-20
2003-04	-11	2	-10	-21	-9	-27
2004-05	7	-19	-24	-33	-6	12
1995-05	**0,05**	**2**	**-13**	**12**	**7**	**-11**
1963-05	**5**	**2**	**0,1**	**6**	**5**	**3**

Table 7 (continued): Percent change of GDP in manufacturing by sector of Greece, 2000 prices

Growth	Printing, Publication	Leather	Rubber, Plastics	Chem.	Petr.- Prod.	Non Met. Minerals
1963-64	-3	-41	-29	31	-19	18
1964-65	9	5	-31	54	-8	21
1965-66	18	18	16	6	29	8
1966-67	7	85	232	-9	48	7
1967-68	14	19	10	9	13	14
1968-69	13	8	37	33	26	12
1069-70	51	1	32	22	-7	28
1970-71	-0,1	14	17	16	14	6
1971-72	7	9	15	14	-42	-3
1972-73	1	20	20	8	202	16
1963-73	**12**	**14**	**32**	**18**	**26**	**13**
1973-74	7	-1	2	10	-12	11
1974-75	18	0,2	17	13	7	3
1975-76	-1	-2	4	2	-11	12
1976-77	6	-9	6	-6	-5	15
1977-78	11	-6	5	13	7	10
1978-79	11	0,3	-2	-3	35	11
1979-80	14	-14	-4	13	5	10
1980-81	1	-14	4	-6	-14	0,1
1981-82	3	2	2	-3	0,4	-7
1982-83	3	4	-2	3	9	-10
1974-83	**7**	**-4**	**3**	**3**	**2**	**6**
1983-84	2	13	-1	6	-4	-1
1984-85	14	-6	7	15	13	2
1985-86	-7	7	-9	-3	0,4	5
1986-87	4	33	3	-5	7	2
1987-88	-1	-25	37	8	17	4
1988-89	-4	-0,1	11	6	1	-7
1989-90	-12	-28	-15	-7	8	3
1990-91	-5	-15	-2	-5	-8	-6
1991-92	0,2	-6	-14	-11	17	-10
1992-93	-1	1	3	3	3	-2
1993-94	6	2	8	8	8	7
1984-94	**-0,3**	**-2**	**3**	**1**	**6**	**-0,2**
1994-95	78	569	-1	21	5	-6
1995-96	20	2	4	1	-14	11
1996-97	-3	-7	-14	-7	18	15
1997-98	4	-1	0,2	2	-1	13
1998-99	12	-7	3	0,1	20	2
1999-00	-8	-10	-2	-11	83	-8
2000-01	21	13	17	0,1	-54	70
2001-02	34	-18	-4	2	11	11
2002-03	7	-10	-2	8	-28	3
2003-04	-8	-17	-29	-28	39	-11
2004-05	24	-27	16	28	52	-5
1995-05	**16**	**44**	**-1**	**1**	**12**	**9**
1963-05	**9**	**13**	**9**	**6**	**11**	**7**

Table 7 (continued): Percent change of GDP in manufacturing by sector of Greece, 2000 prices

Growth	Basic Metals	Metal Prod.	Machinery	Electrical	Transport Eq.
1963-64	7	16	16	26	6
1964-65	-2	7	7	7	6
1965-66	130	17	14	22	9
1966-67	34	3	12	22	-7
1967-68	29	5	9	7	6
1968-69	62	17	16	17	23
1069-70	59	22	12	23	63
1970-71	-15	7	11	26	25
1971-72	-4	18	9	11	1
1972-73	66	26	17	13	20
1963-73	**36**	**14**	**12**	**17**	**15**
1973-74	-1	-5	14	-9	19
1974-75	-7	-15	7	-19	-0,2
1975-76	9	19	6	22	4
1976-77	-19	7	-0,5	-3	10
1977-78	21	5	1	4	3
1978-79	7	6	-7	3	15
1979-80	9	7	-18	12	11
1980-81	-7	-0,3	13	4	7
1981-82	-11	4	0,05	-3	2
1982-83	10	-5	-12	-5	-12
1974-83	**1**	**2**	**0,4**	**1**	**6**
1983-84	11	-0,1	-13	-13	-4
1984-85	8	-6	12	21	-0,01
1985-86	-16	11	-7	5	4
1986-87	-12	-19	-8	-15	4
1987-88	34	17	-1	-9	11
1988-89	4	-9	19	3	0,2
1989-90	-22	-15	-11	-13	12
1990-91	-8	2	1	10	5
1991-92	-13	-3	-8	-5	-2
1992-93	-6	-2	-2	-2	-38
1993-94	9	-2	-2	-2	-2
1984-94	**-1**	**-2**	**-2**	**-2**	**-1**
1994-95	45	22	207	9	-1
1995-96	-15	19	17	-7	8
1996-97	-1	-7	-11	0,03	-1
1997-98	6	9	7	23	11
1998-99	-4	8	-8	5	-8
1999-00	28	-4	1	11	-5
2000-01	12	95	66	80	9
2001-02	15	1	-10	-16	64
2002-03	-11	27	-2	12	-31
2003-04	-16	13	-17	34	-11
2004-05	46	6	8	13	-7
1995-05	**10**	**17**	**23**	**15**	**3**
1963-05	**11**	**8**	**9**	**8**	**5**

AN EVALUATION OF ACTIVE LABOUR MARKET POLICIES: THE CASE OF SPAIN

AINHOA HERRARTE / FELIPE SÁEZ
(UNIVERSIDAD AUTÓNOMA DE MADRID)

1. Introduction

The aim of this paper is to analyse the effects of the main active labour market policies (ALMP) carried out by the Spanish National Employment Institute (INEM) and the regional governments in Spain from 2001 to 2002 (MTAS (2001)). It is customary to develop ex-post evaluation studies using some or a combination of the following variables, or a combination of them, all referring to a specific period after the individuals have participated in one of the LMP measures:
(1) probability of participants finding a job,
(2) actual earnings of participants, and
(3) duration of employment.
However, the key objective of this paper is to estimate the first indicator and the main factors, which also influence its variations.

In its simplest form, the evaluation can be expressed as:

$$\Delta_i = Y_i^1 - Y_i^0 \qquad [1]$$

where Y_i^1 is the outcome for an individual i if he participates in the programme and Y_i^0 is the outcome for the same individual i if he does not participate. The fundamental problem is to determine the labour success rate attained by an individual who took part in a programme as well as the result that the same individual would have reached in the hypothetical absence of ALMP (Heckman et al. (1999), Blundell and Costa-Dias (2000), Caliendo (2006) among others). Since answering this question is impossible, the results for the counterfactual assumption have to be estimated. In order to address this problem and to obtain operational results, we compare the employment ratios of participants for each of the programmes with those achieved by members of a control group (non-participants group). The data used in the evaluation are based on microdata from INEM and from the Spanish Social Security System (SSS) records.

Nevertheless, non-experimental data do lead to a selection bias because the researcher cannot control the decision to participate. The outcome would thus be different even without the programmes (Heckman (1979), Heckman et al. (1999), Eichler and Lechner (2002), Pierre (1999) among others). This means that there are other factors – different from the participation itself – that influence the outcome; for example, variations in skills or age of the individuals that affect their employment probability. These kinds of factors are usually described as observable characteristics. There could also be other kinds of factors, such as motivation, the individual's social environment, social networks, as well as other factors, which researchers cannot observe, that produce a selection bias related to non-observable characteristics (Heckman (1979), Heckman et al. (1999)).

In this paper we have taken great pains to reduce the selection bias produced by the existence of observable characteristics. To that end, we have used a random procedure to construct a control group of the same size and characteristics, matching one-to-one with the treatment group. In this way, we achieve to establish a control group of non-participants that is similar to those of the participants.

The paper is organized as follows: Section 2 describes the procedure used to create the control group. Section 3 describes the analysed programmes and data. Section 4 contains the employment rates for all the programmes and specific collectives (gender, age, etc.). Section 5 estimates a discrete choice model in which the employment status is the endogenous variable and the programme participation and others covariates are the explanatory variables. Section 6 proposes some conclusions and practical recommendations.

2. The control group

In order to analyse the effect of the programme, we have selected a control group of jobseekers that did not participate in any ALMP after April 2001. Our objective was to find a group of jobseekers who were non-participants in any ALMP with the same labour and personal characteristics. Moreover, this control group had to be of the same size as the treatment group.

In order to determine the potential control group members, we have compared the dataset of the participants for each month included in the period of analysis (e.g. 40.705 in April 2001, see table 1) with all the unemployed people registered at the Employment Offices who did not participate in any of the ALMP in that month, or any other month. Thus in April 2001 we selected the members of the control group from the 1.9 million unemployed jobseekers registered at the Employment Offices, excluding the jobseekers who participated in any ALMP. Taking into account this whole database, we proceeded, by a random procedure, to select the definitive members of the control group, imposing the following restrictions: For each individual in the treatment group, we looked for a non-participant with the same labour characteristics (time spent searching for employment and regional labour market, defined

Table 1: Selection of the control group members

	Jobseeker participants in any ALMP (*) (1)	Unemployed registered at the Employment Office (2)	Potential control group members (2) – (1)	Jobseeker non-participants selected as control group
2001.04	40,705	1,910,453	1,869,748	40,705
2001.05	56,232	1,898,285	1,842,053	56,232
2001.06	74,446	1,842,556	1,768,110	74,446
2001.07	76,710	1,835,738	1,759,028	76,710
2001.08	46,096	1,878,513	1,832,417	46,096
2001.09	68,454	1,889,185	1,820,731	68,454
2001.10	92,544	1,940,909	1,848,365	92,544
2001.11	97,171	1,985,857	1,888,686	97,171
2001.12	58,586	1,988,715	1,930,129	58,586
2002.01	51,191	2,075,022	2,023,831	51,191
2002.02	50,236	2,149,908	2,099,672	50,236
2002.03	55,102	2,083,103	2,028,001	55,102
Total	**767,473**	**1,956,520(**)**	**1,892,564(**)**	**767,473**

(*) Not including disabled workers centres, subsidies contracts for disabled workers, self-employment promotion, employment local initiatives, contract subsidies or unemployment subsidies capitalization. – (**) Average period 4/2001 to 3/2002. – Source: Main calculations, Spanish National Employment Institute and MTAS.

by the Spanish *Comunidades Autónomas*), the same human capital (defined by his or her educational level[1]) and the same personal characteristics defined by gender and age (considering groups of ten years). For those cases where we found more than one non-participant who could be a member of the control group, we chose only one of them using a random procedure. The final result is: For each month included in the analysis, we have a control group of the same size and the same observable characteristics as of the treatment group. The detail of the database is shown in Table 1.

3. Programmes and data

The paper focuses on 17 ALMP: i) 6 directed at giving labour orientation to unemployed persons, ii) 3 related to the workers' training processes, iii) 2 promoting employment among disabled and marginalized people and iv) 6 directed at the creation and/or promotion of employment. The

---

[1] We have distinguished among nine different educational level categories in order to select the control group members: Without studies, Primary studies without degree, Primary studies' degree, Vocational training I, Vocational training II, Other vocational training, High School, Medium university studies (less than 3 years), High university studies (3 years and more).

number of participants in each programme analysed is shown in Table 2.

Table 2: Programmes analysed and number of participants

	Number of participants analysed	Number of non-participants analysed
Insertion income (1)	106,110	106,110
General Orientation (2)	10,031	10,031
Individual job-search assistance (2)	214,407	214,407
Personal employment orientation plans (2)	54,957	54,957
Active job-search assistance (2)	29,681	29,681
Entrepreneurial assistance (2)	10,109	10,109
Vocational training (3)	260,155	260,155
Workshop schools (3)	16,454	16,454
Employment workshops (3)	7,201	7,201
Disabled workers centres (*) (4)	3,906	NCG
Contract subsidies for disabled (*) (4)	20,462	NCG
Public employment (Social Activities) (5)	58,368	58,368
Self-employment promotion (*) (5)	15,216	NCG
Employment through local initiatives (*) (5)	1,725	NCG
Contract subsidies (New) (*) (5)	263,764	NCG
Contract subsidies (Old) (*) (5)	14,286	NCG
Unemployment subsidy capitalization (*)(5)	16,233	NCG
Total	**1,103,065**	**767,473**

(*) No control group (NCG). – Source: Spanish National Employment Institute.
(1) Income with the commitment from beneficiaries to collaborate in social activities organised by Public Employment Offices; (2) Orientation and assessment at Public Employment Offices directed at the unemployed; (3) Workers' training programmes; (4) Programmes directed at promoting employment among disabled and marginalized people through subsidies to companies; (5) Programmes directed at the creation and/or promotion of employment through subsidies to companies or self-employed workers.

In this paper we analyse 1,103,065 persons who have participated in any of the ALMP mentioned above from April 2001 to March 2002 ("*Plan de Acción para el Empleo del Reino de España 2001*"). The database was obtained from INEM unemployment records and also includes a further 767,473 individuals selected among those who did not participate in any active labour policies from April 2001 on. The main characteristic of this control group is that all its members are "exactly equal" to the participants in terms of the five types of variables that are available in the administrative records used: gender, age (groups of ten years), educational level (nine categories), duration of unemployment and region (Spanish "*Comunidades Autónomas*").

Table 3 shows the main characteristics of the participants in each of the programmes we have analysed. Regarding the personal characteristics,

61.3% of the participants were women. The average age of the participants was 33 years. 57% of the individuals have only completed their primary education and over 50% were older than 25 years and searching for jobs for less than 12 months before the start of the programmes. 53% were unemployed jobseekers, whereas the other 47% were not unemployed. Finally, 35.6% of the participants were receiving an unemployment subsidy, while 55.9% were not.

Table 3: Distribution by personal and labour characteristics

	Women [in percent]	Age (average) [in years]	Educational level [in %]			
			Without studies	Primary	Secondary	Tertiary
Insertion income	54.7	39.22	36.6	60.1	2.5	0.8
General orientation	60.4	36.37	7.7	62.2	18.3	11.8
Individual job-search assist.	65.9	32.60	5.3	61.7	19.3	13.6
Personal employm. orient. plans	64.6	33.07	2.1	58.8	22.8	16.3
Active job-search assistance	71.2	31.64	4.5	56.1	21.0	18.4
Entrepreneurial assistance	51.2	33.15	1.8	51.5	25.9	20.8
Vocational training	64.3	30.30	0.9	47.8	32.9	18.4
Workshop schools	42.0	19.98	3.4	89.8	6.5	0.3
Employment workshops	58.6	38.54	7.5	69.0	10.6	13.0
Disabled workers centres (*)	32.0	35.60	5.4	78.7	12.0	3.9
Contract subsidies for disabled (*)	42.2	31.61	2.1	66.7	21.8	9.5
Public employment	43.0	38.66	16.0	63.1	10.2	10.8
Self-employment promotion (*)	43.6	33.32	2.3	67.7	19.6	10.4
Employment through local initiat. (*)	48.0	32.70	2.1	62.2	22.0	13.7
Contract subsidies (new) (*)	47.5	29.61	1.5	58.7	20.7	19.1
Contract subsidies (old) (*)	43.8	24.74	0.4	22.5	10.7	66.4
Unemployment subsidy capitaliz. (*)	22.6	31.31	0.0	65.1	21.9	13.0
Total (**)	**61.3**	**33.03**	**8.7**	**57.0**	**20.9**	**13.4**

(*) Programmes without control group. – (**) Only programmes with control group.

Table 3, continued [percentages]

	J-D <25 yrs & <6 months search for job	J-D ≥25 yrs & <12 months search for job	Long term job-seek.	Participants		Non-participants	
				Un-empl.	Not un-empl.	Un-empl.	Not Un-empl.
Insertion income	6.9	77.2	15.9	8.3	91.7	60.6	39.4
General orientation	24.1	67.3	8.6	75.5	24.5	81.3	18.7
Individ. job-search assist.	19.1	51.4	29.5	62.3	37.7	78.9	21.1
Pers. empl. orientation plans	25.5	53.4	21.1	84.3	15.7	85.5	14.5
Active job-search assistance	25.0	49.0	26.0	65.1	34.9	78.0	22.0
Entrepreneurial assistance	12.7	67.8	19.5	62.7	37.3	82.7	17.3
Vocational training	24.4	53.1	22.5	55.3	44.7	80.1	19.9
Workshop schools	57.1	0.8	42.1	24.0	76.0	71.6	28.4
Employment workshops	5.1	69.7	25.2	60.2	39.8	84.7	15.3
Disabled workers centres (*)	-	-	-	-	-	-	-
Contr. subsid. f. disabled (*)	-	-	-	-	-	-	-
Public employment	9.9	70.9	19.2	52.2	47.8	82.0	18.0
Self-employm. promotion (*)	-	-	-	-	-	-	-
Empl. through loc. initiat. (*)	-	-	-	-	-	-	-
Contract subsidies (new) (*)	-	-	-	-	-	-	-
Contract subsidies (old) (*)	-	-	-	-	-	-	-
Unempl. subsidy capitaliz. (*)	-	-	-	-	-	-	-
Total (**)	**19.9**	**56.6**	**23.5**	**52.7**	**47.3**	**77.4**	**22.6**

(*) Programmes without control group. — (**) Only programmes with control group.

Table 3, continued [percentages]

	Participants			Non-participats		
	No subsidy	Sub-sidy	Subsidy finished	No subsidy	Sub-sidy	Subsidy finished
Insertion income	9.9	84.3	5.8	39.0	52.2	8.8
General Orientation	58.9	34.3	6.8	59.0	31.9	9.2
Individual job-search assistance	58.0	33.5	8.5	59.4	30.7	9.9
Person. employm. orientation plans	56.4	35.7	7.9	59.0	31.7	9.2
Active Job-search assitance	60.4	33.1	6.4	63.0	28.0	9.0
Entrepreneurial Assistance	50.1	34.8	15.1	56.4	32.4	11.2
Vocational Training	71.0	21.9	7.2	63.9	26.7	9.4
Workshops Schools	95.7	3.0	1.3	77.7	17.5	4.7
Employment workshops	61.0	19.1	20.0	52.4	35.2	12.4
Disabled Workers Centres (*)	-	-	-	-	-	-
Contracts Subsidies for disabled (*)	-	-	-	-	-	-
Public employments	50.7	28.4	20.8	48.5	39.9	11.6
Self employment Promotion (*)	-	-	-	-	-	-
Employment Local Initiatives (*)	-	-	-	-	-	-
Contract Subsidies (News) (*)	-	-	-	-	-	-
Contract Subsidies (Olds) (*)	-	-	-	-	-	-
Unemploym. Subsidies Capitaliz. (*)	-	-	-	-	-	-
Total (**)	**55.9**	**35.6**	**8.5**	**57.7**	**32.8**	**9.5**

(*) Programmes without control group. — (**) Only programmes with control group.

4. Employment rates: a descriptive analysis

This section shows the employment rates achieved by participants in all the programmes analysed here, differentiated by specific collectives. Additionally, the differences in the employment rate between the treatment group and the control group for all those programmes that need a comparison group can be seen. We assume as a hypothesis that all the differences between participants and non-participants are observables, which means that the recorded information managed by us is only relevant as a way of describing the personal characteristics of unemployed people: i.e. gender, age, educational level, region and the job search duration. Nevertheless, there are other factors that influence the results about which we do not have information. For instance, it was impossible to get information about characteristics such as social and labour integration of workers.

The employment rate is defined as the proportion of individuals that were still affiliated with Social Security in November 2003, which is approximately one-and-a-half years after participation took place. In order to avoid distortions, we have eliminated from the analysis those people who were affiliated with Social Security in November 2003 and were simultaneously receiving an unemployment subsidy. Chart 1 presents the employment rates for *all* the programmes:

As can be observed, the highest employment rates are achieved by those individuals who have participated in *Employment agents and local development* (75.8%), *Local employment initiatives* (70.5%) and *Self-employment promotion* (70.4%), while participants in the *Insertion Income* programme only reach an employment rate of 25% (See notes to Table 2).

As the employment rate for all of the programmes is 48.7%, some differences between collectives can be observed. Men obtain an employment rate which is 11.1% higher than that of women. Also, people from 16 to 24 years of age reach a higher employment rate than members of the other age groups. Individuals with tertiary studies have an employment rate of 61.1%, and this percentage decreases as the individual's educational level decreases. Young people (less than 25 years) who have been searching for a job less than six months also have a higher employment rate (55.6%). Another difference can be observed when we look at the employment situation at the moment of programme participation: unemployed jobseekers reached higher employment rates than non-unemployed jobseekers. Finally, considering whether the individual was receiving an employment subsidy or not, we observe that the highest employment rates are reached by those participants who had finished their subsidy at the moment of participation (60.7%), while those who continued to receive a subsidy have the lowest employment rate (41.3%).

Chart 1: Employment rates by programmes

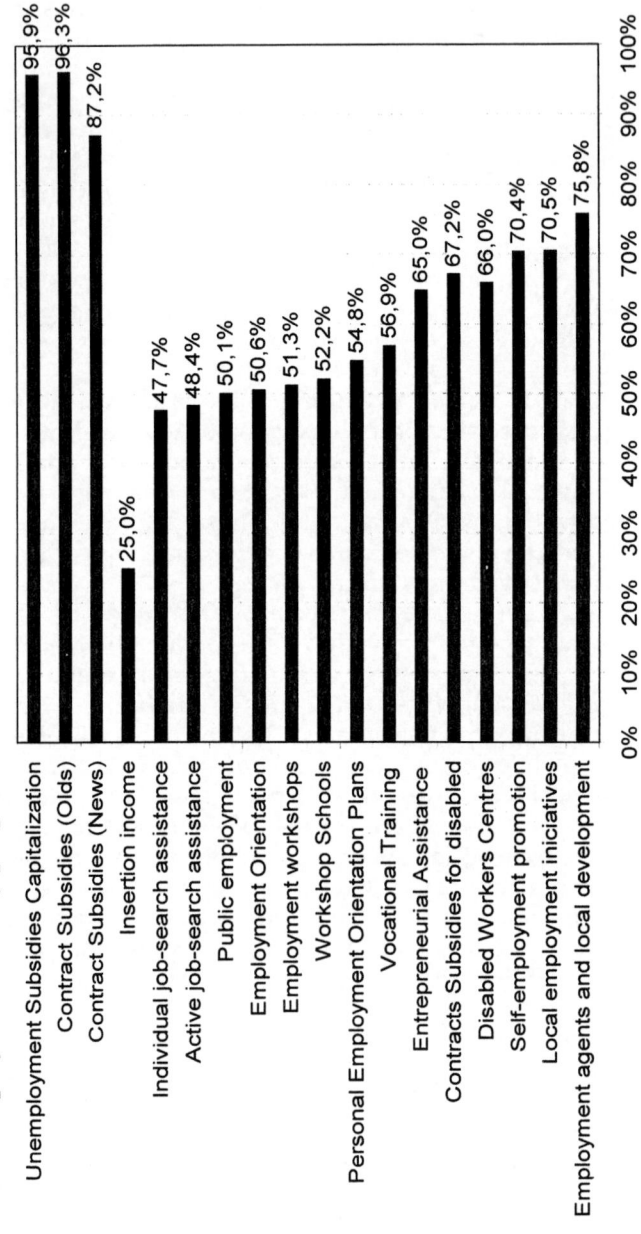

Unemployment Subsidies Capitalization	95,9%
Contract Subsidies (Olds)	96,3%
Contract Subsidies (News)	87,2%
Insertion income	25,0%
Individual job-search assistance	47,7%
Active job-search assistance	48,4%
Public employment	50,1%
Employment Orientation	50,6%
Employment workshops	51,3%
Workshop Schools	52,2%
Personal Employment Orientation Plans	54,8%
Vocational Training	56,9%
Entrepreneurial Assistance	65,0%
Contracts Subsidies for disabled	67,2%
Disabled Workers Centres	66,0%
Self-employment promotion	70,4%
Local employment iniciatives	70,5%
Employment agents and local development	75,8%

Source: Own calculations from the Spanish National Employment Institute (INEM) and Social Security System.

Chart 2: Employment rates by specific collectives. (Only programmes with control group)

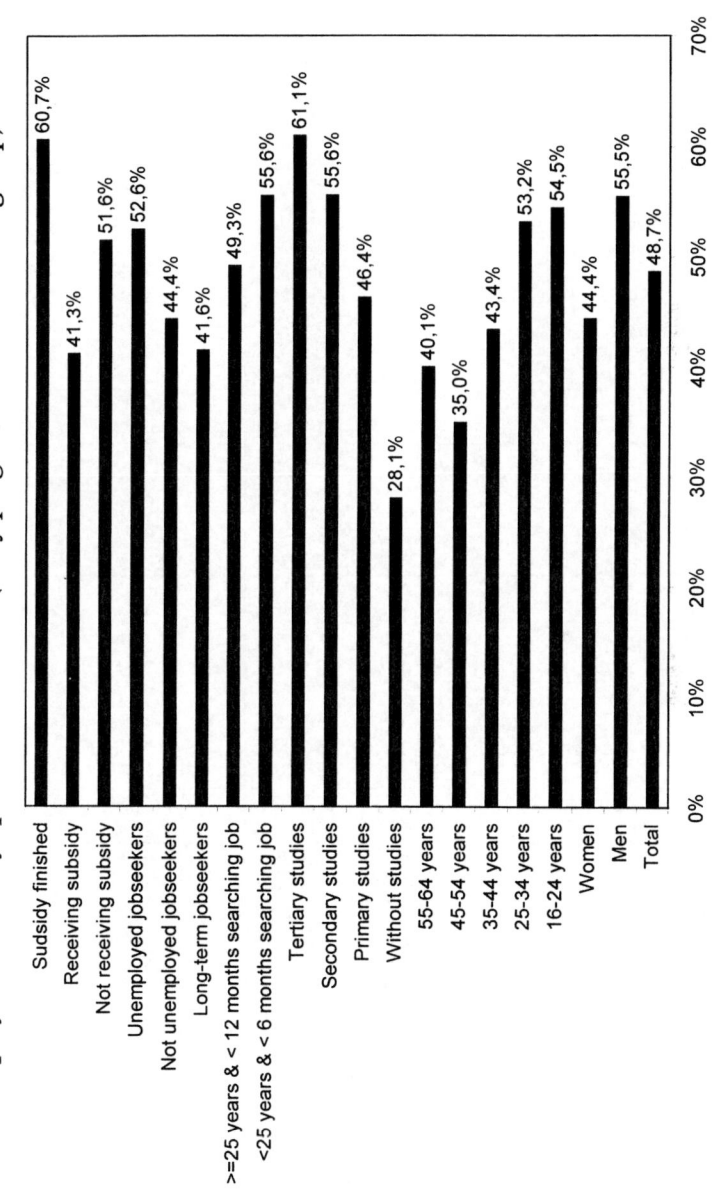

Subsidy finished	60,7%
Receiving subsidy	41,3%
Not receiving subsidy	51,6%
Unemployed jobseekers	52,6%
Not unemployed jobseekers	44,4%
Long-term jobseekers	41,6%
>=25 years & < 12 months searching job	49,3%
<25 years & < 6 months searching job	55,6%
Tertiary studies	61,1%
Secondary studies	55,6%
Primary studies	46,4%
Without studies	28,1%
55-64 years	40,1%
45-54 years	35,0%
35-44 years	43,4%
25-34 years	53,2%
16-24 years	54,5%
Women	44,4%
Men	55,5%
Total	48,7%

Source: Own calculations from the Spanish National Employment Institute (INEM) and Social Security System.

Table 4: Participants' and non-participants' employment rates and statistical differences

	Treatment (Participants)	Control (Non-particip.)	Difference ($ER_{part} - ER_{non-part}$)	Sig. (*)
Total	48.72%	52.25%	-3.53%	0.000
Vocational training	56.91%	56.61%	0.30%	0.028
Insertion income	24.78%	43.04%	-18.26%	0.000
Public employment	50.08%	55.44%	-5.37%	0.000
Employment orientation	50.59%	56.80%	-6.21%	0.000
Individual job-search assistance	47.71%	50.10%	-2.39%	0.000
Personal employment orientation plans	54.75%	53.96%	0.79%	0.008
Entrepreneurial assistance	64.96%	56.16%	8.80%	0.000
Workshop schools	52.16%	52.86%	-0.70%	0.202
Employment workshops	51.31%	51.73%	-0.42%	0.618
Active job-search assistance	48.41%	50.99%	-2.57%	0.000
Men	55.51%	61.48%	-5.98%	0.000
Women	44.45%	46.45%	-2.00%	0.000
16-24 years	54.51%	55.90%	-1.39%	0.000
25-34 years	53.23%	55.57%	-2.34%	0.000
35-44 years	43.44%	49.01%	-5.57%	0.000
45-54 years	35.04%	39.67%	-4.63%	0.000
55-64 years	40.08%	52.86%	-12.79%	0.000
Without studies	28.11%	39.64%	-11.53%	0.000
Primary studies	46.41%	50.88%	-4.47%	0.000
Secondary studies	55.64%	55.50%	0.14%	0.416
Tertiary studies	61.05%	61.25%	-0.20%	0.358
Time searching a job				
<25 yrs. &<6 mon. searching job	55.64%	58.36%	-2.73%	0.000
>=25 yrs.&<12 m. searching job	49.27%	54.94%	-5.67%	0.000
Long term jobseekers	41.60%	40.70%	0.90%	0.000
Not unemployed jobseekers	44.39%	43.36%	1.03%	0.000
Unemployed jobseekers	52.58%	54.84%	-2.25%	0.000
No subsidy	51.59%	50.26%	1.34%	0.000
Subsidy	41.33%	53.45%	-12.12%	0.000
Subsidy finished	60.73%	60.15%	0.58%	0.028
Center of Spain	54.74%	55.29%	-0.55%	0.002
South Spain	40.41%	47.60%	-7.18%	0.000
East (Levante)	57.48%	57.90%	-0.42%	0.035
North Spain	56.19%	56.16%	0.03%	0.872

(*) Significance level Chi-square test — Source: Own calculations from the Spanish National Employment Institute (INEM) and Social Security System.

The comparison of the employment rate of the non-participants (i.e.: the real effect of programmes) is more interesting. Table 4 shows these results. The first and the second columns in Table 4 show the employment rate for the participants in the ALMP programmes and the non-participants respectively. The third column shows the difference in the employment rate between participants and non-participants, and the last column indicates the corresponding statistical significance level.

Comparing the different programmes, we find that only three programmes obtained higher employment rates than the non-participants. Individuals who participated in *Vocational training* reached an employment rate 0.3 percentage points (pp) higher than non-participants. Participants in *Personal employment orientation plans* also have higher employment rates than non-participants; the difference in this case is 0.8 pp. Nevertheless, the most important difference can be observed among the participants in *Entrepreneurial assistance* programmes: Participants reach an employment rate 8.8 pp higher than non-participants.

Although participants in *Workshop schools* and *Employment workshops* have lower employment rates than non-participants, the significance level is much higher than 0.05, so these differences are not statistically significant.

When we look at gender, we observe that employment rates are always higher for non-participants, but the difference is much higher for men. The same occurs when we look at the age of the participants: For every age group the employment rate of non-participants is higher than the participants' employment rate and the difference rises as the age increases. Looking at the educational level, important differences in the employment rate exist for less skilled persons (people without studies and people with only primary studies). Non-participants with tertiary studies also have higher employment rates than participants, but the difference in this case is not statistically significant. A positive difference of 0.14 pp can be observed for those individuals with secondary studies but, once again, the difference is not statistically significant.

In terms of the time spent searching for a job, only the participants who were long-term jobseekers have higher employment rates than non-participants, the difference being 0.9 pp. We can also observe a positive difference in the employment rates for those jobseekers who were not unemployed at the moment of participation.

Finally, an important negative difference in the employment rates can be observed for those people who were receiving the subsidy at the moment of programme participation, while the difference is positive if the individuals do not receive a subsidy or they have finished receiving it. This is an important initial result for determining which persons should participate in active labour market policies. People who are receiving a subsidy have a higher opportunity cost than others and their reserve wage increases consequently, affecting their employment rate negatively (Herrarte, Moral-Carcedo and Sáez (2006)).

Nevertheless, in order to know which variables determine the employment rate, it is necessary to estimate an econometric model controlling for all the relevant explanatory variables as we do in the next section.

5. Econometric model and results

In this section we estimate the employment probability using an econometric model. Our endogenous variable is a binary variable, which is equal to one if a person is employed (has been affiliated with Social Security) in November 2003 (approximately a year and a half after participation) or zero if he or she is not. Taking into account the characteristics of the endogenous variable, and in order to interpret the results as *employment probability*, we have estimated a logit model defined by equation [2]:

$$\operatorname{Prob}(Y_i = 1) = \frac{1}{1+e^{-\alpha-\beta_k X_{ki} - \delta ALMP_i}} \quad [2]$$

where $i = 1, 2, ..., 1,543,175$

The X_{ki} variables considered to be explanatory of the employment probability are: gender, age, educational level, time seeking employment, labour situation at the moment of participation (unemployed or not), whether the individual is receiving a subsidy at the moment of participation, and some regional characteristics such as the province of residence's employment rate and the increase in the employment rate of the province in 2003. Finally, we have included four dummy variables referred to the regional residence zone.

The $ALMP_i$ regressor is a binary variable, which takes the value of 1 if the individual i is a participant in any ALMP and 0 if the individual i is a non-participant. This variable attempts to determine the effect of programme participation in Spain on employment probability.

5.1. Estimation results

First, we estimate the model for the programmes altogether, and afterwards we present the results for each ALMP programme separately. The main results from the logit estimations for all the programmes are shown in Table 5.

Table 5: Logit estimations: Programmes with control group

	B	Sig.	Exp(B)
Women	-0.581	0.000	0.559
Reference: 16-24 years		0.000	
25-34	-0.423	0.000	0.655
35-44	-0.606	0.000	0.545
45-54	-0.922	0.000	0.398
55-64	-0.508	0.000	0.602
Reference: Without studies		0.000	
Primary	0.288	0.000	1.334
Secondary	0.513	0.000	1.670
Tertiary	0.789	0.000	2.202
Reference: <25 years & < 6 months searching job		0.000	
>=25 years & < 12 months searching job	0.369	0.000	1.446
Long-term jobseekers	-0.130	0.000	0.878
ALMP Participation	-0.067	0.000	0.935
Unemployed	0.309	0.000	1.363
Reference: not receiving subsidy		0.000	
Receiving subsidy	0.053	0.000	1.055
Subsidy finished	0.444	0.000	1.559
Province employment rate 01-02	0.031	0.000	1.032
Employment rate change	0.020	0.000	1.020
Reference: Center of Spain		0.000	
South	-0.070	0.000	0.933
East (Levante)	0.021	0.000	1.021
North	0.069	0.000	1.072
Constant	-1.761	0.000	0.172
Number of cases	1,543,175		
Pseudo R2	0.10		
% correct predictions Yi=0	57.92 %		
% correct predictions Yi =1	64.64 %		
% correct predictions	61.31 %		

Source: Own calculations from the Spanish National Employment Institute (INEM) and Social Security System

The first feature to point out is that all variables included in the model have a statistical significance of 99%. Looking at the odds ratio shown in the third column, we can observe that women have a lower probability of being employed than men do (the odds ratio is only 0.55, which implies that the probability for women of being employed is 44% lower than for men). The results also show that any other age group has lower probabilities than the one taken as a reference category (16 to 24 years old). Additionally, the educational level referring to people without studies shows that a higher educational level implies a rise in the employment rate: The odds ratio of people with tertiary studies is 2.2. For young people with fewer than 6 months searching for a job, the variable that measures the time searching for a job shows that those older than 24 years of age with fewer than 12 months searching for a job have higher probabilities of employment: The probability of being employed is 1.44 times higher than that of the reference group. On the other hand, long-term jobseekers have a lower probability of being employed than the reference group.

Being unemployed increases the probability of being employed; the odds ratio in this case is 1.36. Looking at the subsidy variable, we can observe that people who were receiving a subsidy have a higher probability of being employed. The same can be observed for those who had finished their subsidy. Remindable, the effect is much higher for the latter, the odds ratio being 1.55 vs 1.05.

Variables relative to the regional labour market situation show that those provinces with higher employment rates positively affect the probability of employment. Also, if the employment rate increases, we find a positive effect on the employment probability as well. The dummy variable referring to the geographical zone where the programme participation took place shows that, compared to the center of Spain, the employment probability is lower in the South of Spain, but higher in the North and in the Eastern area (Levante).

Finally, the participation programme variable shows a negative coefficient, which implies that the probability of employment is lower for those people who have participated in the programme.

Nevertheless, estimations included in Table 3 do not consider the joint effect of any of the explanatory variables, and the previous descriptive analysis suggests the necessity of considering the interaction between some of these variables. Specifically, we again have estimated the model [2] to include the interaction between gender and programme participation and especially the interaction between the time searching for a job and programme participation. The new estimation results are presented in Table 6. This table contains the estimation for the global sample (all programmes included) and the specific results for each ALMP measure.

Looking at the global estimation for the programmes altogether, the first significant result that can be found is that when we consider the joint action of ALMP participation and the time for seeking an employment, we find a positive effect of participation for the long-term jobseekers' group. This result indicates that for this group of individuals participation in ALMP increases their employment probability (the odds ratio is 1.15). Nevertheless, the effect continues to be negative for jobseekers older than 25 years of age with fewer than 12 months searching for a job. When we look at the interaction of gender and ALMP participation, we also find a positive effect of ALMP participation for women with an odds ratio of 1.15.

Looking at the results for each programme separately, we observe the same effects of many of the variables included: Employment probability is higher for men, young people and individuals with a high educational level. We also find a positive effect on employment probability if the jobseeker was unemployed and if he spent fewer than 12 months searching for a job, while if he is a long-term jobseeker there is a negative effect on employment probability. Living in a province with a high employment rate also affects employment probability positively.

Nevertheless, there are other variables that affect the employment probability in a different manner, depending on the programme. This is the case of the subsidy variable. Although receiving a subsidy increases the employment probability in the majority of the programmes, this does not occur for the *Insertion income* programme or for the *Public employment* programme.

Looking at our interest variables, we can see that ALMP participation has a negative effect for all the programmes except *Entrepreneurial assistance*. More interesting is the interaction between the time for seeking an employment and ALPM participation. Although jobseekers older than 25 with fewer than 12 months searching for a job have a lower probability of employment if they participate in an ALMP programme for the entire sample, this does not occur for the *Vocational training* programme, where we find a positive effect of participation. This also occurs for the *Workshop schools* and for the *Personal employment orientation plans* and, once again, for the *Entrepreneurial assistance* programme, although only the coefficient of the Vocational training programme has a significance level that is high enough.

Being a long-term jobseeker and having participated in any ALMP measure increases an individual's employment probability, except for participants in the *Insertion income* programme. The same occurs for women: Those women who have participated in an ALMP will have higher employment rates.

Table 6: Logit estimations including interactions (*)

	Total			Vocational training			Workshop schools (1)			Empl. workshops		
	B	Sig.	Exp(B)	B	Sig.	Exp(B)	B	Sig.	Exp(B)	B	Sig.	Exp(B)
Women	-0.651	0.000	0.521	-0.467	0.000	0.627	-0.614	0.000	0.541	-0.748	0.000	0.473
Refer.: 16-24 yrs.		0.000			0.000			0.410			0.000	
25-34	-0.421	0.000	0.656	-0.400	0.000	0.670	-0.004		0.996	-0.481	0.007	0.618
35-44	-0.604	0.000	0.547	-0.632	0.000	0.531	-	-	-	-0.483	0.006	0.617
45-54	-0.921	0.000	0.398	-0.974	0.000	0.378	-	-	-	-0.684	0.000	0.505
55-64	-0.505	0.000	0.603	-0.746	0.000	0.474	-	-	-	-0.359	0.054	0.698
Refer.: Without stud.		0.000			0.000			0.000			0.000	
Primary	0.291	0.000	1.337	0.223	0.000	1.250	0.147	0.018	1.158	0.361	0.000	1.435
Secondary	0.515	0.000	1.674	0.346	0.000	1.413	0.343	0.000	1.410	0.537	0.000	1.710
Tertiary	0.792	0.000	2.208	0.627	0.000	1.873	0.940	0.000	2.560	0.900	0.000	2.458
Refer.: <25 yrs. & < 6 months searching job		0.000			0.000			0.000			0.000	
≥25 years & < 12 m. search for job	0.423	0.000	1.527	0.398	0.000	1.489	-0.359	0.577	0.698	0.371	0.074	1.449
Long-term jobseekers	-0.201	0.000	0.818	-0.231	0.000	0.794	-0.211	0.000	0.810	-0.243	0.238	0.784
ALMP participation	-0.125	0.000	0.883	-0.128	0.000	0.880	-0.061	0.109	0.941	-0.365	0.018	0.694
ALMPpart.& ≥25yrs. & <12 m. search for job	-0.111	0.000	0.895	0.050	0.000	1.051	0.306	0.646	1.358	-0.011	0.944	0.989
ALMP part. & long-term jobseekers	0.141	0.000	1.152	0.292	0.000	1.339	0.232	0.000	1.261	0.337	0.048	1.400
Women&ALMP partic.	0.139	0.000	1.150	0.153	0.000	1.166	0.055	0.229	1.057	0.472	0.000	1.603
Unemployed	0.301	0.000	1.352	0.102	0.000	1.107	0.133	0.000	1.143	0.064	0.117	1.066
Ref.: not receiv. subs.		0.000			0.000			0.000			0.000	
Receiving subsidy	0.051	0.000	1.052	0.396	0.000	1.486	0.156	0.000	1.168	0.098	0.021	1.103
Sudsidy finished	0.448	0.000	1.566	0.447	0.000	1.563	0.406	0.000	1.500	0.338	0.000	1.402
Prov. empl. rate 01-02	0.031	0.000	1.032	0.012	0.000	1.012	0.019	0.000	1.019	0.017	0.000	1.017
Employm. rate incr.	0.019	0.000	1.020	0.029	0.000	1.029	0.041	0.006	1.042	0.021	0.305	1.021
Refer.: Center of Spain		0.000			0.000			0.000			0.001	
South Spain	-0.071	0.000	0.932	-0.152	0.000	0.859	-0.083	0.042	0.920	0.079	0.231	1.082

An Evaluation of ALMP: the case of Spain

	Total			Vocational training			Workshop schools (1)			Empl. workshops		
	B	Sig.	Exp(B)	B	Sig.	Exp(B)	B	Sig.	Exp(B)	B	Sig.	Exp(B)
East (Levante)	0.021	0.000	1.022	0.024	0.004	1.024	-0.061	0.220	0.941	0.132	0.017	1.141
North Spain	0.070	0.000	1.072	0.013	0.144	1.014	-0.100	0.014	0.904	0.220	0.000	1.246
Constant	-1.726	0.000	0.178	-0.507	0.000	0.602	-0.790	0.000	0.454	-0.854	0.008	0.426
Number of cases	1.543.175			520.309			32.908			14.402		
Pseudo R2	0.099			0.059			0.042			0.072		
% correct pred. Yi=0	58.75			57.67			52.04			60.61		
% correct pred Yi=1	64.08			59.31			63.19			57.80		
% correct predictions	61.44			58.60			57.89			59.17		

(1) The age variable has been included in this estimation as a numeric variable because all of the participants in this programme are younger than 25 years. – (*) All programmes with control group. – Source: Own calculations from the Spanish National Employment Institute (INEM) and Social Security System.

Table 6 (continued): Logit estimations including interactions (*)

	General orientation			Individual job-search assistance			Personal employment orientation plans			Active job-search assistance		
	B	Sig.	Exp(B)	B	Sig.	Exp(B)	B	Sig.	Exp(B)	B	Sig.	Exp(B)
Women	-0.579	0.000	0.560	-0.674	0.000	0.510	-0.473	0.000	0.623	-0.628	0.000	0.534
Reference: 16-24		0.000			0.000			0.000			0.000	
25-34	-0.438	0.000	0.645	-0.373	0.000	0.689	-0.461	0.000	0.631	-0.441	0.000	0.643
35-44	-0.643	0.000	0.526	-0.505	0.000	0.603	-0.599	0.000	0.549	-0.585	0.000	0.557
45-54	-1.014	0.000	0.363	-0.835	0.000	0.434	-1.064	0.000	0.345	-0.882	0.000	0.414
55-64	-0.437	0.000	0.646	-0.450	0.000	0.637	-0.734	0.000	0.480	-0.535	0.000	0.586
Refer.: Without studies		0.000			0.000			0.000			0.000	
Primary	0.300	0.000	1.350	0.241	0.000	1.272	0.049	0.262	1.051	0.350	0.000	1.420
Secondary	0.476	0.000	1.609	0.433	0.000	1.542	0.186	0.000	1.205	0.587	0.000	1.799
Tertiary	0.717	0.000	2.049	0.723	0.000	2.060	0.390	0.000	1.477	0.849	0.000	2.338
Refer.: <25 years & < 6 m. searching for a job		0.000			0.000			0.000			0.000	
≥25 years & < 12 m. searching for a job	0.381	0.003	1.464	0.325	0.000	1.384	0.389	0.000	1.476	0.396	0.000	1.486
Long-term jobseekers	-0.368	0.002	0.692	-0.317	0.000	0.728	-0.193	0.000	0.824	-0.265	0.000	0.767

Table 6 (continued): Logit estimations including interactions (*)

	General orientation			Individual job-search assistance			Personal employment orientation plans			Active job-search assistance		
	B	Sig.	Exp(B)	B	Sig.	Exp(B)	B	Sig.	Exp(B)	B	Sig.	Exp(B)
ALMP participation	-0.265	0.000	0.767	-0.066	0.000	0.936	-0.022	0.451	0.978	-0.063	0.137	0.939
ALMP part. & ≥25 yrs. & < 12 m. search for job	-0.084	0.228	0.919	-0.084	0.000	0.920	0.011	0.709	1.011	-0.133	0.001	0.875
ALMP part. & long-term jobseekers	0.340	0.004	1.405	0.141	0.000	1.152	0.000	0.998	1.000	0.084	0.080	1.087
Women&ALMP particip.	0.022	0.712	1.023	0.027	0.043	1.027	0.076	0.004	1.079	0.030	0.425	1.031
Unemployed	0.155	0.000	1.168	0.186	0.000	1.205	0.156	0.000	1.169	0.234	0.000	1.263
Refer.: not receiv. subs.		0.000			0.000			0.000			0.000	
Receiving subsidy	0.303	0.000	1.354	0.113	0.000	1.119	0.316	0.000	1.371	0.137	0.000	1.147
Sudsidy finished	0.562	0.000	1.754	0.471	0.000	1.601	0.494	0.000	1.639	0.455	0.000	1.576
Prov. empl. rate 01-02	0.026	0.000	1.026	0.031	0.000	1.031	0.017	0.000	1.017	0.026	0.000	1.026
Employm. rate incr.	0.046	0.005	1.048	0.002	0.581	1.002	0.050	0.000	1.051	0.032	0.001	1.033
Refer.: Center		0.000			0.000			0.000			0.000	
South Spain	-0.210	0.000	0.810	0.025	0.015	1.025	0.094	0.000	1.099	-0.020	0.434	0.980
East (Levante)	0.017	0.850	1.017	-0.016	0.171	0.984	0.041	0.088	1.042	0.050	0.098	1.051
North Spain	0.125	0.000	1.133	0.120	0.000	1.127	-	-	-	0.113	0.001	1.120
Constant	-1.340	0.000	0.262	-1.586	0.000	0.205	-0.767	0.000	0.465	-1.524	0.000	0.218
Number of cases	20.062			428.814			109.913			59.362		
Pseudo R2	0.089			0.089			0.071			0.083		
% correct predic. Yi=0	60.67			61.78			55.63			61.23		
% correct predic. Yi =1	62.52			60.33			62.75			60.40		
% correct predictions	61.66			61.07			59.50			60.82		

	Entrepreneurial Assistance			Insertion income			Publ. Empl. (Soc. Activ.)		
	B	Sig.	Exp(B)	B	Sig.	Exp(B)	B	Sig.	Exp(B)
Women	-0.632	0.000	0.531	-0.860	0.000	0.423	-0.706	0.000	0.494
Reference: 16-24		0.000			0.000			0.000	

(*) All programmes with control group. – Source: Own calculations from the Spanish INEM and Social Security System.

	Entrepreneurial Assistance			Insertion income			Publ. Empl. (Soc. Activ.)		
	B	Sig.	Exp(B)	B	Sig.	Exp(B)	B	Sig.	Exp(B)
25-34	-0.353	0.000	0.703	-0.328	0.000	0.720	-0.256	0.000	0.774
35-44	-0.544	0.000	0.580	-0.415	0.000	0.660	-0.327	0.000	0.721
45-54	-0.949	0.000	0.387	-0.706	0.000	0.493	-0.524	0.000	0.592
55-64	-0.715	0.000	0.489	-0.218	0.000	0.804	-0.050	0.282	0.951
Reference: Without studies		0.000			0.000			0.000	
Primary	0.199	0.077	1.220	0.087	0.000	1.091	0.216	0.000	1.241
Secondary	0.323	0.005	1.381	0.364	0.000	1.440	0.440	0.000	1.552
Tertiary	0.520	0.000	1.682	0.727	0.000	2.068	0.863	0.000	2.370
Ref.: <25 yrs & < 6 months search for job		0.000			0.000			0.000	
≥25 yrs & < 12 months search for job	0.295	0.008	1.343	0.226	0.000	1.253	0.346	0.000	1.413
Long-term jobseekers	-0.301	0.005	0.740	-0.131	0.004	0.877	-0.228	0.000	0.796
ALMP participation	0.342	0.000	1.408	-0.277	0.000	0.758	-0.233	0.000	0.792
ALMP part. & ≥25 yrs.&<12 m. search job	0.058	0.535	1.059	-0.217	0.000	0.805	-0.151	0.000	0.860
ALMP part. & long-term jobseekers	0.090	0.404	1.094	-0.146	0.001	0.864	0.040	0.408	1.040
Women & ALMP participation	0.034	0.576	1.035	0.031	0.125	1.031	0.248	0.000	1.281
Unemployed	0.143	0.000	1.154	0.640	0.000	1.896	0.150	0.000	1.162
Reference: not receiving subsidy		0.000			0.000			0.000	
Receiving subsidy	0.143	0.000	1.154	-0.222	0.000	0.801	-0.122	0.000	0.885
Sudsidy finished	0.473	0.000	1.605	0.407	0.000	1.502	0.365	0.000	1.440
Province employment rate 01-02	0.041	0.000	1.042	0.039	0.000	1.039	0.037	0.001	1.037
Employment rate increase	0.077	0.000	1.080	0.024	0.000	1.024	0.023	0.001	1.023
Reference: Center of Spain		0.000			0.674			0.000	
South Spain	0.037	0.525	1.038	0.003	0.990	1.003	-0.100	0.000	0.905
East (Levante)	-0.014	0.766	0.986	-0.280	0.462	0.756	0.069	0.001	1.072
North Spain	0.384	0.000	1.468	0.250	0.620	1.284	0.148	0.000	1.159
Constant	-2.231	0.000	0.107	-1.982	0.000	0.138	-1.883	0.000	0.152
Number of cases	20.217			212.219			116.735		
Pseudo R2	0.115			0.165			0.107		
% correct predictions Yi=0	61.19			66.64			59.89		
% correct predictions Yi =1	62.92			64.81			63.95		
% correct predictions	62.23			66.02			62.04		

(*) All programmes with control group. – Source: Own calculations from the Spanish INEM and Social Security System.

Finally, Table 7 shows the employment rates observed for all the programmes analysed, differentiating by gender, age, educational level, time searching for a job and whether or not the individual received a subsidy. All the sub-categories for which we observed a higher employment rate for participants are marked by italics. The first feature to point out is that, as the estimation results showed, there are more positive differences for women than for men. Additionally, the majority of programmes, except the *Employment workshops*, *Active job-search assistance*, *Insertion income* and *Public employment*, also show higher employment rates for the long-term jobseekers. With respect to women, the employment rates of participants are always higher for this group. These results underline the necessity of improving the selection of participants in active labour market policies to ensure an increase in their employment probability.

Table 7: Employment rates by programmes and specific groups

		Men				Women			
		Treatment [in %]	Control [in %]	Diff. [in %-points]	Sig.(*)	Treatment [in %]	Control [in %]	Diff. [in %-pts.]	Sig. (*)
Vocational training	16-24 years	58.7	62.3	-3.5	0.000	56.2	55.0	*1.3*	0.000
	25-34 years	66.9	68.8	-1.9	0.000	58.0	54.7	*3.2*	0.000
	35-44 years	62.7	64.5	-1.8	0.002	48.8	47.4	*1.4*	0.000
	45-54 years	52.5	50.6	*1.9*	0.045	40.4	40.1	*0.4*	**0.560**
	55-64 years	52.6	66.8	-14.2	0.000	36.1	49.4	-13.4	0.000
Workshop schools	16-24 years	58.0	59.6	-1.6	0.029	44.2	43.5	*0.6*	0.469
	25-34 years	-	-	-	-	-	-	-	-
	35-44 years	-	-	-	-	-	-	-	-
	45-54 years	-	-	-	-	-	-	-	-
	55-64 years	-	-	-	-	-	-	-	-
Employment workshops	16-24 years	57.7	64.0	-6.3	0.123	53.3	53.3	0.0	1.000
	25-34 years	57.7	67.4	-9.7	0.000	49.9	47.8	*2.1*	**0.258**
	35-44 years	55.7	66.3	-10.6	0.000	48.8	44.5	*4.3*	0.016
	45-54 years	52.7	52.1	*0.6*	**0.824**	44.3	34.1	*10.2*	0.000
	55-64 years	54.7	66.0	-11.4	0.004	45.2	43.8	*1.4*	**0.814**
General orientation	16-24 years	60.1	67.0	-6.9	0.001	52.6	56.3	-3.8	0.036
	25-34 years	64.4	71.1	-6.7	0.005	49.4	54.9	-5.4	0.001
	35-44 years	58.2	65.4	-7.2	0.007	41.2	48.8	-7.5	0.000
	45-54 years	40.6	53.4	-12.8	0.000	32.9	42.5	-9.6	0.000
	55-64 years	67.5	67.7	-0.2	0.933	37.2	42.6	-5.4	0.083
Individual job-search assistance	16-24 years	58.1	59.9	-1.8	0.000	49.5	49.8	-0.3	0.477
	25-34 years	62.5	66.0	-3.5	0.000	44.7	46.4	-1.6	0.000
	35-44 years	57.1	61.3	-4.2	0.000	37.6	40.7	-3.0	0.000
	45-54 years	46.0	45.8	*0.2*	**0.818**	30.5	33.1	-2.6	0.000
	55-64 years	52.2	62.0	-9.8%	0.000	28.7	40.2	-11.5	0.000

An Evaluation of ALMP: the case of Spain

		Men				Women			
		Treatment [in %]	Control [in %]	Diff. [in %-points]	Sig.(*)	Treatment [in %]	Control [in %]	Diff. [in %-pts.]	Sig. (*)
Personal employment orientation plans	16-24 years	62.5	62.5	0.0	0.992	56.8	55.8	1.0	0.153
	25-34 years	66.5	65.8	0.7	0.377	56.7	53.0	3.7	0.000
	35-44 years	65.5	63.2	2.2	0.050	49.9	46.8	3.2	0.000
	45-54 years	48.8	46.6	2.1	0.121	32.8	33.7	-0.9	0.357
	55-64 years	45.2	67.4	-22.2	0.000	28.2	45.0	-16.8	0.000
Active job-search assistance	16-24 years	57.8	60.6	-2.8	0.027	51.1	51.6	-0.4	0.620
	25-34 years	63.1	67.1	-4.0	0.002	47.0	48.2	-1.2	0.127
	35-44 years	63.0	63.1	-0.1	0.967	36.6	41.5	-4.9	0.000
	45-54 years	42.6	50.6	-7.9	0.001	30.3	34.5	-4.2	0.005
	55-64 years	59.5	61.7	-2.2	0.426	27.1	39.7	-12.5	0.000
Entrepreneurial assistance	16-24 years	72.6	61.1	11.5	0.000	60.5	55.6	4.9	0.039
	25-34 years	76.5	70.1	6.4	0.000	61.8	50.8	11.0	0.000
	35-44 years	70.8	62.8	8.0	0.000	53.0	43.5	9.4	0.000
	45-54 years	60.6	48.1	12.6	0.000	46.8	36.1	10.7	0.002
	55-64 years	60.7	63.7	-3.1	0.621	44.4	33.3	11.1	0.167
Insertion income	16-24 years	43.9	59.5	-15.5	0.000	26.5	42.8	-16.3	0.000
	25-34 years	37.1	60.6	-23.5	0.000	18.3	35.3	-17.0	0.000
	35-44 years	32.8	56.7	-23.9	0.000	16.6	33.4	-16.8	0.000
	45-54 years	27.5	44.5	-17.0	0.000	12.8	26.3	-13.5	0.000
	55-64 years	37.7	52.4	-14.7	0.000	16.5	35.9	-19.4	0.000
Public employment (Social Activities)	16-24 years	57.5	61.6	-4.1	0.000	52.4	53.0	-0.6	0.654
	25-34 years	58.8	66.5	-7.7	0.000	48.6	50.6	-1.9	0.008
	35-44 years	52.6	63.5	-10.9	0.000	40.4	43.3	-2.9	0.000
	45-54 years	50.2	52.8	-2.7	0.001	35.1	36.7	-1.6	0.154
	55-64 years	56.2	68.8	-12.7	0.000	38.1	43.0	-4.9	0.008
Vocational training	Without stud.	52.8	55.3	-2.5	0.238	36.8	38.0	-1.3	0.500
	Primary stud.	61.8	64.9	-3.1	0.000	49.5	47.6	1.9	0.000
	Sec. stud.	61.7	63.3	-1.6	0.000	55.6	53.2	2.4	0.000
	Tertiary stud.	65.5	67.6	-2.1	0.000	61.6	60.7	1.0	0.008
Workshop schools	Without stud.	56.7	56.0	0.7	0.836	39.6	33.7	5.9	0.259
	Primary stud.	57.9	59.8	-2.0	0.008	43.4	42.8	0.6	0.497
	Sec. stud.	61.5	56.9	4.7	0.172	50.4	51.8	-1.4	0.607
	Tertiary stud.	80.0	80.0	0.0	1.000	63.6	65.7	-2.1	0.848
Employment workshops	Without stud.	43.7	52.3	-8.7	0.041	36.9	27.7	9.2	0.024
	Primary stud.	55.2	63.6	-8.4	0.000	44.8	41.9	3.0	0.024
	Sec. stud.	57.5	65.0	-7.5	0.069	51.0	49.6	1.5	0.651
	Tertiary stud.	69.9	70.3	-0.3	0.927	65.2	52.7	12.5	0.000
General orientation	Without stud.	36.8	57.2	-20.5	0.000	35.6	33.6	2.0	0.543
	Primary stud.	61.6	66.8	-5.2	0.000	41.2	47.6	-6.4	0.000
	Sec. stud.	60.8	65.6	-4.8	0.065	51.1	57.7	-6.6	0.001
	Tertiary stud.	62.7	66.1	-3.4	0.390	56.2	64.2	-8.0	0.001
Individual job-search assistance	Without stud.	43.6	50.1	-6.6	0.000	26.1	31.7	-5.5	0.000
	Primary stud.	58.2	61.4	-3.1	0.000	38.1	40.7	-2.5	0.000
	Sec. stud.	58.6	60.6	-2.1	0.001	48.7	49.3	-0.6	0.132
	Tertiary stud.	64.0	67.0	-3.0	0.000	55.9	56.5	-0.5	0.248

		Men				Women			
		Treatment [in %]	Control [in %]	Diff. [in %-points]	Sig.(*)	Treatment [in %]	Control [in %]	Diff. [in %-pts.]	Sig. (*)
Pers. employment orient. plans	Without stud.	50.7	60.5	-9.8	0.001	36.3	42.2	-5.9	0.034
	Primary stud.	61.6	61.2	0.3	**0.582**	46.7	45.5	1.2	0.018
	Sec. stud.	62.3	61.9	0.4	**0.712**	55.9	53.0	2.9	0.000
	Tertiary stud.	61.7	65.5	-3.8	0.008	59.4	58.3	1.1	**0.181**
Active job-search assist.	Without stud.	41.6	49.0	-7.4	0.017	24.6	33.8	-9.2	0.000
	Primary stud.	59.6	62.5	-2.9	0.003	38.8	41.7	-2.9	0.000
	Sec. stud.	57.7	61.7	-3.9	0.019	50.2	50.2	0.0	**0.983**
	Tertiary stud.	64.1	66.3	-2.2	0.245	56.3	58.1	-1.8	0.103
Entrepreneurial assistance	Without stud.	50.0	62.0	-12.0	0.102	38.9	30.0	8.9	**0.210**
	Primary stud.	73.0	63.9	9.1	0.000	51.8	42.1	9.7	0.000
	Sec. stud.	72.6	64.6	8.0	0.000	61.6	50.2	11.5	0.000
	Tertiary stu.	73.0	66.8	6.2	0.009	66.1	58.5	7.6	0.000
Insertion income	Without stud.	29.6	46.9	-17.3	0.000	15.0	27.8	-12.8	0.000
	Primary stud.	36.5	59.2	-22.8	0.000	17.1	35.8	-18.7	0.000
	Sec. stud.	41.2	61.7	-20.5	0.000	29.9	47.5	-17.6	0.000
	Tertiary stud.	58.2	70.9	-12.7	0.001	51.9	55.2	-3.4	0.270
Public employment (Soc. Act.)	Without stud.	44.2	55.6	-11.4	0.000	25.5	32.5	-7.1	0.000
	Primary stud.	55.9	63.8	-7.9	0.000	38.3	42.2	-3.9	0.000
	Sec. stud.	60.2	63.1	-2.9	0.033	55.6	53.3	2.3	0.059
	Tertiary stud.	67.8	68.4	-0.6	0.708	65.0	62.2	2.8	0.006
Vocational training	<25 yrs.&<6 m. search for job	58.7	63.7	-5.0	0.000	56.5	56.8	-0.3	0.412
	≥25 yrs & <12 m. search f. job	66.2	68.6	-2.4	0.000	55.8	55.6	0.2	**0.455**
	Long-term jobseekers	55.5	54.0	1.5	0.006	48.0	40.8	7.2	0.000
Workshop schools	<25 yrs.&<6 m. searching job	57.7	61.9	-4.2	0.000	46.5	47.4	-0.9	0.452
	≥25 yrs.&<12 m. search f. job	-	-	-	-	-	-	-	-
	Long-term jobseekers	58.5	55.4	3.0	0.011	41.7	39.6	2.1	**0.078**
Employment workshops	<25 yrs.&<6 m. search for job	57.8	64.8	-7.0	0.102	51.8	56.4	-4.5	0.499
	≥25 yrs.&<12 m. search f. job	57.0	65.2	-8.2	0.000	50.6	48.9	1.7	**0.209**
	Long-term jobseekers	49.0	54.2	-5.2	0.101	42.8	31.1	11.8	0.000
General orientation	<25 yrs.&<6 m. search for job	60.0	68.0	-8.0	0.000	52.5	57.3	-4.8	0.011
	≥25 yrs.&<12 m. search f. job	59.8	66.6	-6.8	0.000	42.9	50.8	-7.9	0.000
	Long-term jobseekers	52.2	48.0	4.2	**0.328**	40.0	37.0	3.0	**0.295**

		Men				Women			
		Treatment [in %]	Control [in %]	Diff. [in %-points]	Sig.(*)	Treatment [in %]	Control [in %]	Diff. [in %-pts.]	Sig. (*)
Individual job-search assistance	<25 yrs.&<6 m. search for job	59.7	62.2	-2.6	0.000	51.7	53.2	-1.5	0.001
	≥25 yrs.&<12 m. search f. job	60.6	65.6	-5.1	0.000	43.9	48.2	-4.3	0.000
	Long-term jobseekers	49.9	49.3	0.6	0.279	35.3	34.0	1.3	0.000
Personal employment orientation plans	<25 yrs.&<6 m. search for job	63.0	62.8	0.2	0.839	57.3	56.8	0.5	0.503
	≥25 yrs.&<12 m. search f. job	65.1	64.6	0.5	0.412	53.7	52.6	1.1	0.033
	Long-term jobseekers	46.3	51.0	-4.7	0.000	38.8	35.6	3.3	0.000
Active job-search assistance	<25 yrs.&<6 m. search for job	58.6	61.9	-3.3	0.018	53.6	53.9	-0.3	0.732
	≥25 yrs.&<12 m. search f. job	61.7	66.1	-4.4	0.000	44.2	49.1	-4.9	0.000
	Long-term jobseekers	51.3	51.4	-0.1	0.946	36.5	36.1	0.4	0.611
Entrepreneurial assistance	<25 yrs.&<6 m. search for job	74.0	64.0	10.0	0.000	63.2	57.7	5.5	0.046
	≥25 yrs.&<12 m. search f. job	74.7	67.4	7.3	0.000	61.7	51.4	10.3	0.000
	Long-term jobseekers	59.9	50.1	9.7	0.000	44.9	35.1	9.9	0.000
Insertion income	<25 yrs.&<6 m. search for job	44.6	61.5	-17.0	0.000	26.4	44.4	-18.0	0.000
	≥25 yrs.&<12 m. search f. job	34.1	55.2	-21.2	0.000	16.8	33.4	-16.6	0.000
	Long-term jobseekers	27.1	46.7	-19.5	0.000	15.1	30.0	-14.9	0.000
Public employment (Social Activit.)	<25 yrs.&<6 m. search for job	58.3	62.4	-4.1	0.000	53.8	55.9	-2.1	0.159
	≥25 yrs.&<12 m. search f. job	56.0	64.6	-8.5	0.000	45.4	49.2	-3.8	0.000
	Long-term jobseekers	45.3	52.0	-6.7	0.000	36.6	34.4	2.2	0.011
Vocational training	Not receiving subsidy	58.5	61.1	-2.5	0.000	51.7	49.5	2.2	0.000
	Receiv. subs.	69.1	69.5	-0.4	0.332	60.4	58.0	2.4	0.000
	Subsidy finish.	70.6	70.4	0.2	0.771	59.8	56.1	3.7	0.000
Workshop schools	Not rec. subs.	57.8	57.6	0.3	0.738	44.0	43.4	0.7	0.456
	Receiv. subs.	60.6	63.9	-3.3	0.332	43.0	42.3	0.7	0.834
	Subsidy finish.	63.5	71.2	-7.7	0.091	51.5	53.5	-1.9	0.754
Employment workshops	Not rec. subs.	56.5	61.4	-4.8	0.009	47.2	40.8	6.4	0.000
	Receiv. subs.	50.5	62.9	-12.3	0.000	44.7	46.3	-1.6	0.491
	Subsidy finish.	58.9	70.6	-11.7	0.000	55.5	50.8	4.7	0.112
General orientation	Not rec. subs.	56.3	62.3	-6.0	0.000	44.7	49.6	-4.9	0.000
	Receiv. subs.	61.0	68.3	-7.4	0.000	41.9	52.1	-10.2	0.000
	Subsidy finish.	67.6	69.9	-2.3	0.493	60.6	59.6	1.0	0.779

		Men				Women			
		Treatment [in %]	Control [in %]	Diff. [in %-points]	Sig.(*)	Treatment [in %]	Control [in %]	Diff. [in %-pts.]	Sig. (*)
Indiv. job-search assist.	Not rec. subs.	56.4	58.6	-2.2	0.000	43.5	43.4	0.1	**0.624**
	Receiv. subs.	57.2	62.2	-5.1	0.000	37.5	44.6	-7.2	0.000
	Subsidy finish.	67.9	67.5	0.5	**0.515**	53.4	51.1	2.3	0.001
Pers. employment orient. pl.	Not rec. subs.	57.7	58.7	-1.0	0.168	49.8	47.6	2.1	0.000
	Receiv. subs.	64.3	65.2	-0.9	0.239	51.9	52.9	-1.0	0.126
	Subsidy finish.	68.5	65.0	3.5	0.020	58.8	53.8	5.0	0.000
Act. job-search assist.	Not rec. subs.	56.5	60.3	-3.8	0.000	45.8	45.7	0.2	**0.767**
	Receiv. subs.	59.9	63.2	-3.3	0.008	39.0	46.9	-7.9	0.000
	Subsidy finish.	70.4	67.7	2.7	**0.260**	53.1	51.9	1.2	**0.514**
Entrepreneurial assist.	Not rec. subs.	69.9	61.3	8.6	0.000	56.9	46.4	10.5	0.000
	Receiv. subs.	70.2	67.3	3.0	0.047	53.9	50.8	3.1	**0.092**
	Subsidy finish.	82.9	68.0	14.9	0.000	72.1	53.0	19.2	0.000
Insertion income	Not rec. subs.	58.7	58.0	0.7	**0.357**	43.1	36.2	6.8	0.000
	Receiv. subs.	27.9	50.5	-22.5	0.000	14.1	29.0	-14.9	0.000
	Subsidy finish.	54.5	66.2	-11.7	0.000	33.6	47.7	-14.0	0.000
Publ. Employment (Social Activit.)	Not rec. subs.	59.5	59.4	0.1	**0.857**	50.8	44.0	6.8	0.000
	Receiv. subs.	40.4	62.9	-22.6	0.000	22.0	47.7	-25.7	0.000
	Subsidy finish.	62.9	70.0	-7.1	0.000	57.0	54.8	2.2	**0.093**

(*) Significance level Chi-square test

6. Conclusions

From a global point of view, the ALMP as a whole and represents an additional value in terms of employment probability for those people who have participated in some of the programmes included in such policies. Generally speaking, women have less probability of being employed than men. The results also show that any age group has lower probabilities than the group of those less than 25 years old. Additionally, the educational level referring to people without studies shows that a higher educational level implies a rise in the employment rate. Finally, the variable that measures the time for searching a job shows that those older than 24 and those who spent fewer than 12 months seeking employment have higher probabilities of being employed; on the other hand, long-term jobseekers have a lower probability of being employed.

The evaluation suggests that there are great differences between programmes in reference to this probability, which are connected not only to the content of each programme but also to the applied criteria in the candidate selection process and with the general management of human and financial resources by the entity responsible for planning and development functions. For participants in programmes that were similar but located in different Spanish regions (*Comunidades Autonomas*), significant differences in the results have been confirmed.

Apart from other statistical sources referring to the labour market evolution, the use of surveys and samples of beneficiaries to collect data directly is one of the most common methods used in Spain to measure the effects of the ESF co-financed programmes. At the same time, the utilization of records of official institutions for similar purposes is quite infrequent, considering that these records are one of the least expensive existing sources of data, and the one with the most potential. Microdata offer not only the possibility of checking the labour itinerary followed by participants in LMP, but it is also the only real way to operate with rigorous control groups.

Experience has shown that the use of control groups also seems very advantageous, especially to analyze the ALMP impact on the labour market and over the ex-post labour insertion of specific groups benefited by these policies. The preparation of such representative groups of non-participants is nevertheless difficult and time consuming, because one must select individuals one-by-one with similar personal and professional characteristics to those who participated in the ALMP. Taking into account these circumstances, the elaboration of these control groups requires a pure, random selection process crossing diverse data records. Nevertheless, the interpretation of these results must be done carefully and under flexible interpretation of the rules for both cases: those with higher results for the objective group versus the control group and those with higher results for the control group.

References

Blundell, R. and Costa-Dias, M. (2000): "Evaluation Methods for Non-experimental Data", Fiscal Studies 21, pp. 427-468

Blundell, R., Costa-Dias, M., Costas, M. and Van Reenen, J. (2001): "Evaluating the employment impact of a mandatory job search assistance program", The Institute for Fiscal Studies WP01/20

Caliendo, M. (2006): Microeconometric evaluation of labour market policies. Springer: Berlin

Eichler, M. and Lechner, M. (2002): "An evaluation of public employment programmes in the East German State of Sachsen-Anhalt", Economic Journal n° 482, vol. 112, pp. 854-893

Gerfin, M. and Lechner, M. (2002): "A microeconometric evalutation of the active labour market policy in Switzerland", The Economic Journal, vol. 112, pp. 854-893

Heckman, J.L. (1979): "Sample selection bias as a specification error", Econometrica. Vol. 47, 1, pp. 153-162

Heckman, J.L., LaLonde, R. J. and Smith, J. A. (1999): "The economics and econometrics of active labor market programs". Handbook of labor economics Vol. III, eds.: O. Ashenfelter/ D. Card

Heckman, J.L. and Smith, J. A. (2003): "The Determinants of Participation in a Social Program: Evidence from a Prototypical Job Training Program", IZA Discussion Paper n° 798

Herrarte, A. and Sáez, F. (2004): "Formación-empleo: una evaluación", Cuadernos de Economía, vol. 27, n° 74, pp. 147-174

Herrarte, A., Moral-Carcedo, J. and Sánchez-Romero (2006): "Desempleo, búsqueda y políticas activas", Revista Presupuesto y Gasto Público, vol. 43, n° 2/2006, pp. 155-178

Herrarte, A. and Sáez, F. (2007): "Labour Market Policy in Spain: Analysis of microdata and main results", in: Labour Market Policy Seminar, Eurostat Methodologies and working papers, pp. 99-118

Lechner, M. and F. Pfeiffer: Econometric evaluation of labour market policies. ZEW Economic Studies 13

Ministerio de Trabajo y Asuntos Sociales (MTAS) (2001): Plan de Acción para el Empleo del Reino de España

– (2000): La evaluación de las políticas de ocupación. Madrid, MTAS, Colección Informes y Estudios

Pierre, G (1999): "A framework for active labour market policy evaluation", Employment and training papers n° 49, International Labour Office Geneva

Sáez, F. and Toledo, I. (1995). "A design including multivariate statistics: Evaluation of ESF training courses", in: Measuring the employment effects of Community Structural Interventions. MEANS, European Union-Regional Policy and Cohesion, Lyon

Sáez, F. (1997). "The monitoring and Evaluation of Employment Policies in Spain", in: Progress in evaluation research, ed.: Wissenschaftszentrum Berlin für Sozialforschung WZB, FS I. Berlin, pp. 97-203

Sáez, F (2004): "Evaluación de la Estrategia Europea de Empleo en las Comunidades Autónomas Españolas". Informe científico-técnico. Madrid: MTAS-INEM, november 2004.

FEMALE VISIONARY-TRANSFORMATIONAL LEADERSHIP AND INNOVATION: THE MODERATING ROLE OF MULTIPLE INTELLIGENCES AND ETHICAL LEADERSHIP

DETELIN S. ELENKOV
(UNIVERSITY OF TENNESSEE, KNOXVILLE, USA)

Introduction

For a variety of reasons, including methodological limitations and the predominance of male researchers, academic research has only recently started paying serious attention to issues related to female visionary-transformational leadership and its effectiveness. Interest in this subject has grown particularly because of the increasing number of women in leadership positions and women in academia. Researchers have started pointing out examples of highly effective female leaders in a variety of domains, including eBay's CEO *Meg Whitman*, Secretary of State *Condoleezza Rice*, and the U.S. Senator *Hillary Rodham Clinton*, to name a few. It has also been recognized that numerous women have found ways to create entrepreneurial ventures that have become profitable and have grown, primarily in the retail business and personal service sectors.

The accelerated pace of innovations and growing diversity of stakeholders are notable characteristics of today's business environment. Accordingly, female executive leaders face a multitude of new critical challenges, including promoting innovation. Under the present circumstances, the effectiveness of female executives appears to depend less on their cognitive abilities in a traditional sense and much more on their possession of multiple intelligences and their practice of ethical leadership.

1. Female Leadership Versus Male Leadership

A number of researchers (e.g., Eagly & Karau, 2002; Rosener, 1990) contend that there are significant differences between male and female leaders. In particular, women leaders focus on the process, while male leaders focus on achievement and closure. Women use more personal power, whereas men use structural power. Besides, female leaders are more flexible, can complete more diverse tasks and, to a greater extent, they rely on value cooperation and relationships. These female qualities are valuable and relevant in organizational leadership. Moreover, female leaders often possess good negotiating skills and the ability to balance, and this makes them soft-skilled executives.

In brief, women are more likely to lead in a style that is effective under present-day conditions. It has also been recognized that women, more than men, face the difficult challenge to prove that they have the high level of ability required to become a leader. Therefore, female leaders face unique challenges that their male counterparts do not.

2. Ethical Dimension of Leadership

There has been a growing interest in individual accountability with respect to ethical decisions, namely the role of leaders regarding the application and endorsement of ethical principles. Consequently, recent research has focused on the topic of ethical leadership behaviors (Brown, Trevino & Harrison, 2005). The latter include demonstrating integrity, considerate and fair treatment of employees, and holding individuals accountable for their behavior. These behaviors promote high levels of trust within the workforce and increased satisfaction with, and commitment to, the organization via identification with goals and mission.

Traditional ethical theories are rational. Ethics theories take into consideration relationships between families, the individual and the society as a whole. In defining the ethical dimensions of leadership, there are two criteria: the character and virtue of leaders and the legitimacy of social processes, defining the leaders' choices.

Economic systems depend on legitimacy. Therefore, trust and values are a necessity for the effective functioning of organizations. Applying this to organizational leadership, there are three ethical dimensions – the leader's motives, the leader's influence strategies, and the leader's character formation – all of which focus on the leader's integrity.

3. Multiple Intelligences

Following Gardner (1983), human intelligence is not a single trait, as supporters of the IQ fad have always claimed. He disagreed with such a narrow and unidimensional view of an individual's capacity for reasoning. Subsequently, he introduced the concept of multiple intelligences essentially emphasizing that human intelligence is multidimensional. In recent years, three kinds of intelligence and related skills – emotional, social, and cultural – have gained increasing popularity.

3.1 Emotional Intelligence

According to Martinez (1997) emotional intelligence can be defined as a set of non-cognitive skills, capabilities, and competencies that influence a person's ability to cope with environmental demands and pressures. Mayer and Salovey (1995) further extended this definition by conceptualizing several categories of emotional intelligence: the assessment and expression of emotions (including perception and empathy), emotional regulation (in self and in others), and utilization of emotions (including flexible planning, creative thinking, and motivation among others).

Goleman (1995), Mayer and Salovey (1995), and Sosik and Megerian (1999) have contended that emotional intelligence is fundamental to leadership effectiveness and to organizational performance. Although the research on this topic has generated a stream of publications, many relevant questions remain unanswered. One of the main questions concerns the specific relationship and possible interaction between emotional intelligence and leader's attributes (e.g., female visionary-transformational abilities) associated with leadership effectiveness.

3.2 Social Intelligence

The notion of social intelligence (SI) has been approached from different standpoints. In particular, some lines of research were concerned with the cognitive aspect of social intelligence whereas others focused on communication and interactive processes. The definition of social intelligence evolved over time. Originally seen as a cognitive ability to understand social interactions and to get along with others, social intelligence has lately been viewed as a much more complex concept encompassing not only the cognitive component of understanding others but also an adaptive behavioral component whereby the individual is able to act in accordance with what the situation dictates.

Marlowe (1986) has been credited for providing the most commonly used definition of social intelligence. He conceptualized social intelligence as the ability to understand the feelings, thoughts, and behaviors of individuals, including their own feelings in interpersonal situations, and to act appropriately upon that understanding. Marlowe (1986) further decomposed social intelligence into five distinct areas:
- prosocial attitude,
- social skills,
- empathy skills,
- emotionality, and
- social anxiety.

Numerous recent studies have focused on the dimensionality of the construct of social intelligence. For example, Kosmitzky and John (1993) categorized that concept into three broad dimensions:
- cognitive (perspective taking, understanding people, knowing social rules, and openness to others),
- behavioral (good at dealing with people, social adaptability, and interpersonal warmth), and
- a separate motivational dimension (manipulating, leading, and motivating others).

However, research in the field is still far from reaching a widely accepted agreement regarding the number and the characteristics of these dimensions.

A growing interest in interpersonal relations in organizations has led to numerous attempts to identify the social skills and traits responsible for increases in performance and for the creation of a positive work climate (Bass, 2001). Leadership, in particular, female visionary-transformational leadership, and motivation represent some of the fields of research in which the notion of social intelligence could play a significant role.

3.3 Cultural Intelligence

Early and Ang (2003) have defined cultural intelligence (CQ) as one's ability to be adaptive and responsive to cultural situations. In addition, they have categorized CQ into three major interrelated components of cognitive CQ, motivational CQ, and behavioral CQ. Cognitive CQ has been conceptualized as the capability to cultivate and develop practical knowledge of cross-cultural cues and schemata of appropriate behavior. It is considered critical for an adequate understanding of specific norms and practices in culturally diverse contexts (Ang, Dyne, Koh, and Ng, 2004). Most recently, Ang and her colleagues have provided evidence in support of the presence of a new distinct component of cultural intelligence, which has been called meta-cognitive CQ. It epitomizes one's cultural self-awareness and ability to modify his or her behavior to adjust to the various situations (Ang, et al. 2004).

Motivational CQ encompasses the inner drive and determination of an individual to learn about cultural similarities and differences. Following Ang, Dyne, Koh and Ng (2004), individuals with high motivational CQ are internally driven to overcome cultural obstacles and to engage in interpersonal exchanges that foster understanding of others in culturally diverse environments. Behavioral CQ refers to one's adaptability and flexibility to take culturally appropriate actions that reflect the specificity of the current situation (Ang, et al. 2004).

4. Visionary-Transformational Leadership and Innovation

Visionary-transformational leadership can be defined as a set of behaviors through which leaders form a vision for the future of the organization and pursue this vision with actions aimed at adequately communicating it to others in the organization, in order to change the basic values, beliefs, and attitudes of followers, so that they will become able and willing to perform beyond the required levels specified by the organization (Elenkov, Judge & Wright, 2005).

One of the recent streams of leadership research has established that visionary-transformational leadership makes a difference – often a big difference – in the success of innovation at the organizational level (e.g., Elkins & Keller, 2003). However, it would be a *faux pas* to consider that any leadership behavior positively affects creativity and innovation. Elenkov and Manev (2005a) have demonstrated that leadership effectiveness in relation to innovation depends on which leadership behaviors are emphasized in a specific cultural context. In addition, Elenkov, Judge, and Wright (2005) have indicated that leadership behaviors, which are closely aligned with a clear and strategically-relevant vision for the organization's future, have the largest potential to promote innovation.

A related stream of recent research on leadership has stressed that, what makes an executive an effective leader, is his or her behavioral profile. Notably, Kouzes and Posner (1987) have introduced a path-breaking conceptual framework consisting of five categories of exemplary leadership practices. These researchers have metaphorically called those practices

"Model the Way",
"Inspire a Shared Vision",
"Challenge the Process",
"Enable Others to Act", and
"Encourage the Heart".

In essence, Kouzes and Posner (1987) have emphasized that visionary-transformational leaders must be models for performing whatever they would like their followers to do; visionary-transformational leaders should inspire their subordinates and encourage them to share the leaders' visions; visionary-transformational leaders ought to try something new and something challenging, as one of their potential main strengths resides in their capacity to support and implement novel ideas; visionary-transformational leaders know that it is next to impossible for a single individual to accomplish great deeds, and, therefore, they should seek cooperation from their followers; and last but not least, visionary-transformational leaders must always encourage their followers to move on, as people tend to give up or withdraw when facing difficulties or confrontations.

Recent research on emotional intelligence proposed that dissimilar levels of emotional intelligence between female and male leaders might explain differences in leadership style and in the likelihood of representatives of each gender displaying specific visionary transformational behaviors (Mandell & Pherwani, 2003). By extension, one may conceptualize that female visionary-transformational leadership may interact with contextual factors to produce complex, but significant, effects on organizational innovation.

5. Research Hypotheses

There is a growing interest in leadership research to study emotional, social, and cultural intelligences as key contributors to effective leadership (e.g., Bass, 2001; Elenkov and Manev, 2005b). For example, a recent study has demonstrated that emotional intelligence is a significant predictor of the adopted leadership style (Sosik and Megerian, 1999). Taking into account the apparent relationship between the adopted leadership style and the female leader's effectiveness, one may argue that emotional intelligence could affect the latter, as it has a proven influence on the former.

Hypothesis 1: Emotional intelligence of female leaders moderates the relationship of these executives' visionary-transformational leadership behaviors with innovation at their organizations.

Female leaders that are socially intelligent should possess the necessary knowledge and skills to detect intricate social cues and accordingly moderate their interactions with followers. Extant research postulated a series of attributes (e.g., understanding of critical aspects of situations, ability to access a vast range of adequate responses, and the capacity to provide socially-appropriate responses) associated with social intelligence of leaders in general. In particular, Bass (2001) has indicated that good communication skills, sociability, and tolerance of stress in interacting with followers and peers are important elements of social intelligence that could conceivably increase the effectiveness of a female leader who possesses these traits.

Hypothesis 2: Social intelligence of female leaders moderates the relationship of these executives' visionary-transformational leadership behaviors with innovation at their organizations.

The ability of a female leader to generate enthusiasm among followers and to support their aspirations, which is called "inspiring the vision," is expected to interact with the motivational component of cultural intelligence, which is the inner drive and determination to accept the challenge of overcoming cultural barriers and obstacles. Moreover, through challenging the process and enabling others to act, female leaders could empower their followers and create an atmosphere conducive for innovation. However, female leaders tend to differ in levels of cultural intelligence. Therefore, the effects of individual female leaders' visionary-transformational behaviors on innovation would also be likely to differ. In formal terms:

Hypothesis 3: Cultural intelligence of female leaders moderates the relationship of these executives' visionary-transformational leadership behaviors with innovation at their organizations.

A number of authors investigated the extent to which women adopt primarily an ethic of care orientation – concern with interpersonal relations and the maintenance of psychological contract – while men adopt an ethic of justice – resolution of conflicting rights and attempt to attain equality (e.g., Peter & Gallup, 1994). The argument with respect to gender differences in ethical decision-making relies on the possibility that men and women leaders have dissimilar value systems and beliefs guiding their decisions. Furthermore, even though the differences found in interpersonal conflict management styles might be attributed to a differing mastery of social skills and gender role orientation (Goleman, 1998), dissimilar patterns of ethical decision-making likely reflect moderating effects of contextual variables that shape priorities, values, and belief systems (Hoffman, 1998). These findings suggest that ethical leadership and the strategic situation associated with specific ethical dilemmas account for differences between female and male leadership effectiveness. Based on this line of reasoning, ethical leadership appears to interact with female leadership to influence important organizational outcomes.

Hypothesis 4: Ethical leadership of female executives moderates the relationship of these executives' visionary-transformational leadership behaviors with innovation at their organizations.

6. Research Methodology and Results

6.1 Sample

One thousand four hundred and sixty nine female respondents residing in 21 countries – the United States, Canada, the United Kingdom, France, Spain, Portugal, Belgium, Italy, Sweden, Norway, Finland, Germany, Austria, Switzerland, Greece, Turkey, Russia, Ukraine, Czech Republic, Slovakia, and Bulgaria – provided data for this study. All of them had formal positions of at least members of the top management teams of their organizations. Two hundred and fourteen of those female leaders were CEOs of their companies. There were also 121 presidents in our research sample. The distribution of respondents within the sample varied from 107 for the United States and 98 for Sweden to 51 for Bulgaria and 46 for Greece.

6.2 Measures

Emotional Intelligence was assessed through International Personality Item Pool (IPIP) Scales for Emotional Intelligence. This instrument consists of seven scales for
- Positive Expressivity,
- Negative Expressivity,
- Attending to Emotions,
- Emotion-based Decision-making,
- Responsive Joy,
- Responsive Distress, and
- Empathic Concern.

Social Intelligence was assessed through the revised International Personality Item Pool (IPIP) Values in Action (VIA) Scale for Social Intelligence. *Cultural Intelligence* (CQ) was operationalized using the instrument developed and substantiated by Ang, Dyne, Koh and Ng (2004). *Leadership Ethics* was measured by using the perceived leader integrity. The concept of perceived leader integrity is based on the utilitarian ethical theory. In essence, perceived leader integrity evaluates female leaders' ethics by measuring the degree to which coworkers see them as acting in accordance with rules that would produce the greatest good for the greatest number of people. The Perceived Leader Integrity Scale (PLIS) (Craig and Gustafson, 1998) is a thirty-item instrument validated by Parry and Proctor-Thomson (2002).

Visionary-transformational Leadership was measured through the Leadership Practices Inventory (LPI), a widely used measure developed and validated by Pozner and Kouzes (1993). We took advantage of the Observer Version of the LPI, in order to avoid any self-report bias. *Innovation* was assessed through the Absolute Innovation Adoption Rate, a measure that Damanpour and Gopalakrishnan (2001) found very useful for projects that attempt to avoid investigating innovation through approaches of a perceptual (as opposed to objective) nature. In fact, we were essentially interested in learning more about how actual innovation was affected by the interaction of female visionary-transformational leadership practices with multiple intelligences and ethical leadership of the respective female executives.

To keep in check possible confounding effects, several control variables were included in this study, namely
- age of the respondents (five categories: from <30 years to >60 years),
- size of the organization for which the respondents worked (three categories from less than 100 employees to more than 1000 employees), and

- industry sector (five categories: natural resource, manufacturing, services, public, and other).

6.3 Results

The research hypotheses were tested through moderated regression analyses with interaction terms, as suggested by Stone and Hollenbeck (1989). The control variables were entered first. Then, the terms for the direct effect of the predictor (female visionary-transformational leadership), the direct effect of the moderators (respectively, emotional, social, or cultural intelligence and ethical leadership), and interaction terms (products of the predictor variable with, respectively, each of the moderators) were entered.

The interaction terms explained a significant amount of the variance in the rate of innovation adoption in the cases of
- emotional intelligence ($\Delta R^2 = .12$, $F = 18.73$, $p < .001$),
- social intelligence ($\Delta R^2 = .10$, $F = 13.35$, $p < .001$),
- cultural intelligence ($\Delta R^2 = .13$, $F = 23.21$, $p < .001$), and
- ethical leadership ($\Delta R^2 = .11$, $F = 15.34$, $p < .001$).

Thus, the statistical results of the study provided qualified support to H1, H2, H3, and H4.

In summary, female visionary-transformational leadership proves to be a critical factor for successful innovation. As changes in organizations are beginning to make it easier for women to reach senior managerial positions, and as women are taking more strategic leadership positions, there are new opportunities to achieve more effective innovation-related outcomes. Besides, the combination and dynamic interaction of female visionary-transformational leadership with multiple (emotional, social, and cultural) intelligences and ethical leadership prove to further enhance innovation results. The implications of the findings presented in this section for academic research and business practice are discussed more extensively in the final part of this article.

7. Conclusions

Based on the findings of our study, emotional, social, and cultural intelligences of female leaders moderate the relationship of these executives' visionary-transformational leadership with innovation. Besides, ethical leadership proves to interact with female visionary-transformational leadership in relation to the effects of the latter on innovation.

In addition, the research results provide some direction for business practice. For example, female leaders wishing to enhance the effects of innovation processes at their organizations should look for ways to further develop their multiple intelligences. Acquiring advanced emotional intelligence, social intelligence, and cultural intelligence appears to hold a great promise for increasing the effectiveness of female visionary-transformational leadership in relation to innovation in various contexts. As Earley and Peterson (2004) have indicated, the elusive "cultural chameleon" could be tamed through new approaches to intercultural training. The same conclusion applies to developing further emotional and social intelligences of female leaders.

Moreover, ethical leadership may also enhance the effects of female visionary-transformational leadership on innovation. The former factor proves to be critically important for achieving a proper balance in modern organizations, while female visionary-transformational leadership has emerged as a crucial determinant of organizational effectiveness.

The main limitation of the current study is the non-random sample of female respondents used to obtain the research data, but the relatively large sample size and the number of countries from which the research sample was drawn does assure the external validity of the study findings. To be sure, more research should be conducted in future, in order to investigate both direct and interaction effects of female visionary-transformational leadership, other psychological and behavioral factors and their correlates and/or moderators on innovation and other strategically important variables.

References

Ang, S., Van Dyne, L., Koh, C., and Ng, K.Y. "The Measurement of Cultural Intelligence", Paper Presented at 2004 Annual Meetings of the Academy of Management, New Orleans, LA, 2004

Bass, B. "Cognitive, Social, and Emotional Intelligence of Transformational Leaders" in R. Riggio, S. Murphy, and F. Priozzolo (Editors), Multiple Intelligences and Leadership, Mahwah, NJ: Lawrence Earlbaum and Associates, 2001, pp. 54-77

Brown, M.E., Trevino, L.K., and Harrison, D.A. "Ethical leadership: A social learning perspective for construct development and testing", Organizational Behavior and Human Decision Processes, Vol. 97, 2005, pp. 117-134

Craig, S. B. and Gustafson, S. B. "Perceived Leader Integrity Scale: An instrument for assessing employee perceptions of leader integrity", Leadership Quarterly, Vol. 9 (2), 1998, pp. 127-145

Damanpour, F. and Gopalakrishnan, S. "The dynamics of the adoption of product and process innovations in organizations", Journal of Management Studies, Vol. 38 (1), 2001, pp. 45-65

Eagly, A. H., and Karau, S. J. Role congruity theory of prejudice toward female leaders. Psychological Review, Vol. 109, 2002, pp. 573–598

Earley, P. C. and Ang, S. Cultural Intelligence: Individual Interactions Across Cultures. Stanford, CA: Stanford Business Books, 2003

Earley, C., and Peterson, R. "The Elusive Cultural Chameleon: Cultural Intelligence as a New Approach to Intercultural Training for the Global Manager", Academy of Management Learning & Education, Vol. III (1), 2004, pp. 100-115

Elenkov, D., Judge, W., and Wright, P. "Strategic Leadership and Executive Innovation Influence: An International Multi-Cluster Comparative Study," Strategic Management Journal, Vol. XXVI (7), 2005, pp. 665-682

Elenkov, D. and Manev, I. "Top Management Leadership and Influence on Innovation: The Role of Socio-Cultural Context", Journal of Management, Vol. XXXI (3), 2005a, pp. 381-402

Elenkov, D. and Manev, I. "Social Culture Intelligence, Top-Level Leadership and Innovation Influence: An International Study", Academy of Management Best Paper Proceedings, Honolulu, HI, 2005b, IM F1-F6

Elkins, T. and Keller, R.T., "Leadership in research and development organizations: A literature review and conceptual framework." The Leadership Quarterly, Vol. XIV, 2003, pp. 587-606

Gardner, H. Multiple intelligences: The theory in practice. New York: Basic Books, 1993

Goleman, D. Emotional intelligence. New York: Bantam Books, 1995

Goleman, D. Working with emotional intelligence. New York: Bantam Books, 1998

Hoffman, J.J. "Are women really more ethical than men? Maybe it depends on the situation", Journal of Managerial Issues, Vol. 10 (1), 1998, pp. 60-74

Kosmitzky, C. and John, O. P. The implicit use of explicit conceptions of social intelligence. Personality and Individual Differences, Vol. XV (1), 1993, pp. 11-23

Kouzes, J. M., and Pozner, B. Z. The Leadership Challenge. San Francisco: Jossey Bass, 1987

Mandell, B. and Pherwani, S. "Relationship between emotional intelligence and transformational leadership style: A gender comparison", Journal of Business and Psychology, Vol. 17 (3), 2003, pp. 387-404

Marlowe, H. "Social Intelligence: Evidence of Multidimensionality and Construct Independence", Journal of Educational Psychology, Vol. 78 (1), pp. 52-58

Martinez, M. "The Relation of Emotional Intelligence with Selected Areas of Personal Functioning", Imagination, Cognition and Personality, Vol. XVII (1), 1997, pp. 3-13

Mayer, J. D. and Salovey, P. "Emotional Intelligence and the Construction and Regulation of Feelings", Applier and Preventive Psychology, Vol. IV (3), 1995, pp. 197-208

Parry, K. W. and Proctor-Thomson, S. B. "Perceived integrity of transformational leaders in organizational settings", Journal of Business Ethics, Vol. 35, 2002, pp. 75-96

Peter, E. and Gallup, R. "The ethic of care: A comparison of nursing and medical students", Image, Vol. 26 (1), 1994, pp. 47-51

Pozner, B. Z., and Kouzes, J. M. "Psychometric properties of the Leadership Practices Inventory", Educational and Psychological Measurement, Vol. 53, 1993, pp. 191-199

Rosener J. "Ways Women Lead", Harvard Business Review, November-December, 1990, pp. 119-125

Sosik, J. and Megerian, L. "Understanding Leader Emotional Intelligence and Performance: The Role of Self-Other Agreement on Transformational Leadership Perceptions", Group and Organization Management, Vol. XXIV, 1999, pp. 367-390

Stone, E. and Hollenbeck, J. "Clarifying Some Controversial Issues Surrounding Statistical Procedure for Detecting Moderator Variables: Empirical Evidence and Related Matters", Journal of Applied Psychology, Vol. 74 (1), 1989, pp. 3-10

WHAT DO OPTIMUM CURRENCY AREA CRITERIA TELL US ABOUT THE READINESS OF CENTRAL AND EAST EUROPEAN COUNTRIES TO JOIN THE EUROZONE?

GUERGANA STANOEVA
(SOFIA UNIVERSITY "ST. KLIMENT OHRIDSKI", BULGARIA)

The Central and East European countries (CEE countries) which joined the European Union (EU) in 2004 and 2007 must also join the European Monetary Union (EMU) when ready. The fulfilment of the Maastricht criteria implies, among other considerations, that these countries have to maintain stable nominal exchange rates vis-à-vis the Euro. Therefore, it is not only of scientific interest, but also of practical importance to study the degree of exchange rate volatility of the CEE countries and verify if there is any relationship between this volatility and the criteria established by the Optimum Currency Areas (OCA) theory. This could provide us with a useful insight into the spheres where more restructuring efforts are needed in order to better prepare for the Euro adoption, all of this, from the perspective of the OCA theory.

The first part of the study in hand is directed at the discussion of some important points of the OCA theory and presents the methods of evaluation of the OCA criteria which have been applied to ten CEE countries. These are Bulgaria, the Czech Republic, Estonia, Hungary, Latvia, Lithuania, Poland, Romania, Slovakia and Slovenia. I have applied this estimation for the period before and after EU entry[1] in order to check whether this major event has contributed to the acceleration of the convergence process with respect to these criteria. The findings could contribute to the debate on the exogenous or endogenous character of the OCA criteria as put forward, for example, by Frankel and Rose (1996: 1-33).

In the second part, we shall deal with the development of a simple econometric model that helps to verify the presumed relationship between the nominal exchange rate behaviour of the respective CEE countries and the OCA criteria. For this purpose I have run regressions, which are applied to each country taken apart from the others. Then pooled estimations are used in order to verify this relationship for groups of countries, chosen according to the similarity of their exchange rate regime choice and for all CEE countries as a whole.

---

[1] Since 8 of the 10 countries joined the EU in 2005, that year has been chosen as a reference year. It should be noted, however, that Bulgaria and Romania became part of the EU in January 2007 when Slovenia joined the EMU. Due to the short period of time that has elapsed from these events, 2007 has not been used as a reference year in this study.

The conclusion sums up the major findings of this piece of work.

1. OCA criteria, methods of evaluation and CEE countries

The OCA theory comes into light in the sixties with a seminal article by Robert Mundell (Mundell 1961: 657-665). The author defines a currency area as a "domain within which exchange rates are fixed" (Mundell 1961: 657). According to Mundell two countries are interested in establishing a currency area if between them the factor mobility of capital and labour is high. This stems from the necessity of adjustment to asymmetric shocks. Countries prone to such shocks are disadvantaged on their way to forming a currency area. This is all the more true for transition CEE countries which come out of a system of planned economyies, gravitating around the former USSR. These countries are developing market economies that will bring them closer to the EU. The more the countries are exposed to asymmetric shocks, the less useful appears adopting fixed exchange rate regimes.

Real shocks (SDY_{ij}) can be measured in their magnitude as follows[2]:

$$SDY_{ij} = \left| SD\ln\left(\frac{GDP_i^t}{GDP_i^{t-1}}\right) - SD\ln\left(\frac{GDP_j^t}{GDP_j^{t-1}}\right) \right|$$

Where i = CEE country; j = EMU (12 countries); GDP = GDP at constant prices.

The magnitude of real shocks in period t is measured as the absolute value of the difference of the standard deviations (SD) of the logarithms of the GDP ratios for countries i and j for two consecutive periods t and $t-1$.

The results for the ten CEE countries are shown in Table 1[3]. Results are arranged in ascending order and those marked by bold italics indicate progress with respect to the OCA criteria since July 2005. To eliminate any possible bias due to the length of the period under consideration, the period before and after the EU entry contains equal numbers of observations.

The results show that 6 out of 10 countries have improved their performance after the EU enlargement. In the same time, and as a whole (2003 – 2007), the magnitude of asymmetric shocks is relatively more impor-

---

[2] Most of the proposed measures are personal adaptations of measures widely used in the economic literature. See, for example, Bayoumi and Eichengreen (1998: 191-209) and Bénassy-Quéré and Lahrèche-Révil (1998: 3-27).

[3] For all the estimations quarterly data have been used, taken from the database DATASTREAM (Datastream Advance Version 4.0 SP5 Copyright © 1995-2004: Thomson Financial Limited).

tant in Bulgaria and Romania than in the other CEE countries included in the sample. This suggests that the business cycles of these two countries are less harmonized with the EMU than those of Latvia and Slovenia. This could be a problem notably for Bulgaria which operates in a Currency Board system since July 1997 and cannot use the exchange rate as a means of adjustment to such shocks. Therefore the country should improve its factor mobility and introduce more price and wage flexibility to avoid adjustment through reductions in the employment and production levels in case of negative shocks.

Table 1: Magnitude of real asymmetric shocks between CEE countries and the EMU

Country	2003:Q3 – 2005:Q1	2005:Q3 – 2007:Q1
Latvia	0.0158	0.0182
Slovenia	0.0159	0.0268
Czech Republic	0.0507	*0.0427*
Slovakia	0.0548	0.0564
Estonia	0.0590	*0.0516*
Lithuania	0.0894	*0.0880*
Poland	0.0900	0.0986
Hungary	0.0966	*0.0915*
Bulgaria	0.2479	*0.2028*
Romania	0.3083	*0.3081*

Data source: DATASTREAM (Datastream Advance Version 4.0 SP5 Copyright © 1995-2004: Thomson Financial Limited)

The degrees of openness and size are other important criteria put forward by the OCA theory (McKinnon 1963: 717-725). In fact, McKinnon develops further an old idea of J. St. Mill[4] that the creation of more and more currencies in the world diminishes the utility of any given national currency as a unit of account and medium of exchange. Analogously, McKinnon suggests that for a small open country, the utility of its own national currency increases if it is linked with the other currencies through a fixed exchange rate system.

The intensity of trade between CEE countries and the EMU is measured as follows[5]:

---

[4] Quoted by Mundell (1961: 662).
[5] We do not estimate the size of the countries since in general bigger countries are less open and *vice versa*. In the same time there is no unique measure of size: sometimes GDP (per capita) is appropriate but estimates of population as a proxy for the country's potential are also used.

$$TR_{ij} = Average\left(\frac{Exp_i^{t,j} + Exp_j^{t,i}}{NGDP_i^t}\right)$$

Where TR_{ij} = degree of openness of country i relative to country j (j = EMU) in what concerns the exports and imports of goods (at current prices) between the two regions; $NGDP^t_i$ = GDP at current prices for the period t.

The results are shown in Table 2.

Table 2: Trade of goods between CEE countries and the EMU (in percent)

Country	2003:Q3 – 2005:Q1	2005:Q3 – 2007:Q1
Slovakia	34.97	*40.78*
Czech Republic	32.27	*35.31*
Estonia	31.29	*33.55*
Hungary	28.17	*31.92*
Slovenia	24.90	*29.17*
Latvia	20.34	*21.37*
Lithuania	20.24	*22.05*
Bulgaria	18.98	*21.01*
Romania	17.83	15.03
Poland	15.49	*17.28*

Data source: DATASTREAM (Datastream Advance Version 4.0 SP5
Copyright © 1995-2004: Thomson Financial Limited)

As expected, Poland and Romania – which are the most populated countries and both of relatively important size – are the least open countries towards the EMU. At the same time, 9 out of 10 countries have intensified their trade since the accession in the EU. This gives some credit to the argument that OCA criteria can be fulfilled *ex post* rather than *ex ante*. It should be noted that the estimations do not take into account the trade in services and that is why for all countries the results underestimate the magnitude of the trade relations with the EMU. Moreover, the more the production and trade composition of goods and services is diversified, the better. According to Kenen (1969), asymmetrical shocks do not affect the whole industrial tissue of a country but rather one or more particular sectors of the economy. Thus, the more the production structure of a given country is diversified, the smaller the repercussions of the shock will be on the economy of the country as a whole.

Among the more "modern" considerations relative to the formation of an OCA we find the degree of financial development of the candidate country[6]. A stable and developed financial system facilitates the absorption of asymmetric shocks by the country with a fixed exchange rate system and thus limits the pressures on the exchange rate stability.

The economic literature offers a few measures of financial development. The most frequently used one estimates the ratio of a large monetary aggregate to the GDP of the respective country. But here this measure has not been used because of the non-harmonised definitions of monetary aggregates of the CEE countries, which impairs any comparison among the obtained results.

An alternative measure of financial development considers the part of the credit given to private enterprises in the global sum of the domestic credit. Far from being perfect, this measure (which we identify as FC_i) makes possible the unambiguous comparisons among the CEE countries:

$$FC_t = Average\left(\frac{PC_t^i}{TDC_t^i}\right)$$

where PC_i = credit (at current prices) distributed to private enterprises in country i during period t; TDC_i = total domestic credit (at current prices) distributed in country i during period t.

Table 3: Financial development (in percent)

Country	2003:Q3 – 2005:Q1	2005:Q3 – 2007:Q1
Bulgaria	97	*99*
Romania	89	*97*
Lithuania	88	*89*
Slovenia	86	*88*
Poland	82	*86*
Latvia	81	*86*
Hungary	76	*82*
Slovakia	74	*78*
Czech Republic	69	*85*
Estonia	64	*87*

Data source: DATASTREAM (Datastream Advance Version 4.0 SP5
Copyright © 1995-2004: Thomson Financial Limited)

---

[6] The traditional OCA literature primarily considered the structural characteristics of the countries willing to form a currency area. More recent developments add other arguments that take into account, apart from the degree of financial development, for example, the search of exchange rate regime credibility and the adverse effects of an unsustainable exchange rate policy (Isard 1997).

The results (cf. Table 3) show a net progress in this measure of financial development in all ten CEE countries. The percentage is close to 100% in Bulgaria and Romania where virtually all domestic credit is obtained by private enterprises. These results should be taken with the necessary precaution since they show only one aspect of the degree of financial development. Countries willing to join a currency area need to have functioning banking systems and capital markets. Several CEE countries have experienced profound banking system crises during the transition years. Among these we can cite Bulgaria as a glaring example, but banking problems plagued also the Czech Republic, Estonia and Lithuania. Other countries like Hungary, for example, have had less problems of this type, because a two-tier banking system (even if rudimentary) existed already before the fall of the Berlin wall. In other words: Many of the banking system problems of the transition economies were in part predetermined by the lack of experience and prudential regulations at the beginning of the nineties. Nowadays, the domestic banking system in many of the CEE countries is dominated by foreign-owned banks, which lessens the liquidity crisis probability. As for the capital markets and the use of diverse financial instruments, however, though existing, they are not as sophisticated as their European counterparts.

2. Nominal exchange rate stability and the OCA theory

The predictions of the OCA theory were underestimated for a long time, in part because of a lack of sufficient empirical work. Nevertheless, the theory has experienced a renewed interest with the formation of the EMU. Thus, this study was inspired in part by previous work (Bayoumi and Eichengreen 1998: 191-209, Bénassy-Quéré and Lahrèche-Révil 1998: 3-27) which renders the theory operational. More precisely, Bayoumi and Eichengreen find out that the theory explains well exchange rate volatility and intervention. Bénassy-Quéré and Lahrèche-Révil adapt the cross-section estimation method proposed by Bayoumi and Eichengreen to show that the CEE countries are interested in adopting the Euro as a nominal anchor of their currencies rather than the US dollar or the Yen. Our objective is to verify whether OCA criteria and exchange rate volatility are empirically related in the case of the CEE countries. If so, policy makers should care more about the respect of these criteria in their attempt to prepare the CEE countries for the euro.

Now we turn to a test of the following econometric model:

$Y_T = c + a_1 X_{1T} + a_2 X_{2T} + a_3 X_{3T} + u_T$

where:

$$Y_T = \left| \ln \frac{S^t_{ij}}{S^{t-1}_{ij}} \right|$$

S_{ij} is the nominal market exchange rate of currency i (of a CEE country) vis-à-vis the currency j (*i.e.* the Euro);

$$X_{1T} = \left| \ln\left(\frac{GDP^t_i}{GDP^{t-1}_i}\right) - \ln\left(\frac{GDP^t_j}{GDP^{t-1}_j}\right) \right|$$

GDP is the GDP at constant prices;

$$X_{2T} = \left[d\left(\frac{Exp^{i,j}_i + Exp^{i,j}_j}{Cons^t_i} \right) \right]$$

Exp^j_i are exports of country i (CEE country) to country j (EMU),
Exp^i_j are exports of country j (EMU) to country i (CEE country),
$Cons_i$ is the final private consumption of country i (CEE country);

$$X_{3T} = \left[d\left(\frac{PC^t_i}{TDC^t_i} \right) \right]$$

PC_i is credit (at current prices) distributed to private enterprises in country i,
TDC_i is total domestic credit (at current prices) distributed in country i.

All data are quarterly and are obtained through the database DATASTREAM and the official sites of the CEE Central banks. Private consumption is used in the expression of trade at the place of GDP at current prices to avoid any collinearity problems. All series are seasonally adjusted and stationary at first difference (ADF unit root tests). If we find any autocorrelation of the residual U_T for lags 1, 2, m, when analyzing the correlograms, the tested equation has to be transformed into an AR(1, 2, m) process:

$$Y_T = b_1 Y_{T-1} + b_2 Y_{T-2} + b_m Y_{T-m} + c + a_1 X_{1T} + a_2 X_{2T} + a_3 X_{3T} + \varepsilon_T$$

Apart from eliminating the autocorrelation of the residual we suppose that it has a normal distribution. The estimation method used is ordinary least squares. The final result is corrected to avoid eventual heteroskedasticity problems. The procedure is applied when testing the model for different countries, taken separately, as well as in the pooled estimations. In the latter case we determine a common AR(1, 2, m) process and different fixed effects in order to take into account the specificities of each of the CEE countries.

Finally, we expect that the coefficients a take the following signs: $a_1>0$, $a_2<0$ and $a_3<0$ with all a significant.

The results for each CEE country are represented in Table 4.

In 70% of the cases the coefficients have the expected signs and 40% of the results concerning the coefficients a are significant. Exchange rate variability increases in the presence of asymmetric real shocks and decreases with the increase of trade and financial development. In the cases of Latvia and Romania, however, increasing trade contributes to the instability of the nominal exchange rate. This troubling result could probably be explained with the intense utilisation of the US dollar in the commerce of these countries. It also seems that the proposed measures do not explain the behaviour of the exchange rate in Slovenia.

Table 4: Nominal exchange rate variability and OCA criteria: Estimation results

Country	Number of observations	Constant	a1	a2	a3	R2 adj. %	Model
Bulgaria	39	0.01	*0.125***	*-0.217**	-0.024	21	-
Czech Rep.	36	0.01***	0.113	-0.004	*-0.103**	8	-
Estonia	44	0.01	0.001	-0.002	*-0.009**	31	AR(1,2)
Hungary	45	0.03***	-0.079	-0.002	*-0.333****	25	AR(2)
Latvia	25	0.01*	0.044	0.158***	0.220	16	AR(1)
Lithuania	42	0.01	0.037	-0.030	*-0.064**	43	AR(1,4)
Poland	34	0.03***	*0.112***	*-0.490****	0.096	24	AR(2,5)
Romania	29	0.07***	*0.169**	0.677**	0.311	18	AR(2)
Slovakia	36	0.01	*0.282****	-0.028	0.007	4	AR(6)
Slovenia	40	0.01	-0.029	-0.002	0.009	8	AR(1,3)

Significance level: ***1%, **5%, *10%.
Data source: DATASTREAM (Datastream Advance Version 4.0 SP5
    Copyright © 1995-2004: Thomson Financial Limited)

The ambiguity of some results could be explained, as well, by the relatively small number of observations by country (between 25 and 45). Bulgaria and Poland are the only countries where two out of the three OCA criteria seem to be in significant (and with the expected sign) relationship with the exchange rate variability[7]. These are countries that either show serious real asymmetries with the EMU (Bulgaria) or are large and with relatively less intensive trade (Poland). All in all, the most significant results concern the importance of real shocks and financial developments.

---

[7] Exchange rate data for all countries is based on the market, not the official exchange rate. Thus, even a country with a Currency Board system like Bulgaria can experience limited exchange rate variations.

Table 5: Importance of the OCA criteria in the countries with Currency Board systems (Bulgaria, Estonia, Lithuania)

Dependent variable: Y – Sample (adjusted): 1997:Q2 – 2006:Q3 – Total panel (balanced) observations: 114 – White Heteroskedasticity-Consistent Standard Errors & Covariance				
Coefficient	Coefficient value	Std. Error	t-Statistic	Prob.
A1	0.008300	0.019297	0.430146	0.6680
A2	-0.029643	0.048388	-0.612619	0.5414
A3	**-0.043793**	**0.028721**	**-2.028531**	**0.0422**
Constant:				
Bulgaria--C	0.001772	Model	R^2=0.29	
Lithuania--C	0.000340	AR(1)	Adjusted R^2 0.25	F-statistic 14.57273
Estonia--C	0.017609		D-Watson stat 1.19	Prob (F-stat) 0.00000

Table 6: Importance of the OCA criteria in countries with floating and managed floating exchange rate systems (Poland, Czech Republic, Slovakia, Romania)

Dependent variable: Y – Sample (adjusted): 1999:Q2–2005:Q4 – Total panel (balanced) observations: 104 – White Heteroskedasticity-Consistent Standard Errors & Covariance				
Coefficient	Coefficient value	Std. Error	t-Statistic	Prob.
A1	0.023097	0.037723	0.612289	0.5418
A2	-1.73E-05	4.13E-05	-0.417572	0.6772
A3	-0.000403	0.041033	-0.009828	0.9922
Constant:				
Poland--C	0.035124	Model	R^2=0.27	
Czech Rep--C	0.017181	AR(1)	Adjusted R^2 0.21	F-statistic 11.96816
Slovakia--C	0.013901		D-Watson stat 2.10	Prob (F-stat) 0.00000
Romania--C	0.037418			

Next, according to the existing exchange rate regimes, pooled estimations have to be performed. Two groups of countries can be distinguished: those with Currency Board systems and those with (managed) floating exchange rate regimes. Results are shown in Tables 5 and 6 respectively.

The results for countries with Currency Board systems all take the expected signs with only the degree of financial development being with a significant coefficient (Table 5). This suggests that in such countries the improvement of the financial market structure is of special importance for the stability of the exchange rate. As for the group of countries with flexible regimes (Table 6), however, none of the OCA criteria have a significant importance in spite of the fact that all coefficients have the predicted signs. The weakness of this result could be probably explained by the significant differences between the specific floats of these countries as well as possible divergence between *de jure* exchange rate policies and *de facto* exchange rate variability.

Table 7: Importance of the OCA criteria in the 10 CEE countries

Dependent variable: Y – Sample (adjusted): 2002:Q2 – 2005:Q4 – Total panel (balanced) observations: 230 – White Heteroskedasticity-Consistent Standard Errors & Covariance				
Coefficient	Coefficient value	Std. Error	t-Statistic	Prob.
A1	0.023333	0.026225	0.889727	0.3746
A2	-5.31E-06	2.11E-05	-0.251385	0.8018
A3	**-0.005399**	**0.026632**	**-2.027397**	**0.0451**
Fixed effects for each country				
			R^2=0.42	
			Adjusted R^2 0.39	F-statistic 79.3057
			D-Watson stat 1.73	Prob (F-stat) 0.00000

Finally, we consider all CEE countries, actual members of the EU in one single group. The results are shown in Table 7.

In this case, the measure of financial development, which has been used here, confirms its statistical importance, although its effect diminishes relative to the case with Currency Board systems. All in all, however, the pooled estimations provide less important results than the tests run for each country taken apart. This could be explained by the different stages of development of the 10 CEE countries, which present different structural characteristics, and seem to affect the respective nominal exchange rates through different channels. Consequently, it may be better to consider the CEE countries apart rather than as a homogeneous group when trying to explain the effect of OCA criteria on their exchange rates.

3. Conclusion

Traditional OCA theory puts an emphasis on the structural characteristics of countries and the existence of asymmetric shocks as important conditions for the creation of an OCA. The empirical studies in hand help to reveal which countries satisfy best the OCA criteria with respect to the Eurozone. These are Latvia and Slovenia (smallest magnitude of the asymmetric shocks), Slovakia and the Czech Republic (highest intensity in trade with goods) and Bulgaria and Romania (financial development). The results that we have seen show that different countries excel in different spheres. This could explain the relatively weak global importance of OCA criteria for the nominal exchange rate stability in the CEE region as a whole. The results seem to be globally significant only with respect to the stabilising properties of financial development. It seems necessary to verify this result by using different measures for assessing the financial development.

The country-by-country analysis reveals the importance of the magnitude of asymmetric shocks for the stability of the exchange rates in the cases of Bulgaria, Romania, Poland and Slovakia. Financial development seems to be important for the Czech Republic, Estonia, Hungary and Lithuania. Openness to trade seems of less importance for the stability of the exchange rate.

The existence of shocks suggests that countries should develop shock absorbers such as the flexible movement of productive capital and labour between the affected regions. The results suggest that the harmful effects of asymmetric shocks can be reduced with the acceleration of the financial development and the trade links with the members of the EMU. The good news is that entry in the EU has accelerated trade and financial development of the CEE countries. This implies that some OCA criteria may be endogenous. Business cycles, however, will probably need more time to harmonize as suggested by the results concerning the evolution of asymmetric shocks. With the increase of the number of observations by country, results of this type may become more significant in future.

References

Bayoumi, T./B. Eichengreen 1998: Exchange Rate Volatility and Intervention: Implications of the Theory of Optimum Currency Areas, in Journal of International Economics, vol. 45, pp. 191-209

Bénassy-Quéré, A./A. Lahrèche-Révil 1998: Pegging the CEEC's Currencies to the Euro, in CEPII, document de travail, n°98-04, pp. 3-27

DATASTREAM Advance Version 4.0 SP5, Copyright © 1995-2004: Thomson Financial Limited

Frankel, J./A. Rose 1996: The Endogeneity of the Optimum Currency Area Criteria, in NBER Working Paper n°5700, pp. 1-33

Isard, P. 1997: Exchange Rate Economics, Cambridge: Cambridge University Press

Kenen, P. 1969: A Theory of Optimum Currency Areas: An Eclectic View, in R. Mundell et A. Swoboda (eds): Monetary Problems of International Economy, Chicago: University of Chicago Press

McKinnon, R. 1963: Optimum Currency Areas, in American Economic Review, vol. 53, pp. 717-725

Mundell, R. 1961: A Theory of Optimum Currency Areas, in American Economic Review, vol. 51, pp. 657-665

SUPERSTARS AS WINNERS OF THE COMMON MARKET
- THE ROLE OF THE MASS MEDIA -

HORST SCHELLHAASS
(UNIVERSITY OF COLOGNE, GERMANY)

1. Problem

Labour mobility of article 39 EU Treaty allows workers to take advantage of higher wages in other member states. The higher wage level might reflect a higher living standard, a shortage of labour in a specific sector, or a higher individual productivity by using a more capital intensive technology. Though labour mobility formally applies to all employees, the income gains of migrating workers are quite different for different types of workers.

On the one hand, there are the normal workers. As migration follows the wage differentials, in principle all member states of the EU can be a destination of migration. It can easily be that a small country like Luxembourg has a higher income level than a large country. Market size doesn't matter here, as the individual productivity is never high enough to serve the whole market.

On the other hand, there are the stars of show business, in arts as well as in sports. What is important here, is that market size matters, as here we find the configuration of "the winner takes it all markets". Superstars can exploit the mass media to enlarge their market shares. Sports markets in Europe are still national markets with the effect that the TV-audience in a small country necessarily produces fewer receipts than the TV-audience in a big country. Labour mobility allows the foreign superstars to participate at the rents of the larger market. Therefore, only the larger member states can be the destination of migrating superstars.

Rosen (1981) and Adler (1985) have analyzed in their seminal papers the factors of a very skewed income distribution on labour markets where superstars are present. In this paper, I add a regional component to the superstar phenomenon. The member states of the European Union have different comparative advantages or disadvantages with regard to the mass media leverage effect which is the basis for the high superstar incomes. Our analysis will derive some contra-intuitive results with regard to superstars.

2. Labour mobility of normal workers: arbitrage gains

The main financial incentive for migrations is the existence of arbitrage gains. For example, the German wages for the average of all professions in 1996 have been about three times as high as the Polish wages (Sinn et al. 2001, p. 46). This difference should induce a significant migration from Poland to Germany. In practice however, we cannot observe anything like that. This is not only caused by the fact that Poland has not been a member of the EU at that time, but labour mobility between long time EU members is low as well. Can the wage gap between EU member states be persistent without inducing migration?

Transaction costs can explain persistent wage differentials. If we consider the transportation costs of goods or the moving costs of workers, the usual assumption of no transaction costs might not be too restrictive. But migrating workers have to bear other losses which we cannot neglect. When crossing the border, the human capital is depreciated, sometimes to a dramatical extent. Becker (1964) differentiates between *general* and *specific human capital*. *Specific human capital* is only productive in that company where it has been acquired. Every separation depreciates the value of specific human capital to zero, irrespective whether it is an interregional or an international migration. We should therefore expect about the same income differences between member states as we can now observe between different regions in Germany or France.

Regarding international migrations, we have the additional phenomenon that not only the specific, but also a fraction of the general human capital is depreciated. *General human capital* increases the productivity of a worker in many domestic firms, but not necessarily in foreign firms, as it is imperfectly portable across countries (Möller 2002, chapter 4). Prone to depreciation when crossing a border are those components of the human capital which are specific for a region or a nation. To a large extent it is the tacit knowledge of social norms which gives a domestic worker a comparative advantage over a foreign worker. A good command of the national language belongs also to those components of the human capital which are depreciated by a migration to a foreign country. As an employer cannot expect that these disadvantages disappear within a fairly short time, he will be reluctant to hire foreign workers if more than basic qualifications are required.

When general human capital is acquired from schooling either at a university or by an apprenticeship, there exists an additional barrier to entry. Formal certificates on the successful completion of a certain training often are not acknowledged in a foreign country. This means that a migrating worker often cannot practice the profession he was trained for in his home country. From an economic point of view, he cannot exploit the full range of his abilities as a result of regulatory restraints. This is not only an income loss for the worker, but also a loss for the receiving country as it does not use the full capacity of its resources.

The proportion of the human capital which is lost when the new work place is in a foreign country differs according to its portability. The more comparable the technology used in different countries and the less relevant formal certificates, the easier it is to transfer acquired human capital. Therefore, construction workers or nurses easily find adequate jobs in other EU states. In these professions we can expect a tendency for an equalization of wages. At the other end of the scale we find lawyers for example. Since, as the legal system differs significantly from country to country, for a lawyer even an excellent knowledge of German law doesn't help much if he migrates to France or Spain. For most lawyers the market value of their acquired human capital is nearly zero in a foreign country; that means there is no transferability of the human capital. This might change a little bit with the completion of the Common Market, because for the preparation of contracts as well as for an eventual litigation of the other party it is useful to have experience in several legal systems.

Some depreciation of the general human capital of migrating workers is unavoidable, but must this be reflected in the worker's income? When a worker voluntarily moves *within* a nation, his *specific* human capital is totally depreciated. But the new employer expects that he will acquire the required specific human capital either by learning on the job or by participating at formal training courses. As a rule, the new employer bears the investment costs for the specific human capital, and the employee will not suffer an income loss. Can we assume that the same principle applies to international labour mobility?

With regard to *national* migrations, it is the *specific* human capital which must be renewed; according to Becker (1964) this should be financed by the *employer*. With regard to *international* migrations, *general* human capital must be renewed. In this case, the employer has the chance to recruit national applicants with all the required qualifications instead of a foreign worker with a lower stock of useable human capital. Therefore, the *immigrant* has to finance the accumulation of his human capital out of his own resources. As bank loans are not available for these investments, for most normal workers the acquisition of compensating human capital is not a feasible option. The employer expects this and therefore he is not willing to pay the usual wage.

Thus it is not very useful to compare the wages paid to national employees when analyzing the financial incentives for international migrations. We have to deduct the depreciations of human capital from the wage difference. There exists a positive incentive for migration, if the income with the depreciated human capital in the country of destination is higher than the income in the country of origin where the worker can use the full amount of his human capital. Only this difference can be considered as a realizable arbitrage gain. This implies that the wage per unit of human capital must be considerably higher in the new country than in the old country (see Möller 2002, p. 70 ff.).

The factor price equalization theorem tells us that in perfect markets wages tend to be equalized even if there is no international mobility of factors. In the common European market we have not only a free movement of goods and services, but we have also labour mobility. In a low income country, there will be eventually a shortage of labour which will result in a more than proportionate increase of wages. In a high income country, the market forces will work in the opposite direction: the increasing supply of qualified workers will keep down the wage increases. Of course, the factor price equalization cannot equalize the wages within the European Union, but it can eliminate the realizable arbitrage gains; for professions in which a large part of the human capital is not portable across countries, there will be a persistence of considerable wage differences.

3. Labour mobility of superstars: capturing rents

The international migration of superstars is governed by the same motivation that is relevant for normal workers, namely by income maximization. Superstars in sports or in show business have the great advantage that they can easily transfer their skills from one country to another, as the same rules of the game apply all over the world. As they do not have to learn new rules, the internationalization of professional sports clubs is much more advanced than that of "normal" professions. The same applies to show business: An appearance of a singer or of a conductor in Germany doesn't differ significantly from an appearance of the same artist in France or Spain. With regard to the command of the foreign language, superstars seem to have the same problems as normal workers. But in practice, language problems are for these professions no important impediment for a good performance on the field or on the stage. A reason is that a sportsman does not have to be fluent in the foreign language, but he must only be able to understand his instructor and his team mates. This requires only a limited vocabulary and therefore no big investment with respect to time or money.

With regard to the *specific human capital*, sportsmen are in no better position than normal workers. Sportsmen have to adapt to potentially different tactics of a foreign team, but this is also necessary if they change to another club within their own country. In principle, every migrant has the chance to replace the depreciated human capital by acquiring new abilities. For most normal workers this is only a theoretical possibility, because they do not have the financial reserves to invest in new human capital. This is totally different in team sports as the employer finances the investments into the human capital of his players. The club does not only pay for the coach and other staff members, but it also often finances a language course for his superstars. It is for this reason that it is relatively easy for superstars in sports or in show business to act on an international plane. As the employer knows from experience that the depreciation of the human capital is compensated by new skills within a fairly short time, superstars will not suffer an income loss when they change to a foreign club.

The decisive difference between the normal labour market and the segment of superstars is the impact of market size on the determination of the wage. A nurse, for example, can care for the same number of people in Poland or in Germany. The physical output of a construction worker may be somewhat higher in Germany than in Poland, because the German construction industry uses a more capital intensive technology. Both effects have nothing to do with the size of both countries. C.p. our construction worker can earn the same wage in the small country of Luxembourg as in Germany. Therefore, a normal worker can potentially realize arbitrage gains in every member state of the European Union.

A star in sports or in show business does not change to a more capital intensive technology, but he takes advantage of the larger market. A football superstar migrating from Bulgaria to Germany can produce with the same 90 minutes of high effort entertainment for 80 millions instead of 8 millions inhabitants. It is here that market size matters. The modern mass media – especially TV and internet – have produced a leverage by which entertainment programmes can be offered to a significantly larger audience than before at very low marginal costs. Before the Bundesliga was founded in 1963, a spectator had to commute to the stadium. Ticket sales were nearly the only source of income for the clubs. The economic value of the commercials on the barriers of the playing field was low as only the spectators in the stadium could take notice of them. For geographical reasons the fan basis of a team was limited to those inhabitants who lived in a circle around the stadium of about 60 to 80 kilometres. At that time, each team has had its regional superstars. A player, no matter how good he was, could serve only a limited number of people. Even outstanding players could earn only a moderate salary as the size of each club's market was small. The result was an income distribution where the difference in salaries between stars and average players was small.

The path breaking innovation for the professional team sport has been the TV coverage of the league competitions. Superstars in sports or in show business are operating on "the winner takes it all markets". What

TV-stations can pay to the clubs for the transmission rights depends on the size of the audience for commercials for the private TV-stations and on the number of households for the public TV-stations, as they are financed by radio and TV licence fees. The sponsoring earnings from ads on the barriers of the playing field or on the jerseys of the players depend directly on the number of visitors in the stadiums and of the spectators in front of the TV screens. These innovations are relevant for the income of superstars in a twofold manner: On the one hand, it increased dramatically the number of potential spectators. In former days, the capacity of the stadiums limited the number of spectators to about 300,000 persons for the weekend's matches. Since the introduction of TV transmissions a capacity constraint does not exist any more; this medium is used by about six million spectators per weekend. Today, the TV receipts are a very important income source for all teams. They do not necessarily change the income distribution between the teams, as the supply-side conditions have been improved for all clubs in the same manner.

The second effect of TV coverage has been more dramatic, as it intensified the competition among the clubs for spectators. For most inhabitants of Germany – with the exception of North-Rhine-Westfalia – only one or two Bundesliga clubs are situated in that geographical area within which a visit of home matches is feasible. Traditionally, one of these nearby clubs became the favourite club of a spectator. The TV recipient, however, can choose between all Bundesliga clubs to select his favourite club. It were TV transmissions which enabled the consumers to consume the best quality. The best description how a superstar emerges in a professional sports league has been given by MacDonald (1988), who describes the emergence of a talent in the performing arts as a dynamic process. He argues that every team is capable of producing either a good or a bad performance. The difference in talent is seen in the probability that a particular match will be won by the favourite team. That means that also a top team like Bayern München will lose a number of matches but the win probability will be higher than, for example, that of SC Karlsruhe. Spectators like to identify themselves with clubs with a high win probability. TV coverage makes it possible that the suppliers of entertainment are no longer tied as strictly as before to certain market segments defined by time and geographical constraints. Now a fan of a Bundesliga club can live somewhere in Germany and watch the match of his favourite team on TV.

The mass media leverage effect has a dramatic impact on the distribution of incomes if the consumers cannot perfectly substitute better quality for lower quality (Rosen 1981). Top teams can ask for higher ticket prices, but only to the extent to which their quality is above the average quality of the league. The same reasoning applies to fan articles. These slightly higher prices for tickets and fan articles cannot explain the observed differences in income between top clubs and average clubs of a league. If the spectator prefers a high quality match, a top club like Bayern München may find fans in the home areas of Cottbus, Wolfsburg or Karlsruhe. We need the mass media leverage effect to explain why even small differences in the performance of teams can generate huge income differences. Superstars do not earn much more money per spectator, but it is the much larger crowd in the stadiums or the larger number of buyers of fan articles which multiply a slight quality advantage of the top teams into huge income differences (Rosen 1981).

We can observe the superstar phenomenon in the national leagues as well as in international competitions. This has foreseeable effects on the regional allocation of players. Even if the living standards in Germany and Bulgaria should be equalized in some future, the income of football stars in Bulgaria would nevertheless be significantly lower than in Germany, due to the mass media leverage effect. It is no surprise that the big five European nations in football are countries with a large population (England, France, Germany, Italy and Spain). As the high earnings in the big five nations are distributed among approximately the same number of players as the lower earnings in Bulgaria, there is a huge income gap. Income maximization requires a migration to one of the big five leagues. It is the market size which counts.

Since the high drawing leagues could not recruit for legal reasons as many highly qualified foreign players as they wanted to get, until 1995 the allocation of players among the European countries was not optimal. The Bosman rule of the European Supreme Court (1995) has enforced labour mobility in professional sports. Most sports associations have extended the labour mobility of players from the European Union and the associated states to the whole world. The mass media leverage effect gives a clear direction to the international migration of superstars: It is from low drawing to high drawing leagues while the size of the population of a country is a good approximation for the drawing power of a league. Winners of the single common market are the best qualified players of low income countries, who are now recruited by the most successful clubs in Europe. Nowadays, qualification instead of nationality determines who is employed by the high paying teams. Especially the clubs of the big five nations substituted domestic players by foreign ones.

On the other hand, the average players and especially the young talents in the high income countries are the losers of the Bosman rule. As the teams are internationalized, the positions available for national players become more scarce. The negative effects for active players might be limited: They are still employed by their clubs, but they are only occasionally sent onto the playing field; they lose the variable components of their salary. For young talents the situation is much worse. The coach has the alternative either to send an inexperienced young talent or an experienced foreign player onto the field. In order to minimize the risk to lose the match, he normally prefers the experienced player. In effect, the clubs have reduced the number of minutes when young talents can play as members of the professional team under competitive conditions (Kummer 2008). Without this practical experience it is nearly impossible for them to be recruited by another professional team. As the fans have accepted the internationalization of the teams, the managers can recruit the best players available somewhere on the world. It is not their job to take into account the negative effects which a smaller number of national superstars might have on the performance of the national teams of the big five nations.

Now we turn to the long run effects of international migration on the incomes of superstars. Low income countries steadily lose their superstars, while high income leagues increase the quality of their product at the same time. This gain in reputation and team strength determines the success probability in the European competitions of the Champions League and the UEFA cup. The top clubs are able to recruit the best players of the world. Therefore we have the surprising result that – contrary to the factor price equalization theorem – the *income differentials on sports markets increase* as a result of the international migration of superstars. We find that the reallocation of players in the Common European Market increases the quality of those leagues which already have the advantage of the mass media leverage effect. Both effects together will result in a more skewed income distribution among the European leagues.

We have shown that migrating superstars exploit the rents of larger markets. To a large extent it is a redistribution of income from domestic to foreign players and to a small extent the cake is increased insofar as the better quality attracts additional spectators. In the next chapter, we will see that foreign superstars can do even better by enlarging the market of a sports league.

4. Labour mobility of superstars: enlarging markets

The American professional leagues cover the whole territory of the US and Canada; there are no professional league competitions on the level of states. In Europe however, we have separated sports markets with the result that each spectator pays highest attention to his own national league. Given this constellation, it is rational to broadcast the national leagues only in their own territories. Even the matches of the European competitions – with the exceptions of the semi-finals and finals – are often broadcasted only in the countries of the two participating teams. As a result of the dominance of the national leagues, we have no hierarchical league structure in Europe. We can observe the rare phenomenon that the top clubs play in two leagues at the same time, namely in a national league and a European competition.

Nowadays, the mass media leverage effect generates economic incentives to enlarge the markets of league competitions. As the transmission signal for all matches is produced anyway, the summary of the weekend's matches can be supplied to other nations at low marginal costs. For some countries, an additional transponder on a satellite must be rented, and in nearly all cases the moderation must be translated into the language of the country of destination. As long as there was a scarcity of frequencies, the transmission of a foreign league was possible only if the league summary replaced the regular programme of the foreign TV station. If a sufficient number of channels is available, the sports programme can be an addition to the regular TV programme. By this way the opportunity costs of the introduction of a new programme are reduced. The rising transmission capacities via TV and internet allow it now to exploit the mass media leverage effect on a European level.

The most spectacular plan stems from the American NBA. It supposedly plans to expand the basketball league to Europe by founding and licensing some new clubs in the European Union. This might be an answer to the disappointing quotas, which are realized at live transmissions of the national basketball league though Dirk Nowitzki is a very popular superstar. It is difficult to evaluate the chances of such a strategy. It shows, however, very clearly that league commissioners do not consider any more national frontiers as natural boundaries for the sale of league competitions.

For Europeans the actual question is not: "Will football or any other sport win the European market?", but it is: "Which football league will win the European market?". If there is a network externality of social communication, consumers prefer the most popular sports discipline – in Europe, that is football. No other professional league has a chance to entice audiences away from football (Adler 2006, p. 899). Currently a handful of football associations are vigorously trying to sell their TV rights to foreign broadcasting stations – in Europe and in Asia. From a technical point of view, the supply of a Europe-wide instead of a nation-wide TV coverage of a football league is no problem. The real problem exists on the demand side, where a sufficient number of spectators has to be found.

The problem to be solved can be described as follows: How can we persuade a spectator, for example in Bulgaria, to switch to a foreign sports event? This might be relatively easy with regard to figure skating, because here the interest of the spectator is directed toward the technical perfection of the performance. It is the aesthetics which fascinate. Nobody, however, watches a football match just to observe and analyze the technical abilities of the players. Most sportive competitions are demanded because the spectator wants to be in a fever of excitement during the matches of his team. This requires that the spectator identifies himself with one of the teams. Identification requires knowledge of the rules, of the modalities of the competition, of the players, and of the teams (Schellhaass 2002). A sports competition is an "experience good" for which the spectator needs a lot of ex ante information to fully understand it. Stigler/Becker (1978) have named this bundle of information "consumption capital".

The critical point for the strategy to expand TV transmissions into other countries is how the accumulation of a sufficient amount of consumption capital can be organized. The normal fan has a lot of consumption capital on his own national league, but he has only a faint idea about foreign leagues. He knows the reputation of some teams and of a few superstars, especially if they have participated several times in European competitions. If a Bulgarian spectator should be persuaded successfully to switch from the transmission of the Bulgarian national league to the summary of the German Bundesliga, he could still use his knowledge of rules and techniques. But his knowledge of the Bulgarian teams and players would have no further value for him. At the same time, his knowledge on the German teams and players is still moderate with the result that it is very difficult for him to identify himself with a Bundesliga team. We can derive the conclusion that the utility from watching the foreign league is initially lower than the utility level of other available alternatives.

The only reason to prefer the German Bundesliga is that our spectator expects that the utility of the TV transmissions increases over time. Our Bulgarian spectator has to consider the switching process as an investment. It is profitable for him if the loss of utility during the period while he is accumulating new consumption capital on a foreign league is more than compensated by the higher utility in later periods. The investment process of consumption capital has a great advantage insofar, as it is accumulated automatically when watching matches. After a while our spectator has eventually enough information on the foreign league that he derives greater utility from watching a foreign football match than from the regular domestic TV programme.

As the utility derived from the identification with the foreign league must finally be higher than that from the domestic league, only high quality European leagues can expand their TV coverage into foreign countries. In the economics of superstars of Rosen (1981) it is assumed that it is possible to identify unambiguously the best European leagues or teams. As consumers prefer higher quality to lower quality, the best league in Europe will win the vast majority of all TV spectators. In this scenario all spectators who are considering a switching to a foreign league are well advised to acquire consumption capital on the best European league; let us assume that this is the English Premier League. If the other big five nations want to sell their TV rights in foreign countries, they have to replace the Premier League at the top position in the performance ranking. This will become more and more difficult as time goes on. All big football nations have comparable home markets, but only the Premier League has in our example the additional income from the foreign TV rights. This enables it to buy the best players of the world which guarantees it a persistent dominant position. It is the mass media leverage effect which transforms an initial small performance advantage into long lasting income advantages.

On a national level, it is fairly easy for a top club to augment its fan basis. We have a complete TV coverage of all matches, so Bayern München, for example, can gradually penetrate into the home areas of its competitors at no additional cost. If, instead, a league tries to expand into foreign markets, we have the problem of sunk costs. As long as the TV signal of the Bundesliga is not transmitted in Bulgaria, nearly nobody is interested in the German Bundesliga. The number of fans can only increase if the TV signal is transmitted. This requires not only the costs for the transmission of the TV signal, but also the decision to substitute a reputated regular programme for the summary of the Bundesliga. The foreign TV station will lose an established audience for its regular programme while it gains only a low number of spectators for the German Bundesliga. Should an additional channel be available, the economic loss is smaller, as it is not necessary to cannibalize an established programme. But even in this constellation, the foreign broadcaster has to decide whether he will allocate the foreign football league or an additional TV movie to the additional channel. It is not surprising that in most cases this decision will be in favour of the established programme categories and against the transmission of a foreign league, even if the TV rights of the Bundesliga are given for free to the foreign station.

An expansion to foreign markets is only possible, if the difference in performance outways the popularity disadvantage. The national league has always a popularity advantage in its own country; this can only be compensated if a foreign league has a sufficiently high advantage in performance. It seems that the markets of the big five nations in football are natural monopolies, where the combination of high performance and high popularity is a very effective protection against the entrance of competitors. There are differences in quality, but they are not high enough to outweigh the popularity advantage of the domestic league. The small countries, however, have a permanent disadvantage in sports, as there the mass media leverage effect will always be smaller than in the big five nations. This offers a chance for the best European leagues to expand into these countries.

Nevertheless, they have to find a way to increase the number of spectators within a fairly short period. Adler (1985) has extended the arguments of Rosen (1981) by pointing out that a spectator does not only derive utility from the event itself, but also from the communication before, during and after the match. It is a well known phenomenon that football matches are often consumed together with friends. We are also familiar with the social value of discussions in offices or at other meetings, when the football matches of the weekend are discussed. The social communication is the most important factor for people, who are not really interested in football, nevertheless to watch the TV transmissions. This observation shows us a kind of network externality in the centre of which we find the personalities of the superstars.

A condition for positive network externalities is that each participant in the discussion has acquired at least a minimal amount of consumption capital of the sports discipline in discussion. It is nearly impossible to begin a discussion on Badminton or Hockey on Monday morning since nobody else has seen the weekend matches of these sports. Social communication requires that nearly all participants in the discussion have seen the same matches. It is therefore rational for young people to specialize in those disciplines which have already been chosen by the majority of the population. This is the reason, why football has such a constant popularity, irrespective of the results of the national team or of the top clubs in the European competitions. As soon as a discipline is a factor of social communication, the performance is no longer as important as in the initial phases, when the reputation of the discipline has to be built up. Social communication is possible whether the team has won or lost.

If a league with a weaker performance was successful in penetrating into foreign markets, it must have had some advantages in gaining popularity in comparison to the competitors from the other big football nations. At this point a weakness of the German Bundesliga becomes a competitive advantage. Germany has specialized in hiring "cheap" players from smaller countries, especially from Eastern Europe. Their popularity in their home countries is a door opener for the marketing activities of the Bundesliga. In this case, the success arises from a chance event: consumers in foreign countries select one of the big five leagues at random when they add a new professional league to their consumption basket.

If social communication is an important factor for the interest in a specific discipline, the superstars do not need to supply a higher quality than their competitors (Adler 1985). This is the chance for the German Bundesliga which does not have a top position in the five years performance ranking of the UEFA. If talent and market success are untied, the reputation of the superstar is most important for the development of new markets. Let us assume that a Bulgarian superstar is hired by a German team. The Bulgarian newspapers and TV stations will continue to report on his successes and failures – but now in the context of the German Bundesliga. A good example are the continuing reports on Michael Ballack, who is now playing for Chelsea in the English premier league. The German reader is not only kept informed on the development of Michael Ballack, but – at no additional cost – his consumption capital on the English league accumulates.

The Bulgarian superstar hired by a German team is the focal point for social communication in Bulgaria. Some of the Bulgarian readers and spectators will begin to identify themselves with the new club of their superstar and eventually also with the Bundesliga. If a critical mass of spectators is achieved, it becomes profitable to sell the TV rights of the Bundesliga to Bulgarian broadcast stations. With regard to the removal of barriers of entry to foreign markets a foreign superstar might have a higher economic value for a Bundesliga club than an equally qualified German superstar. If the club can sell the TV rights to foreign countries, it will receive additional receipts from the ads on the barriers of the playing field or on the jerseys of the players. Experience tells us that most of the value added will increase the income of the superstars. Therefore they will be the winners of the European integration.

5. Conclusion

Europe has developed a strange organisation for its team sports. Normally, a team plays in one and only one league. But the European top teams play in their own highest national league as well as in a European competition. In such a situation, the top clubs have full stadiums in their national leagues and additionally the receipts from the European competitions. The economic reason for this constellation is that the majority of the spectators has accumulated only a moderate amount of consumption capital on foreign clubs. It is therefore foreseeable that a European league cannot fill the stadiums week for week.

Table 1: European Clubs and their Fans (in Millions)

1.	FC Barcelona	50,3
2.	Real Madrid	45,9
3.	Manchester United	32,8
4.	FC Arsenal	22,9
5.	AC Mailand	22,2
6.	Bayern München	19,9
7.	FC Chelsea	19,7
8.	FC Liverpool	19,4
9.	Juventus Turin	17,7
10.	Zenit St. Petersburg	15,3
.		
.		
.		
20.	Werder Bremen	4,4
25.	Borussia Dortmund	3,6
26.	FC Schalke	3,3
27.	Hamburger SV	3,2
Season 2007/08		

Quelle: „Die Welt" 13.03.2008

Things begin to change. The free movement of superstars within the European Union increases the knowledge of foreign leagues. More and more top clubs will become known in all member states of the European Union (see table 1) We see that those clubs which play regularly in the Champions League have a much higher fan basis than those clubs which are very well known in a national context, but which are not very successful in the European competitions. This endangers the dominant position of the national leagues. The accumulation of consumption capital on foreign clubs might give rise to the foundation of a European league on top of all national leagues. A hierarchical structure of leagues in Europe will become profitable as soon as the receipts from a common European league are higher than the aggregated receipts of the top clubs from the national leagues and their participation in European competitions. This requires that the stadiums are fully booked up not only for matches of the top clubs against each other, but for practically all matches.

In this case, "a global culture, with a global set of superstars, is replacing local cultures with local stars" (Adler 2006, p.905). For consumers and sportsmen this means that a relatively small number of players can serve the whole European market. As a consequence, their incomes will increase even further – at the expense of the players in the national leagues. Then the latter will be indisputably in the second rank with the result that they will lose reputation and income. According to the theory of the economics of superstars the income difference between the European league and the national leagues will be much higher than the difference in performance. The common European league will be the final step to maximize the incomes of superstars in team sports. The marketing of a common European league in Asia or in the Middle East will be much more profitable than the competitive sale of different national leagues – the mass media leverage effect will not stop at the boundaries of Europe.

References

Adler, M. 1985: Stardom and Talent. American Economic Review 75, pp. 208-212

Adler, M. 2006: Stardom and Talent. In: Ginsburgh, V.A.; Throsby, D. (Ed.): Handbook of the Economics of Art and Culture Vol. 1. Elsevier B.V., pp. 896-906

Becker, G.S. 1964: Human Capital. New York

Europäischer Gerichtshof (EuGH) 1995: Urteil vom 15.12.1995, Rs. C-415/93 (Bosman), Slg. 1995, I-4921 ff.

Franck, E. 2001: Warum gibt es Stars? Drei Erklärungsansätze. Wirtschaftsdienst 1, S.59-64

Hafkemeyer, L. 2003: Die mediale Vermarktung des Sports. Strategien und Institutionen. Deutscher Universitätsverlag, Wiesbaden

Kummer, N. 2008: Spielermarktdesign für Nationalmannschaften: Eine anreizökonomische Analyse. Books on Demand GmbH, Norderstedt

MacDonald, G. 1988: The Economics of Rising Stars. American Economic Review 78, pp. 155-166

Möller, D. 2002: Migration und ihre Arbeitsmarkteffekte in Deutschland. Peter Lang Verlag, Frankfurt

Rosen, S. 1981: The Economics of Superstars. American Economic Review 71, pp. 845-858

Schellhaass, H.M. 2008: Sport als Ware und Kulturgut: Die Fußballweltmeisterschaft im Programm der Deutschen Welle. In: Kops, M. (Hrsg.): Die Aufgaben des öffentlich-rechtlichen Auslandsrundfunks in einer globalisierten Medienwelt. DW-Schriftenreihe 6, VISTAS Verlag Berlin, S. 109-123

Schellhaass, H.M. 2002: Wie kommt der Sport ins Fernsehen? - Eine wettbewerbspolitische Analyse. Bundesinstitut für Sportwissenschaft 8/2002, Sport und Buch Strauß, Köln

Sinn, H.-W.; Flaig, G.; Werding, M.; Munz, S.; Düll, N.; Hofmann, N. 2001: EU-Erweiterung und Arbeitskräftemigration: Wege zu einer schrittweisen Annäherung der Arbeitsmärkte. In: ifo Beiträge zur Wirtschaftsforschung, Nr. 2, München

Stigler, G.J. /Becker, G.S. 1977: De Gustibus Non Est Disputandum. The American Economic Revue 67, pp. 76-90.

Chapter three:

GLOBAL AND GENERAL ASPECTS OF ECONOMIES

DYNAMIC EQUILIBRIUM STABILITY OF TWO MARKETS
GEORGE CHOBANOV
(SOFIA UNIVERSITY "ST. KLIMENT OHRIDSKI", BULGARIA)

1. The moving power of a neoclassical economic system

Researchers often consider an object under investigation like a system with specific structure and components interacting via links under the pressure of a moving power. Here, we consider a human society like an economic system with economic subjects performing economic activities under formal regulations. The economic subjects are people performing economic activities in order to satisfy their need of goods. Therefore, the moving power of the economic system is considered to be generated by the behavior of the people involved in the human society under consideration. The behavior of a human being is a consequence of its behavioral norms. The behavioral norms of a human being consist of internal, genetically inserted codes; on the other side, norms of behavior may be externally imposed by the human society or by the individual itself under the influence of the surrounding environment or its health state. The basic instincts are the self-saving or self-protecting instinct, reproduction instinct (sex), the conservation instinct (life for ever) and the domination instinct. The externally imposed norms of behavior are the moral, ethics, religion, any kind of dogmas, habits, traditions. The set of behavioral norms of an individual essentially influents its decision making process by its propensity for undertaking an economic activity or action, or by its preference in choice of different opportunities in order to satisfy its needs of goods.

The economic theory postulates the behavioral norms of economic subjects by setting up axioms.

The behavioral axiom of the neoclassical theory is called the personal utility axiom. It sets up that the decision making system of an economic subject or an individual is totally directed to its personal utility. Furthermore, the personal utility axiom means that the economic subject does not only undertake utility *bringing* activities, but even utility *maximizing* activities. An economic subject is called *homo oeconomicus*, if its economic activities are completely subordinated with respect to the personal utility axiom. The power engine of a neoclassical economic system is moving its mechanisms via the basic principles:

I. Principle of optimization

The behavioral norms of every economic subject contain the propensity for optimization according to the personal utility axiom, maximizing utility and minimizing costs.

II. Principle of market regulation

All the individual's activities and decisions are regulated by the exchange mechanism of markets and by the price as the mechanism for the allocation and distribution of resources.

The price is influencing the behavior of economic subjects, but its equilibrium value is determined by supply and demand on the other side.

III. Principle of market equilibrium

The conditions of a good market order contain a mechanism for moving the market towards an equilibrium state. For market mechanisms are properly functioning only under a market order, which means market rules and institutions insuring property rights, transparency, freedom of making contracts, freedom of economic activities etc.

The theorem of Say is basic for the neoclassical analysis of the equilibrium. A simple version of this theorem says that every supply requires its demand. As a consequence, in the long run supply and demand will be equalized, which means that the market will reach an equilibrium state.

2. The general equilibrium of an economic system

The basics of the general equilibrium theory of economic systems were set up by Leon Walras (1874) at the end of 19th century. The more detailed elaboration and development of the theory came nearly a century later, in the second part of 20th century, when mathematical techniques for rigorous description and quite powerful calculation methods have been developed. The development of the general equilibrium theory of economic systems is going on, now finding its publicity in classical textbooks on microeconomics like the one by Andreu Mas-Colell, Michael D. Whinston and Jerry R. Green (1995) and in a variety of monographs and papers.

The core of the general equilibrium theory of economic systems is concentrated in the Walras theorem of market system equilibrium.

Let us consider an economic system of I households, denoted by $i = 1,2,...,I$, demanding according to the personal utility axiom the quantities $x^{(i)} = (x_1^{(i)}, x_2^{(i)}, ..., x_G^{(i)})$ of G goods denoted by $g = 1,2,...,G$ and supplying for enterprises the quantities $\lambda^{(i)} = (\lambda_1^{(i)}, \lambda_2^{(i)}, ..., \lambda_L^{(i)})$ of L production factors, denoted by $l = 1,2,...,L$. According to the personal utility axiom, in the economic system, J enterprises, denoted by $j = 1,2,...,J$, are supplying the quantities of goods $y^{(j)} = (y_1^{(j)}, y_2^{(j)}, ..., y_G^{(j)})$ and are demanding the quantities of factors $z^{(j)} = (z_1^{(j)}, z_2^{(j)}, ..., z_L^{(j)})$. The existing quantities of goods $\bar{x}^{(i)} = (\bar{x}_1^{(i)}, \bar{x}_2^{(i)}, ..., \bar{x}_G^{(i)})$ and of production factors $\bar{\lambda}^{(i)} = (\bar{\lambda}_1^{(i)}, \bar{\lambda}_2^{(i)}, ..., \bar{\lambda}_L^{(i)})$ with the newly produced G goods denoted by $g = 1,2,...,G$ at prices $p = (p_1, p_2, ..., p_G)$, and L production factors, denoted by $l = 1,2,...,L$ at prices $w = (w_1, w_2, ..., w_L)$ are supplied. For reasons of simplicity, let us suppose, production factor equipment of enterprises do not change during the economic cycle. Enterprises are owned by households. Let's denote by $\delta_j^{(i)}$ the share of enterprise j, owned by household i. The shares are situated in a matrix $\Delta = [\delta_j^{(i)}]$ with dimensions $I \times J$, with:

$$\sum_{i=1}^{I} \delta_j^{(i)} = 1 \qquad (1)$$

The profits of enterprises are situated in a vector $\pi = (\pi_1, \pi_2, ..., \pi_J)$. Household i receives the share $\delta_j^{(i)} \pi_j$ of the profit π_j of enterprise j. The budget restriction of household i:

$$\sum_{g=1}^{G} p_g x_g^{(i)} \le \sum_{g=1}^{G} p_g \bar{x}_g^{(i)} + \sum_{l=1}^{L} w_l \bar{\lambda}_l^{(i)} + \sum_{j=1}^{J} \delta_j^{(i)} \pi_j \qquad (2)$$

Given prices $p = (p_1, p_2, ..., p_G)$ of goods and prices $w = (w_1, w_2, ..., w_L)$ of production factors, enterprise j is selecting a production plan $(y^{(j)}, z^{(j)}) = (y_1^{(j)}, y_2^{(j)}, ..., y_G^{(j)}, z_1^{(j)}, z_2^{(j)}, ..., z_L^{(j)})$ from the set $Y^{(j)}$ of all admissible plans, which maximizes its profit. Choosing production plan $(y^{(j)}, z^{(j)})$, enterprise j is indeed selecting production factors $(z^{(j)}) = (z_1^{(j)}, z_2^{(j)}, ..., z_L^{(j)})$, for producing the quantities of goods $(y^{(j)}) = (y_1^{(j)}, y_2^{(j)}, ..., y_G^{(j)})$, solving its optimization problem:

$$MAX \quad \pi^{(j)} = py^{(j)} - wz^{(j)}, \qquad (3)$$

The maximum is among all $(y^{(j)}, z^{(j)}) \in Y^{(j)}$. This mathematical problem could be solved for bounded, closed and convex $Y^{(j)}$.

Solving its optimal production problem, enterprise j is indeed determining its:
- supply function $y_g^{(j)}(p, w)$ of good $g = 1,2,...,G$
- demand function $z_l^{(j)}(p, w)$ of production factor $l = 1,2,...,L$
- profit function $\pi^{(j)}(p, w)$.

Supply, demand and profit functions generally should have to depend on all prices $(p, w) = (p_1, p_2, ..., p_G, w_1, w_2, ..., w_L)$, of goods and factor prices.

Every household $i = 1,2,...,I$ determines its supply of production factors and its demand of consumption goods, selecting a consumption plan $(x^{(i)}, \lambda^{(i)} - \bar{\lambda}^{(i)}) = (x_1^{(i)}, x_2^{(i)}, ..., x_G^{(i)}, \lambda_1^{(i)} - \bar{\lambda}_1^{(i)}, \lambda_2^{(i)} - \bar{\lambda}_2^{(i)}, ..., \lambda_L^{(i)} - \bar{\lambda}_L^{(i)})$ from the set $X^{(i)}$ of all admissible consumption plans, and maximizing its utility function $u^{(i)}(x^{(i)}, \lambda^{(i)} - \bar{\lambda}^{(i)})$. Household $i = 1,2,...,I$ is indeed finding:

$$MAX \quad u^{(i)}(x^{(i)}, \lambda^{(i)} - \bar{\lambda}^{(i)}) \tag{4}$$

among $(x^{(i)}, \lambda^{(i)} - \bar{\lambda}^{(i)}) \in X^{(i)}$, under the budget restriction

$$px^{(i)} \leq p\bar{x}^{(i)} + w\lambda^{(i)} + \sum_{j=1}^{J} \delta_j^{(i)} \pi^{(j)} \tag{5}$$

for $i = 1,2,...,I$. The budget restriction is said to be full, if:

$$px^{(i)} = p\bar{x}^{(i)} + w\lambda^{(i)} + \sum_{j=1}^{J} \delta_j^{(i)} \pi^{(j)} \tag{6}$$

The profit $\pi^{(j)}(p,w)$ of enterprise $j = 1,2,...,J$ is used by households, which own the enterprise for consumption.

For a set $X^{(i)}$ of consumption plans of household $i = 1,2,...,I$ with $\bar{\lambda}_l^{(i)} \leq \lambda_l^{(i)}$ for $l = 1,2,...,L$, being closed, bounded and convex, and for increasing utility function, the household $i = 1,2,...,I$ can solve its optimization problem to find out
 - the demand function $x_g^{(i)}(p,w)$ of good $g = 1,2,...,G$ and
 - the supply function $\lambda_l^{(i)}(p,w)$ of production factor $l = 1,2,...,L$.

The prices (p,w) of goods and production factors influence the behavior of supplier and demander for the determining the quantities of supply and demand. Price changes generate contradictory tendencies, inducing moving powers, which could bring the prices (p,w) in the system of markets to the equilibrium state (p^*, w^*), simultaneously satisfying all the participants in the market system. This state is said to be the **general equilibrium** or **Walras equilibrium** state of the economic system and is mathematically determined as a solution of the equations

$$x_g(p^*, w^*) = \bar{x}_g + y_g(p^*, w^*) \tag{7}$$

for $g = 1,2,...,G$

$$\lambda_l(p^*, w^*) = z_l(p^*, w^*) \tag{8}$$

for $l = 1,2,...,L$.

A function $f(X)$ of the economic variable X is said to be invariant with respect to scale or the unit of account or homogeneous of order 0, if

$$f(\rho X) = f(X) \tag{9}$$

for all $\rho > 0$.

A function $f(X)$ is homogeneous of order n, if

$$f(\rho X) = \rho^n f(X). \tag{10}$$

Particularly, $f(X)$ is homogeneous of order 1, if

$$f(\rho X) = \rho f(X). \tag{11}$$

Prices of goods and production factors are homogeneous of order 0, because the change of the unit of account does not change the value.

I) The supply function $y_g^{(j)}(p,w)$ of good $g = 1,2,...,G$ and the demand function $z_l^{(j)}(p,w)$ of production factor $l = 1,2,...,L$ of enterprise $j = 1,2,...,J$ are homogeneous of order 0 with respect to prices:

$$y_g^{(j)}(\rho p, \rho w) = y_g^{(j)}(p,w) \text{ for } g = 1,2,...,G \tag{12}$$

$$z_l^{(j)}(\rho p, \rho w) = z_l^{(j)}(p,w) \text{ for } l = 1,2,...,L \tag{13}$$

II.) The profit function $\pi^{(j)}(p,w)$ of enterprise $j = 1,2,...,J$ is homogeneous of order 1:

$$\pi^{(j)}(\rho p, \rho w) = \rho \pi^{(j)}(p,w) \tag{14}$$

III.) The demand function $x_g^{(i)}(p,w)$ of good $g = 1,2,...,G$ and the supply function $\lambda_l^{(i)}(p,w)$ of production factor $l = 1,2,...,L$ of household $i = 1,2,...,I$ are homogeneous of order 0 with respect to prices:

$$x_g^{(i)}(\rho p, \rho w) = x_g^{(i)}(p,w) \text{ for } g = 1,2,...,G \tag{15}$$

$$\lambda_l^{(i)}(\rho p, \rho w) = \lambda_l^{(i)}(p,w) \text{ for } l = 1,2,...,L \tag{16}$$

Markets are the sites of the economic system, where the property of goods and factor prices change. At given prices (p,w) the exchange of good $g = 1,2,...,G$ results in an excess demand we denote by $\varphi_g(p,w)$, similarly the exchange of production factor $l = 1,2,...,L$ is resulting in its excess demand, denoted by $\psi_l(p,w)$ and being correspondingly equal to:

$$\varphi_g(p,w) = \sum_{i=1}^{I} x_g^{(i)}(p,w) - \sum_{i=1}^{I} \bar{x}_g^{(i)}(p,w) - \sum_{j=1}^{J} y_g^{(j)}(p,w), \quad g = 1,2,...,G \tag{17}$$

$$\psi_l(p,w) = \sum_{j=1}^{J} z_l^{(j)}(p,w) - \sum_{i=1}^{I} \lambda_l^{(i)}(p,w), \quad l = 1,2,...,L \tag{18}$$

The Walras law states that, with full budget restriction $px^{(i)} = p\bar{x}^{(i)} + w\lambda^{(i)} + \sum_{j=1}^{J} \delta_j^{(i)} \pi^{(j)}(p,w)$, the sum of excess demands of goods and production factors equals zero:

$$\sum_{g=1}^{G} p_g \varphi_g(p,w) + \sum_{l=1}^{L} w_l \psi_l(p,w) = 0 \tag{19}$$

The Walras law shows that a full budget restriction economic system is closed. Goods and production factors can exchange their properties, keeping the same total amount.

Consequence: In a full budget restriction economic system the equilibrium of all markets with one exception is implying the equilibrium of the exceptional one.

3. Relativity of prices.

Among other functions, money is serving as a unit of account. Based on the unit of account one can introduce a scale for measuring the value of goods and production factors. The scales we use are called currencies and are based on euro, dollar, pound, lev, etc. as units of account. For passing from one currency to another, one has to multiply the relevant amount by the exchange rate. More generally, for changing the unit of account of an economic variable X one has to multiply it by a common factor ρ, for getting the new measure $X' = \rho X$ of the same variable. Some variables do not change, being multiplied by a common factor: $X' = X$. This is the case of a configuration of $(p^{(0)}, w^{(0)}) = (p_1^{(0)}, p_2^{(0)}, ..., p_G^{(0)}, w_1^{(0)}, w_2^{(0)}, ..., w_L^{(0)})$ of goods and production factors. Multiplying it by a common factor ρ, we get an equivalent configuration $(\rho p^{(0)}, \rho w^{(0)}) = (\rho p_1^{(0)}, \rho p_2^{(0)}, ..., \rho p_G^{(0)}, \rho w_1^{(0)}, \rho w_2^{(0)}, ..., \rho w_L^{(0)})$:

$$\rho(p^{(0)}, w^{(0)}) \approx (p^{(0)}, w^{(0)}) \qquad (20)$$

Multiplying by arbitrary $\rho > 0$, we get infinite many configurations being equivalent to configuration $(p^{(0)}, w^{(0)}) = (p_1^{(0)}, p_2^{(0)}, ..., p_G^{(0)}, w_1^{(0)}, w_2^{(0)}, ..., w_L^{(0)})$. This means, that it does not make much sense to say that the price of bread is one, five or thousand Euro without comparing it with other prices. Thus, relative prices have an economic sense, but not nominal ones. Relative prices show more realistic values of goods and production factors by comparing them with each other. Every price could be a base for comparison.

Case 1. The prices of configuration $(p_1, p_2, ..., p_G, w_1, w_2, ..., w_L)$ are compared with price p_1 of good 1, multiplying them by $\rho = \frac{1}{p_1}$, and getting the configuration of real prices $(1, \frac{p_2}{p_1}, ..., \frac{p_G}{p_1}, \frac{w_1}{p_1}, \frac{w_2}{p_1}, ..., \frac{w_L}{p_1})$, with the price of good 1 being 1 and playing the role of a unit of account, and all other prices are compared, related with the nominal price of good 1.

Case 2. The prices of configuration $(p_1, p_2, ..., p_G, w_1, w_2, ..., w_L)$ are compared with price w_1 of production factor 1, multiplying them by $\rho = \frac{1}{w_1}$, and getting the configuration of real prices $(1, \frac{p_2}{w_1}, ..., \frac{p_G}{w_1}, \frac{w_1}{w_1}, \frac{w_2}{w_1}, ..., \frac{w_L}{w_1})$, with the price of production factor 1 being 1 and all other prices compared with the nominal price of production factor 1.

Case 3. The prices of configuration $(p_1, p_2, ..., p_G, w_1, w_2, ..., w_L)$ are compared with their sum $\sum_{g=1}^{G} p_g + \sum_{l=1}^{L} w_l$, getting real prices

$(p'_1, p'_2, ..., p'_G, w'_1, w'_2, ..., w'_L)$, for $p'_g = \dfrac{p_g}{\sum\limits_{g=1}^{G} p_g + \sum\limits_{l=1}^{L} w_l}, g = 1, 2, ..., G$,

$w'_l = \dfrac{w_l}{\sum\limits_{g=1}^{G} p_g + \sum\limits_{l=1}^{L} w_l}, l = 1, 2, ..., L$. In this case $\sum\limits_{g=1}^{G} p'_g + \sum\limits_{l=1}^{L} w'_l = 1$.

Case 4. The prices of configuration $(p_1, p_2, ..., p_G, w_1, w_2, ..., w_L)$ are compared with the sum of prices of goods $\sum\limits_{g=1}^{G} p_g$, getting real prices $(p'_1, p'_2, ..., p'_G, w'_1, w'_2, ..., w'_L)$, for $p'_g = \dfrac{p_g}{\sum\limits_{g=1}^{G} p_g}, g = 1, 2, ..., G$, $w'_l = \dfrac{w_l}{\sum\limits_{g=1}^{G} p_g}, l = 1, 2, ..., L$. In this case $\sum\limits_{g=1}^{G} p'_g = 1$.

Case 5. The prices of configuration $(p_1, p_2, ..., p_G, w_1, w_2, ..., w_L)$ are compared with the sum of production factor prices $\sum\limits_{l=1}^{L} w_l$, getting the real prices $(p'_1, p'_2, ..., p'_G, w'_1, w'_2, ..., w'_L)$, for $p'_g = \dfrac{p_g}{\sum\limits_{l=1}^{L} w_l}, g = 1, 2, ..., G$,

$w'_l = \dfrac{w_l}{\sum\limits_{l=1}^{L} w_l}, l = 1, 2, ..., L$. In this case $\sum\limits_{l=1}^{L} w'_l = 1$.

The formation of prices of goods and production factors is a complicated process including interactions between all the markets. These interactions make prices more or less correlated with each other. For measuring correlations between prices, correlation coefficients can be used. Some correlation coefficients could be closer to zero, showing lower interdependence of some prices of goods. Correlation coefficients closer to one would express a closer relationship between prices, which could be even linear. Such prices we call sticky prices. A factor price and a price of a good could be sticky, because an increase of production factor prices usually implies an increase of prices of goods.

4. Equilibrium stability of a dynamic economic system

The state of an economic system is expressed by *economic parameters* depending on time *t*.

$$X(t) = (x_1(t), x_2(t), ..., x_n(t)), \text{ for } t \geq 0$$

We have to calculate the values of the parameters $(x_1(t), x_2(t), ..., x_n(t))$ in every moment of time $t > 0$, proposed the values of the parameters are known at the initial moment $t=0$.

One way to do this is to describe the dynamics of the system by differential equations. The rate of change or velocity of change $\dot{X} = (\dot{x}_1(t), \dot{x}_2(t), ..., \dot{x}_n(t))$ of the state $X = (x_1(t), x_2(t), ..., x_n(t))$ is expressed by a system of differential equations:

$$\dot{x}_1(t) = f_1(x_1(t), x_2(t), ..., x_n(t), y_1, y_2, ..., y_m)$$
$$\dot{x}_2(t) = f_2(x_1(t), x_2(t), ..., x_n(t), y_1, y_2, ..., y_m)$$
$$...$$
$$\dot{x}_n(t) = f_n(x_1(t), x_2(t), ..., x_n(t), y_1, y_2, ..., y_m)$$
(21)

where $f_1, f_2, ..., f_n$ are functions and $y_1, y_2, ..., y_m$ exogenous parameters, giving the outside conditions of the system. The parameters $X(t) = (x_1(t), x_2(t), ..., x_n(t))$ of the system are called endogenous parameters, particularly

$$\dot{x}_1(t) = a_{11}x_1(t) + a_{12}x_2(t) + ... + a_{1n}x_n(t) + b_1$$
$$\dot{x}_2(t) = a_{21}x_1(t) + a_{22}x_2(t) + ... + a_{2n}x_n(t) + b_2$$
$$...$$
$$\dot{x}_n(t) = a_{n1}x_1(t) + a_{n2}x_2(t) + ... + a_{2n}x_n(t) + b_n$$
(22)

where a_{ij} for $i, j = 1, 2, ..., n$ and $b_k = b_{1k}y_1 + b_{2k}y_2 + ... b_{mk}y_m$ for $k=1, 2, n$ are coefficients.

Matrix form:
$$\dot{X}(t) = AX(t) + B$$
(23)

denoting:

$$A = \begin{bmatrix} a_{11} & a_{12} ... a_{1n} \\ a_{21} & a_{22} ... a_{2n} \\ ... \\ a_{n1} & a_{n2} ... a_{nn} \end{bmatrix}, \quad B = \begin{bmatrix} b_1 \\ b_2 \\ ... \\ b_n \end{bmatrix}, \quad X(t) = \begin{bmatrix} x_1(t) \\ x_2(t) \\ ... \\ x_n(t) \end{bmatrix}, \quad \dot{X}(t) = \begin{bmatrix} \dot{x}_1(t) \\ \dot{x}_2(t) \\ ... \\ \dot{x}_n(t) \end{bmatrix}$$

Equilibrium states and their stability

Definition 1. The state $X^* = \begin{bmatrix} x_1^* \\ x_2^* \\ ... \\ x_n^* \end{bmatrix}$ is an equilibrium state for the dynamic system (1), if there is $X(t)$, such that:

$$X(t) \equiv X^* \text{ т.е. } \begin{vmatrix} x_1(t) \equiv x_1^* \\ \dots \\ x_n(t) \equiv x_n^* \end{vmatrix}$$

For all $t \geq 0$.

If $X(t) \equiv X^*$, then $\dot{X}(t) \equiv 0$. Therefore
$$AX^* + B = 0$$
$$X^* = -A^{-1}B$$

An economic system stays in equilibrium since it will be forced to move out of ist equilibrium under the pressure of exogenous parameters $y_1, y_2, \dots, y_m$, changing the outside conditions of the economic system, which is called a shock.

What happens when the system is put out of equilibrium? It could converge to equilibrium again, or it could diverge away of equilibrium. Thus possible cases are the following.

The *Equilibrium* could be:
- *Globally stable*, for every $X(0)$, $X(t) \to X^*, t \to \infty$.
- *Partially stable*, if for some initial states $X(0)$, $X(t) \to X^*$ for $t \to \infty$.
- *Globally instable*, if for all $X(0)$ different from X^*, is divergent $X(t)$, when $t \to \infty$.
- *Periodic*, if independently of the initial state $X(0)$, the system $X(t)$ periodically passes through state X^*.

There is a variety of monographs and papers devoted to the methodology of investigation of the dynamic equilibrium stability of economic systems. Here, we would refer to Martin Braun 1978, Giancarlo Gandolfo 1997, Akira Takayama 1994.

5. The equilibrium stability of two markets

We consider a dynamic system of two markets denoted by 1 and 2. On market 1 the good or production factor 1 at price P_1 is offered and on market 2 the good or production factor 2 at price P_2 is given. The quantity of demand $Q_1^{(d)}(P_1, P_2)$ and of the supply $Q_1^{(s)}(P_1, P_2)$ of good 1 on market 1 depends on the price P_1 of good 1, but on price P_2 of the good 2 as well. Similarly, the quantity of demand $Q_2^{(d)}(P_1, P_2)$ and of supply $Q_2^{(s)}(P_1, P_2)$ of good 2 on market 2 depend on price P_2 of good 2 and on price P_1 of good 1. Suppose the dependence is linear:

$$Q_1^{(d)} = \delta_{10} - \delta_{11} P_1 + \delta_{12} P_2 \tag{24}$$

$$Q_1^{(s)} = \sigma_{10} + \sigma_{11}P_1 - \sigma_{12}P_2 \qquad (25)$$

$$Q_2^{(d)} = \delta_{20} + \delta_{21}P_1 - \delta_{22}P_2 \qquad (26)$$

$$Q_2^{(s)} = \sigma_{20} - \sigma_{21}P_1 + \sigma_{22}P_2 \qquad (27)$$

where $\delta_{ij}, \sigma_{ij}, i = 1,2; j = 0,12$ are positive.

Equilibrium prices $\overline{P} = (\overline{P_1}, \overline{P_2})$ are derived, when $Q_i^{(d)}$ equals $Q_i^{(s)}$:

$$\overline{P_1} = \frac{\det\begin{bmatrix} \delta_{10} - \sigma_{10} & -(\delta_{12} + \sigma_{12}) \\ \delta_{20} - \sigma_{20} & \delta_{22} + \sigma_{22} \end{bmatrix}}{\det\begin{bmatrix} \delta_{11} + \sigma_{11} & -(\delta_{12} + \sigma_{12}) \\ -(\delta_{21} + \sigma_{21}) & \delta_{22} + \sigma_{22} \end{bmatrix}} = \frac{(\delta_{10} - \sigma_{10})(\delta_{22} + \sigma_{22}) + (\delta_{20} - \sigma_{20})(\delta_{12} + \sigma_{12})}{(\delta_{11} + \sigma_{11})(\delta_{22} + \sigma_{22}) - (\delta_{12} + \sigma_{12})(\delta_{21} + \sigma_{21})} \qquad (28)$$

$$\overline{P_2} = \frac{\det\begin{bmatrix} \delta_{11} + \sigma_{11} & \delta_{10} - \sigma_{10} \\ -(\delta_{21} + \sigma_{21}) & \delta_{20} - \sigma_{20} \end{bmatrix}}{\det\begin{bmatrix} \delta_{11} + \sigma_{11} & -(\delta_{12} + \sigma_{12}) \\ -(\delta_{21} + \sigma_{21}) & \delta_{22} + \sigma_{22} \end{bmatrix}} = \frac{(\delta_{20} - \sigma_{20})(\delta_{11} + \sigma_{11}) + (\delta_{10} - \sigma_{10})(\delta_{21} + \sigma_{21})}{(\delta_{11} + \sigma_{11})(\delta_{22} + \sigma_{22}) - (\delta_{12} + \sigma_{12})(\delta_{21} + \sigma_{21})} \qquad (29)$$

Determining the dynamics of the two markets, we could consider the velocity of change $\dot{P_i}$ of price $P_i = P_i(t)$, $i = 1,2$ to be proportional to the gap between demand and supply $Q_i^{(d)} - Q_i^{(s)}$:

$$\begin{aligned} \dot{P_1} &= \theta_1(Q_1^{(d)} - Q_1^{(s)}) \\ \dot{P_2} &= \theta_2(Q_2^{(d)} - Q_2^{(s)}) \end{aligned} \qquad (30)$$

where $\theta_i > 0$. Inserting (24)-(27) in (30) we get:

$$\begin{aligned} \dot{P_1} &= \theta_1(\delta_{10} - \delta_{11}P_1 + \delta_{12}P_2 - \sigma_{10} - \sigma_{11}P_1 + \sigma_{12}P_2) \\ \dot{P_2} &= \theta_2(\delta_{20} + \delta_{21}P_1 - \delta_{22}P_2 - \sigma_{20} + \sigma_{21}P_1 - \sigma_{22}P_2) \end{aligned} \qquad (31)$$

$$\begin{aligned} \dot{P_1} &= -\theta_1(\delta_{11} + \sigma_{11})P_1 + \theta_1(\delta_{12} + \sigma_{12})P_2 + \theta_1(\delta_{10} - \sigma_{10}) \\ \dot{P_2} &= \theta_2(\delta_{21} + \sigma_{21})P_1 - \theta_2(\delta_{22} + \sigma_{22})P_2 + \theta_2(\delta_{20} - \sigma_{20}) \end{aligned} \qquad (32)$$

$$\begin{bmatrix} \dot{P_1} \\ \dot{P_2} \end{bmatrix} = \begin{bmatrix} -\theta_1(\delta_{11} + \sigma_{11}) & \theta_1(\delta_{12} + \sigma_{12}) \\ \theta_2(\delta_{21} + \sigma_{21}) & -\theta_2(\delta_{22} + \sigma_{22}) \end{bmatrix} \begin{bmatrix} P_1 \\ P_2 \end{bmatrix} + \begin{bmatrix} \theta_1(\delta_{10} - \sigma_{10}) \\ \theta_2(\delta_{20} - \sigma_{20}) \end{bmatrix} \qquad (33)$$

Dynamic Equilibrium Stability of Two Markets

Denoting

$$A = \begin{bmatrix} -\theta_1(\delta_{11}+\sigma_{11}) & \theta_1(\delta_{12}+\sigma_{12}) \\ \theta_2(\delta_{21}+\sigma_{21}) & -\theta_2(\delta_{22}+\sigma_{22}) \end{bmatrix}, \; B = \begin{bmatrix} \theta_1(\delta_{10}-\sigma_{10}) \\ \theta_2(\delta_{20}-\sigma_{20}) \end{bmatrix}, \; P = \begin{bmatrix} P_1 \\ P_2 \end{bmatrix} \quad (34)$$

We get

$$\dot{P} = AP + B \quad (35)$$

Equations (33) and (35) are the equations of the dynamic system of the two markets.

Dynamic equilibrium:

$$\begin{bmatrix} \dot{P}_1 \\ \dot{P}_2 \end{bmatrix} = \begin{bmatrix} 0 \\ 0 \end{bmatrix} \quad (36)$$

$\bar{P} = (\bar{P}_1, \bar{P}_2)$ coincides with (28) and (29). Stability of the equilibrium depends only on matrix A and is:

I. *Globally stable*, if and only if: $traceA < 0$, $det A > 0$
II. *Globally unstable*, if and only if: $traceA > 0$, $det A > 0$
III. *Focus point*, if and only if: $traceA = 0$, $det A > 0$
IV. *Saddle point*, if and only if: $det A < 0$

Do to

$$traceA = -(\theta_1(\delta_{11}+\sigma_{11}) + \theta_2(\delta_{22}+\sigma_{22})), \quad (37)$$
$$det A = \theta_1\theta_2((\delta_{11}+\sigma_{11})(\delta_{22}+\sigma_{22}) - (\delta_{12}+\sigma_{12})(\delta_{21}+\sigma_{21})) \quad (38)$$

We get

I. . *Globally stable*, if and only if:
$$traceA = -(\theta_1(\delta_{11}+\sigma_{11}) + \theta_2(\delta_{22}+\sigma_{22})) < 0, \quad (39)$$
$$det A = \theta_1\theta_2((\delta_{11}+\sigma_{11})(\delta_{22}+\sigma_{22}) - (\delta_{12}+\sigma_{12})(\delta_{21}+\sigma_{21})) > 0 \quad (40)$$

II. *Globally unstable*, if and only if:
$$traceA = -(\theta_1(\delta_{11}+\sigma_{11}) + \theta_2(\delta_{22}+\sigma_{22})) > 0, \quad (41)$$
$$det A = \theta_1\theta_2((\delta_{11}+\sigma_{11})(\delta_{22}+\sigma_{22}) - (\delta_{12}+\sigma_{12})(\delta_{21}+\sigma_{21})) > 0 \quad (42)$$

III. *Focus point*:
$$traceA = -(\theta_1(\delta_{11}+\sigma_{11}) + \theta_2(\delta_{22}+\sigma_{22})) = 0, \quad (43)$$
$$det A = \theta_1\theta_2((\delta_{11}+\sigma_{11})(\delta_{22}+\sigma_{22}) - (\delta_{12}+\sigma_{12})(\delta_{21}+\sigma_{21})) > 0 \quad (44)$$

IV. *Saddle point*, if and only if:
$$det A = \theta_1\theta_2((\delta_{11}+\sigma_{11})(\delta_{22}+\sigma_{22}) - (\delta_{12}+\sigma_{12})(\delta_{21}+\sigma_{21})) < 0 \quad (45)$$

Because $\delta_{ij}, \sigma_{ij}, i=1,2; j=0,12$ are positive and $\theta_i > 0$ we get:

$$traceA = -(\theta_1(\delta_{11}+\sigma_{11}) + \theta_2(\delta_{22}+\sigma_{22})) < 0 \quad (46)$$

Therefore, we have only two cases:

Case I: $det A = \theta_1\theta_2((\delta_{11}+\sigma_{11})(\delta_{22}+\sigma_{22}) - (\delta_{12}+\sigma_{12})(\delta_{21}+\sigma_{21})) > 0$ global stability and case IV: $\det A = \theta_1\theta_2((\delta_{11}+\sigma_{11})(\delta_{22}+\sigma_{22})-(\delta_{12}+\sigma_{12})(\delta_{21}+\sigma_{21})) < 0$.

For a more detailed analysis let us consider:

$$q_1^{(d)}: Q_1^{(d)} = \delta_{10} - \delta_{11}P_1 + \delta_{12}P_2 \tag{47}$$

$$q_1^{(s)}: Q_1^{(s)} = \sigma_{10} + \sigma_{11}P_1 - \sigma_{12}P_2 \tag{48}$$

$$q_2^{(d)}: Q_2^{(d)} = \delta_{20} + \delta_{21}P_1 - \delta_{22}P_2 \tag{49}$$

$$q_2^{(s)}: Q_2^{(s)} = \sigma_{20} - \sigma_{21}P_1 + \sigma_{22}P_2 \tag{50}$$

On figure 1 the convergence of prices of good 1 and good 2 towards the equilibrium prices $\bar{P}_1$ and $\bar{P}_2$ is shown under the pressure of the contracting power $\sigma_{11}+\delta_{11}$ and $\sigma_{22}+\delta_{22}$, correspondingly, determining the speed of convergence. When $\sigma_{11}+\delta_{11} > 0$ ($\sigma_{22}+\delta_{22} > 0$) markets 1 (2) are contracting towards $\bar{P}_1$ ($\bar{P}_2$), with speed proportional to $\sigma_{11}+\delta_{11} > 0$ ($\sigma_{22}+\delta_{22} > 0$). Correspondingly, when $\sigma_{11}+\delta_{11} < 0$ ($\sigma_{22}+\delta_{22} < 0$) markets 1 (2) are going away from $\bar{P}_1$ ($\bar{P}_2$).

Since we have $\sigma_{11}+\delta_{11} > 0$ and $\sigma_{22}+\delta_{22} > 0$, then $traceA = -(\theta_1(\delta_{11}+\sigma_{11})+\theta_2(\delta_{22}+\sigma_{22})) < 0$. Whether this contracting power will be enough to keep the equilibrium stable or partially stable depends on the interacting power of the markets.

The second market is pulling the first one with power proportional to $\delta_{12}+\sigma_{12} > 0$. Similarly, the first market is pulling the second one with power proportional to $\sigma_{21}+\delta_{21} > 0$. If the pulling powers are not too strong, then

$$\det A = \theta_1\theta_2((\delta_{11}+\sigma_{11})(\delta_{22}+\sigma_{22})-(\delta_{12}+\sigma_{12})(\delta_{21}+\sigma_{21})) > 0,$$

and the equilibrium will be globally stable.

Figure 1: The convergence of markets to equilibrium separately

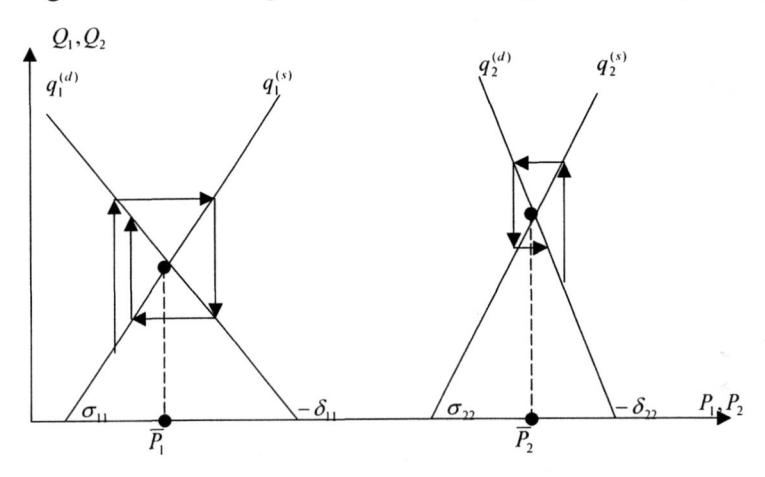

Figure 2: The pulling interaction between markets

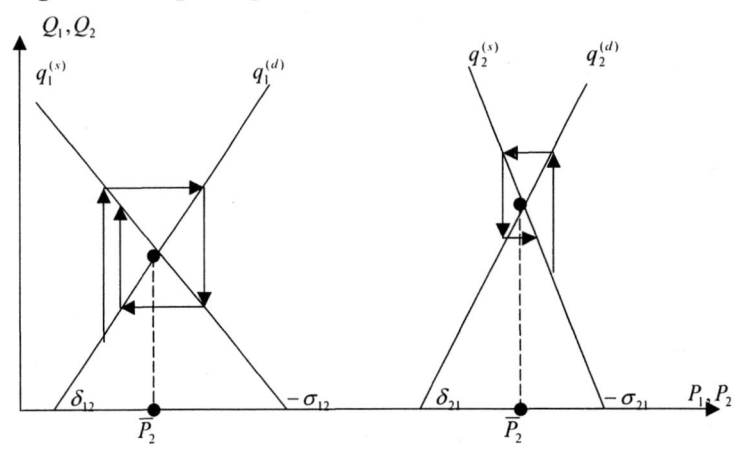

If the „pulling powers" $\delta_{12} + \sigma_{12} > 0$, $\sigma_{21} + \delta_{21} > 0$ are so strong, that
$$\det A = \theta_1 \theta_2 ((\delta_{11} + \sigma_{11})(\delta_{22} + \sigma_{22}) - (\delta_{12} + \sigma_{12})(\delta_{21} + \sigma_{21})) < 0,$$
then the system will be destabilized and from stable one it will be transformed into an only partially stable one (saddle point stability).

Figure 3: Global stability

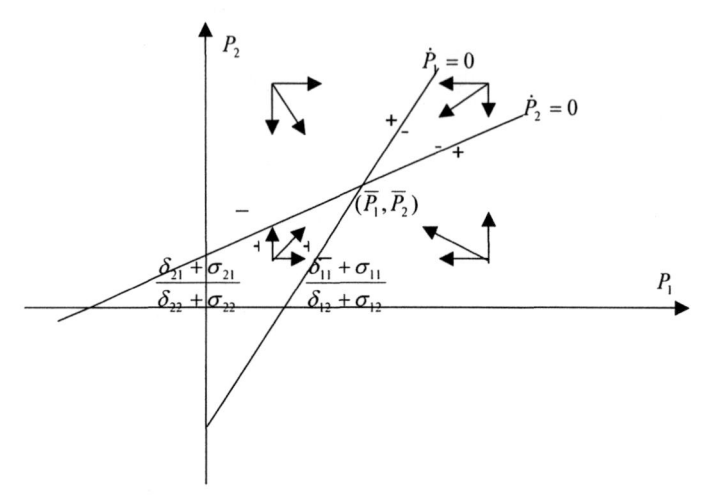

Figure 4: Saddle point stability

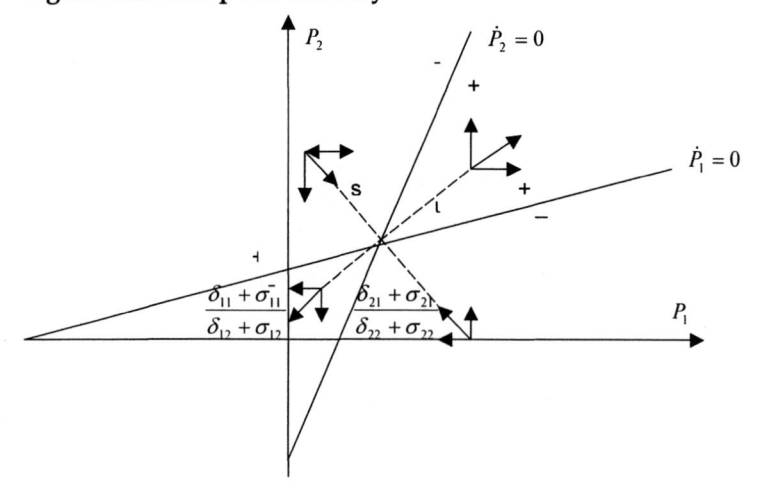

Calculating the equation of the saddle point line s in figure 4:

$$P_2 = \frac{\lambda_2 + \theta_1(\delta_{11} + \sigma_{11})}{\lambda_1 + \theta_1(\delta_{11} + \sigma_{11})} P_1 + \frac{\theta_1(\delta_{10} - \sigma_{10})(\lambda_2 + \theta_1(\delta_{11} + \sigma_{11})) - \theta_1\theta_2(\delta_{10} - \sigma_{10})(\delta_{21} + \sigma_{21})}{\lambda_1(\lambda_1 + \theta_1(\delta_{11} + \sigma_{11}))} \quad (51)$$

for
$$\lambda_1 = -\frac{\theta_1(\delta_{11}+\sigma_{11})+\theta_2(\delta_{22}+\sigma_{22})}{2} +$$
$$+\sqrt{(\frac{\theta_1(\delta_{11}+\sigma_{11})+\theta_2(\delta_{22}+\sigma_{22})}{2})^2 - \theta_1\theta_2((\delta_{11}+\sigma_{11})(\delta_{22}+\sigma_{22})-(\delta_{12}+\sigma_{12})(\delta_{21}+\sigma_{21}))}$$
$$\lambda_2 = -\frac{\theta_1(\delta_{11}+\sigma_{11})+\theta_2(\delta_{22}+\sigma_{22})}{2} -$$
$$-\sqrt{(\frac{\theta_1(\delta_{11}+\sigma_{11})+\theta_2(\delta_{22}+\sigma_{22})}{2})^2 - \theta_1\theta_2((\delta_{11}+\sigma_{11})(\delta_{22}+\sigma_{22})-(\delta_{12}+\sigma_{12})(\delta_{21}+\sigma_{21}))}$$

$\lambda_2 < \lambda_1$, because $\theta_1, \theta_2, \delta_{11}, \sigma_{11}, \delta_{22}, \sigma_{22}$ positive.

Equation (51) gives the relationship of prices to be held on for the equilibrium stability of a two market system for linearly depending prices.

6. Concluding remark

Due to the uncertainty of the surrounding world, there is a desire for a more balanced and stable economic systems. Here, we concentrate our attention on the equilibrium stability of two markets, we find most essential, even though the economic system could consist of more than two markets.

We could find as essential examples for couples of markets:
   (a) goods market – money market;
   (b) goods market – labor market.

In order to keep the equilibrium stability of the markets under consideration, the calculated relationships between the parameters determining the markets and the equilibrium market prices have to be hold. Particularly, if we like to keep the balance of the saddle point stability, the relationship (51) between the equilibrium prices P_1 of maket 1 and P_2 of market 2 has to be hold. As an example, P_1 could be the price level of consumer goods and P_2 the price level of labour, which means the level of wages. In this case, the relationship between prices and wages has to be kept according (51), which takes the productivity of labor into account.

References

Braun, Martin 1978: Differential Equations and Their Applications. Springer-Verlag. New York, Heidelberg, Berlin

Gandolfo, Giancarlo 1997: Economic Dynamics. Springer-Verlag. Berlin, Heidelberg, New York

Mas-Colell, Andreu/Mihael D. Whinston/Jerry R. Green 1995: Microeconomic Theory. Oxford University Press. New York, Oxford

Takayama, Akira 1994: Analytical Methods in Economics. Harvester Wheatsheaf. New York

Walras, Leon 1874: Elements d'economie politique pure. Corbaz. Lausanne

THE MEASUREMENT OF THE EFFICIENCY OF TRANSACTION COSTS

JEAN-PIERRE GERN

(NEUCHÂTEL, SWITZERLAND)

Transaction costs play an increasing role in modern economies. The development of production techniques and of scales of production decreases constantly the share of employment in production proper (even within production enterprises). The counterpart is the emergence of ever increasing transaction costs. Their burden is becoming so high that it raises questions: How far are they efficient? How far do they contribute to the availability of goods and services, and even more to social welfare? A clear answer needs measurement; but is it possible to measure? What is to be measured? On the ground of which concepts? How can the measurement be organised?

1. The definition of transaction costs

Until the 19th century economic theories considered the role of transaction costs – at least parts of them. For that period, the considerations about commercial costs in the theory of the "Physiocrates" are typical. With the classical economists and even more with the general equilibrium theory, transaction costs as such disappeared; either they were ignored, as did David Ricardo in his theory of international trade (Ricardo 1970: 97-114) or they were considered as a creation of value, as did David Ricardo in his theory of value (Ricardo 1970: 24-25) or of utility (Léon Walras 1952: 180) just as productive activities, their contribution being measured by the income they raise, on the assumption that in the general equilibrium the income of a factor of production or of an activity is equal to its marginal productivity.

Transaction costs are not a clear concept; what they include varies greatly among economists. We shall not choose one definition of transaction costs. It is more fruitful to use and compare different definitions. As background, we refer to the article published in the "Dictionnaire d'analyse économique" by Bernard Guerrien[1] (Guerrien 1996), but broaden it.

We may first consider transaction costs within the productive sector:
  1. The narrowest and most evident definition is to make the distinction among the cost borne by the economic agents themselves between

those which are relevant to production and those which concern exchanges; transaction costs have to be found inside the productive units as well as in the trade sector.
2. A second approach, which is methodologically different but has a similar objective, consists of the comparison of the cost of production on one side and the price for the consumer on the other side.

But transaction costs may be defined in a wider way:
3. To the costs borne by the economic agents, the cost of organising the market, of providing legal security ... may also be included. Taking such costs into account invites us to a broader definition. It is not easy to set its limits: Is it between the activities, which by themselves contribute directly to the supply of goods and services to the consumer, and those which do not? Or between activities which are directly useful, indirectly useful or not useful at all?

But transaction costs are not only costs of activities. They may also consist of indirect effects of economic and other activities on the society.
4. Nowadays there is a great debate about who should bear an increasing amount of costs previously ignored: the economic agents, the consumers, the state? Such costs generally do not correspond to an activity; they may be a loss, a burden (like pollution or noise, queuing for services ...).
5. An economic analysis made by the World Bank, which attempted to include all social costs (use of not renewable resources, deterioration of living conditions, loss of opportunity for future generations...) came to astonishing conclusions: the very profitable external trade of Brazil became a dramatic drain on national resources, when such costs were included. This is the broadest definition. In our time, when conscientiousness for environmental and social costs is increasing, it cannot be ignored, though it is very difficult to assess. The study of the World Bank shows the way.

2. The definition of efficiency

Similarly the concept of efficiency may be approached in different ways. It may refer to efficiency in the framework of the productive sector only:
1. The narrowest and most obvious definition is to consider a specific activity, the expenses of which are considered as transaction costs, and to analyse how efficient the combination of resources in that activity would be.

2. But the purpose of that activity cannot be ignored. Higher transaction costs may make them more efficient if they allow a greater increase in the performance of productive activities. With the development of technology and transportation, an increase in the efficiency of productive activities has been obtained through larger transaction costs. Important items are the concentration of production or its spatial distribution to obtain lower production costs. In such a context has not the efficiency to be appraised in a combined way for both? Equally, mass production requires a large and secure market, which implies constant marketing and publicity. How can the measurement of efficiency take that problem into account?

The first two approaches consider only the efficiency from the viewpoint of the supply side. But we may also consider the efficiency for the consumer:

3. Despite some ideological statements, marketing is not information. It often tends to destroy the transparency of the market (e.g. nowadays in telecommunications). As the supports for publicity develop, in order to maintain their share of the market producers need to increase constantly their presence in the media. What is the result if all of them do so? If we try to imagine a marketing, which is consumer oriented, with an optimal allocation of resources for that purpose, wouldn't it be far from the present situation? Can we measure efficiency in such a perspective?

The definition of efficiency implies valuation. And the definition of values has best to be based on utility. How do we appraise utility, even if we are not able to measure it?

4. Vilfredo Pareto used to make a distinction between utility and "ophélimité"(Pareto 1896/97). The latter is the appreciation by the individual, the former the real utility for society. On which basis should we consider efficiency?

5. We may also confront the concept of utility of the marginal school with the concept of Gossen (Gossen 1983: 6, 13, 14), which has been unduly forgotten. In his approach the quantity, which offers the maximum satisfaction is not the consumption which brings the marginal utility to zero as in the general equilibrium theory. He does not consider total utility as the generating function of marginal utility. When marginal utility comes to zero, the total satisfaction is also that low. Considering the optimal use of resources in his perspective might be very relevant in the context of a limited environment.

Could it be used for the measurement of efficiency under our present economic conditions?

The previous definitions refer to efficiency in a microeconomic approach. Alternatively efficiency may be considered in a systemic context:

6. When we consider the efficiency of every single category of transaction costs, we make the assumption of "ceteris paribus". Optimizing efficiency in such a perspective would not be globally optimal. To consider the interrelations between all activities we need a systemic approach. The systemic theory has raised great interest, as it is more relevant than a sum of partial analyses, but that interest has apparently weakened, when the problem of application has come on the table. Nevertheless, conceptually we may consider a society with a given productive capacity, whose needs are not under the influence of publicity and marketing, neither conditioned by institutions. (The influence of culture we cannot exclude.) Under such conditions we may raise the question: How well could it live with its productive capacity, if all activities classified as transaction costs in the broader sense were optimally organised for social welfare? It would be the most significant reference for the measurement of the efficiency of transaction costs, if it could be sufficiently defined to be used for the purpose. Nevertheless, it might be a relevant approach for a development policy, a tool for the elaboration of long term strategies.

3. The unit of measurement

Measuring efficiency requires an appropriate tool. The first question is: How do we measure the value of goods and services, how do we measure costs?

It is generally assumed that prices are a good expression of both. Such a belief is founded on the basic assumptions of the general equilibrium theory. But older theories suggest that we should be more careful. In the real world price determination is far from the expression of marginal cost and utility. We are in a world where everyone tries to impose himself on the market and to drain as much income as he can. Some have more power than others; and transaction costs reflect largely that inequality in the draining of income. Many institutional and organisational factors also intervene.

Prices are a doubtful reference. It surely is so for all problems; but in our case it is more disturbing than in most others: indeed the relation between what is paid for productive activities and for transaction ones scarcely reflects the amount of human and physical resources attributed to both.

Besides, according to the issue, the most relevant measurement may be in real terms or in monetary terms – or even in the relation between both of them.

When a measurement in real terms is essential, reference to physical quantities may be opportune, especially if a reference to labour is involved.

4. The purpose of measuring

Considering the very wide range of questions raised by the various approaches mentioned above, it is necessary to define the purpose of measurement and accordingly the ways of measuring in order to answer them. The list of purposes mentioned here is in no way exhaustive; its aim is to show how, according to the purpose chosen, the definition of both transaction costs and efficiency as well as the methodology to follow are fundamentally different.

1. We may aim at the pursuit of the best allocation of human and physical resources. It is especially pertinent in a world where the resources dedicated to production and to consumer services are a smaller and smaller share of all resources, an increasing share being absorbed by the transaction costs of enterprises, of consumers, of the State and by hidden losses (in natural and social capital).
2. On the footpath of the "Physiocrates" we may consider that transaction costs are largely a burden on the economy and a hindrance to development, that consequently the productive sector would be more dynamic, if transaction costs could be restricted (both in real and in monetary terms).
3. We may be preoccupied with the fact that transaction costs (in their wider definition) are heavier in old industrialized countries than in new ones, that consequently they are a key element in the economic relations between the West and Asia in particular.
4. A large share of the transaction costs of enterprises is due to their struggle for the domination of the market and a hindrance to an efficient competition between enterprises.
5. Enterprises tend to shift as much as possible the transaction costs to either the State, the consumers, poorer economic partners or future

generations. A measurement of such phenomena may be a useful tool for economic policies.
6. As far as some transaction costs represent a drain from the economic flows, not only do they hinder prosperity, but they also create social injustice. The present accumulation of capital in a small number of hands and the growing poverty even in richer countries are signs of such a problem.

5. Suggested measurements

5.1. For the best allocation of resources

For such a measurement, we may use a strict definition of transaction costs, or broader ones. With a strict definition it is a question of the efficiency of the productive sector. With the rapid structural changes due to new technologies, lower transportation costs and larger markets, new opportunities have emerged in the location and organisation of productive activities, in services to enterprises, in trade between enterprises or on the way to the consumers. In such a transition period, competition has not developed its full impact on efficiency; but in the long run its impact may not be sufficient either.

Presently, national accounts show that the share of commercial activities tend to surpass that of production in the national income, though it does apparently not include commercial activities internal to productive units. The reasons for it need investigation. Two elements may have to be considered:

- in real terms: the excessive and often irrational development of transportation of goods, of commercial surfaces and personnel, as well as the growing weight of publicity, marketing and other services or intermediaries,
- in monetary terms: the fact that the development of world trade has opened vast possibilities of making large profits thanks to the disparities in world prices and consequently an accumulation of financial resources. In order not to overestimate the weight of transaction costs in real terms, such a financial drain of income should not be taken into consideration in the measurement.

The difficulty of measurement comes from the necessity of differentiating between the use of real resources and the drainage of income, which is also worth measuring for its own sake.

Besides, the decrease of the direct costs of production due to rapid technological progress has opened a gap between production costs and consumer prices on the market (typical in telecommunications). It allowed the development of parasitic activities. For instance, financial activities are more and more lucrative, but does their contribution to the availability of goods and services increase in proportion? If not, their increasing share of national income has to be considered as inefficient transaction costs. It is in the present ideology that all activities, which can be a source of income, have a social utility; it is consequently difficult to appraise such phenomena without preconceptions.

But we may also refer to a broader definition of transaction costs: enterprises tend to avoid covering costs, which can be borne by others: by the consumers (queues for services ...), by the state (health cost of overstressed personnel, costs of infrastructures for excessive movements of goods in the production and commercialisation process ...) or by future generations (costs of damages to the environment ...). If we take such costs into account to measure the efficiency of transaction costs in the perspective of the best allocation of resources, a complex analysis of the economic system will be necessary.

5.2. For optimizing economic growth

Point 5.1. considered the burden of transaction costs on the available human and natural resources, which is in itself a weight on economic development. But as development is a dynamic process in the lapse of time, which is conditioned by the dynamism of economic flows, econometric models may reveal that transaction costs, even when they do not imply the use of real resources, may be a hindrance to development if the exchanges among producers are made less profitable because of the excessive income of the traders (Quesnay 1958: 565), if the circularity of economic flows is broken (Boisguillebert 1966: 173-239) or if it is a source of hoarding (John Maynard Keynes 1955: 129).

This analysis requires an approach of the economic system in terms of economic flows and not of equilibrium. In a very condensed form Cantillon (Cantillon 1952: 25-28, 70-73) and the "Tableau économique" of the Physiocrates (François Quesnay 1969) opened the way to dynamic flows analyses. To measure the impact of transaction costs in that perspective requires extensive econometric models.

5.3. For international competition

Currently, there is a strong competition between economic areas, which have quite different institutional, economic, and social systems. There are many historical examples of the advantage of newcomers over well establishes industrial systems. The weight of transaction costs is an important, though largely ignored element of this advantage. In this case, the key elements to consider are:

- the legal and institutional system,
- the organisation of the productive sector (industry and trade)
- the organisation of governmental, institutional and other activities,
- the maintenance of infrastructures of all kind,
- the institutional and spatial structures of activities,
- the social system.

To face such a competition, enterprises of old industrialised countries try to decrease their costs to the detriment of the individuals and of other institutions, including the State – which is no long term solution. But not all such transaction costs can be compressed; under the pressure of enterprises some are even increased (additional services from the state). Delocalisations increase the weight of transaction costs on remaining enterprises.

More than a measurement a complete study of the transaction costs involved and of their consequences may suggest some improvements in their efficiency.

5.4. For a better management of competition

A large part of transaction costs of enterprises aim at maintaining or developing their share of the market, or even at dominating it. Patents, trade marks, publicity and marketing in all its ways are heavy on their budget. Exclusivity and other rules imposed to the trade sector add to that burden. They may serve the production process: the large acceptance of Windows is a positive example; but the restrictions imposed today by Microsoft may not be. The losses imposed on the economy by such transaction costs could only be measured if a model of an alternative system could be drawn.

Many products which may be produced locally by small producers are practically monopolised by big ones through an aggressive marketing. It is typical in the food industry. In such cases transaction costs have a double negative effect: their own burden and the distorted organisation of production, which also implies costs of administration, transportation..., which could be avoided.

An analysis for some products, for which the concentration of production in large enterprises has no technical reason, may cast some light on the issue.

5.5. True prices

At present there are strong movements fighting for true prices, requiring that all the costs of production be borne by the producer, especially in environmental policies and in international trade. They bring to light the burden of largely overlooked transaction costs. Except if they are borne by the state, those costs do not appear in statistics and need special enquiries. They are easily excessive as they are not borne by those who create them.

Efforts are being made to trace such transaction costs, even to appreciate their importance though they are not easy to be quantified; it may open the way to meaningful evaluations, if not to proper measurements.

5.6. Social justice

In a world of small producers, nobody would exchange *two* hours of work against only *one* (A. Smith 1970: 26). But in the following century, the development of mass production has created crying inequalities and produced a dual society (England, mid-19th century). A century of social fighting has restored the balance to a certain degree. But nowadays, with new technologies the direct cost of production is a small part of the price. Indirect costs and especially transaction costs take the greater share. The mechanisms of the past to maintain an adequate level of social justice are no more operative. Profits against wages and salaries in the enterprise is no more the main issue. New mechanisms are to be developed in order to face the increase of poverty in richer countries. The weight of transaction costs is to be analysed in this perspective.

In this case, transaction costs appear mainly as a drainage of income. To trace them, a refined analysis of income distribution through statistics and surveys may produce the necessary basic information. Then it is necessary to identify the mechanisms, which produce such income discrepancies through the increase of transaction costs.

6. Conclusion

We started with various definitions of transaction costs and of efficiency. As the spectrum is very wide, approaches to measurement need to be oriented. For that purpose, we tried to identify for which objectives it may be useful to consider measuring the efficiency of transaction costs. There are many; we only gave a few examples.

It appears that according to the question to be answered, the choice of definition has to be adapted. Not the same elements have to be included in transaction costs, if the question is one of best allocation of human and physical resources, economic growth, management of competition, "true prices", international competition or social justice.

To some questions – rather seldom - the measurement of well identified items is possible and meaningful, in most cases it requires an econometric analysis or some more extensive research in the operation of the economic system.

Notes

(1) Bernard Guerrien, Dictionnaire d'analyse économique: microéconomie, macroéconomie, théorie des jeux, etc., Paris, La Découverte 1996, p. 118:

«**Coûts de transaction:** Coûts provoqués par toutes les procédures – ou opérations – qui rendent possibles des échanges mutuellement avantageux, entre deux ou plusieurs individus. Pendant longtemps, les coûts de transaction ont été assimilés aux *coûts de coordination* des choix d'unités de décision autonomes – choix guidés par un système de prix lui-même considéré comme autonome. Dans ce cas, l'étude des coûts de transaction dépend de la forme d'organisation sociale des échanges qui est envisagée – notamment en ce qui concerne le contenu donné à la notion de MARCHÉ; elle nécessite aussi une réflexion sur le rôle de la MONNAIE, en tant qu'intermédiaire privilégié dans les échanges. On peut se faire une idée de l'importance des coûts de coordination en calculant la différence entre le prix payé pour un bien par le consommateur final et ce que touche le producteur (différence qui rémunère toute la chaîne d'intermédiaires, qui assurent en fait – et plus ou moins bien la coordination).

Les coûts de transaction en tant que coûts de coordination supposent un (relativement) grand nombre de participants. Toutefois, dans les années soixante-dix, théoriciens néo-classiques se sont de plus en plus intéressés aux RELATIONS BILATERALES et aux CONTRATS qui souvent les codifient. L'habitude a alors été prise – à commencer par Oliver Williams et le courant NÉO-INSTITUTIONNALISTE dont il est le chef de file – d'appeler« coûts de transaction » l'ensemble des coûts qui résultent de la relation contractuelle; soit, pour l'essentiel :

    1. *les coûts qu'entraînent pour chaque partie la recherche et l'énumération de toutes les éventualités qui peuvent survenir pendant la période où le contrat s'exécute;*

2. *les coûts provoqués par les négociations entre les parties*, en tenant compte de chaque éventualité; à cela s'ajoutent les frais qui résultent de la rédaction puis de la mise en forme du contrat qui en résulte;
3. *les coûts inhérents à la recherche et au fonctionnement de systèmes – légaux ou autres – qui garantissent que chacun respectera ses engagements* (car, sans eux, il se peut qu'il n'y ait pas de contrat, chacun se méfiant de l'autre).

Pris ensemble, ces coûts sont loin d'être négligeables; ils peuvent même théoriquement devenir infinis, si le nombre d'éventualités envisageables l'est, ou si les négociations ne s'arrêtent jamais, faute d'accord. Quant au système de garanties, il fait à un moment ou à un autre appel à l'État et à son appareil de contrôle et de répression, dont les coûts de fonctionnement peuvent être importants.

Alors que les coûts de transaction du premier type (liés à la coordination) sont inhérents à l'organisation même du système, ceux du second type sont essentiellement dus aux comportements des individus – à leur «opportunisme» ou à leur RATIONALITÉ LIMITÉE, selon le cas. En règle générale, les NÉO-CLASSIQUES préfèrent mettre l' accent sur les seconds («C'est la faute à l'homme, par nature égoïste et paresseux») que sur les premiers (qui seraient faibles si on «laisse faire le marché»). Ainsi, dans le modèle de référence néo-classique, le modèle d'équilibre général d'ARROW-DEBREU, rien n'est dit sur les coûts de transaction ; mais ils sont en fait totalement pris en charge, et de façon bénévole, par le COMMISSAIRE-PRISEUR.»

References

Boisguillebert, Pierre le Pesant Sieur de 1966: Le détail de la France (1697), in: Les principaux économistes, réimpression del'édition 1846, tome 1, Zeller, Osnabrück

Cantillon, Richard 1952: Essai sur la nature du commerce en général (1755), INED, Paris

Gossen, Hermann Heinrich 1983: The laws of human relations and the rules of human action derived therefrom (1854)

Guerrien, Bernard 1996: Dictionnaire d'analyse économique: microéconomie, macroéconomie, théorie des jeux, etc., La Découverte, Paris

Keynes, John Maynard 1955: Théorie générale de l'emploi, de l'intérêt et de la monnaie (1936), Payot, Paris

Pareto, Vilfredo 1896/97: Cours d'économie politique.

Quesnay, François 1969: Tableau économique des Physiocrates (1758), Calmann-Levy, Paris

Quesnay, François 1958: Hommes (1768) INED Paris

Ricardo, David 1970: Principes de l'économie politique et de l'impôt (1817), Calmann-Levy, Paris

Smith, Adam 1970: The Wealth of Nations (1776), Dent, London

Walras, Léon 1952: Eléments d'économie politique pure (1874-1877), LGDJ, Paris

E-BUSINESS – PERSPECTIVES AND CHALLENGES IN GLOBAL COMPETITION

LIANA BADEA / NICOLAE NEDELCU
(ACADEMY OF ECONOMIC STUDIES, BUCHAREST - ANGHEL SALIGNY COLLEGE, ROSIORI DE VEDE, ROMANIA)

1. "E-business"– definition, typology and some characteristics

E-business (electronic business), derived from such terms as "e-mail" and "e-commerce", is the conduct of business on the Internet, not only buying and selling but also servicing customers and collaborating with business partners. One of the first to use the term was IBM, when, in October, 1997, it launched a thematic campaign built around the term. Today, major corporations are rethinking their businesses in terms of the Internet and its new culture and capabilities. Companies are using the Web to buy parts and supplies from other companies, to collaborate on sales promotions, and to do joint research. Exploiting the convenience, availability, and world-wide reach of the Internet, many companies, such as Amazon.com, the book sellers, has already discovered how to use the Internet successfully.

E-business is just business using electronic networks to transform a business process or business system to create superior value for current or potential customers. E-business is more than e-commerce, even though the terms are often used interchangeably (www.epsilonium.com). The latter is focused on buying and selling products and services, using network technologies. E-business goes beyond mere transactions. It facilitates new types of connections among a broad range of entities. It enables any type of business activity over the network[1].

E-business changes the meaning of the word "firm". The boundaries of the firm are blurring to the point that the enterprise transcends the firm to also encompass partners, suppliers, and customers - the extended enterprise, a business without boundaries. The linking of these entities makes possible new applications to build, manage and strengthen relationships among them.

E-business represents in fact a number of processes. For example, you may:
- Communicate with customers, clients or suppliers via email.

---

[1] Just to name a few - communicating, collaborating, learning, innovating, planning, and recruiting.

- Send emails to other businesses to order products and services.
- Sell products or services via website.
- Use the Web to find information, such as prices, phone numbers and reviews of products.
- Use the Web for research (such as the latest industry trends) and provide information about products and services.
- Use the website as a means of managing information in business.
- Use the Internet for online banking and paying bills (http://www.e-businessguide.gov.au).

What e-Business is not
- E-business is not a bolt-on to the business; rather it is an integral component of it.
- E-business is not about technology.
- E-business is not a middle-management initiative – It is the CEO's job.
- E-business is not tied to a particular department or functional area.
- E-business is not a fixed target. – It is about adapting and keeping up with changes around.

The intensity and impact of electronic business depend on the business activities of companies, and on the configuration of the value system in which these companies operate. In manufacturing sectors, companies focus on procurement processes, optimizing supply chain management and integrating retail and distribution. In a project-oriented business such as construction, applications supporting project management have a high potential. In tourism, online information and reservation services have become a commonplace. In telecommunications, it is hardly possible to make a clear distinction between the use of e-business by telecom firms themselves and the provision of related services to customers. Hospitals aim at improving the efficiency of their internal processes as well as document exchanges within the health system by means of ICT, thus cutting costs.

Companies are increasingly using Information and Communication Technologies to link together their business processes and systems:

⇒ internally: hooking departments together to provide better products and more responsive services more efficiently;
⇒ with those of their suppliers, distributors and other partners, increasing efficiencies even further;
⇒ with public authorities;

⇒ with their customers, allowing them to respond more directly to market trends and sell worldwide.

E-business therefore allows new forms of partnership, and improves both, the way companies work and the products and services they offer.

When we speak about electronic business, we speak about some new issues, such as:
- business-to-consumer (B2C): online transactions are made between businesses and individual consumers;
- business-to-business (B2B): businesses make online transactions with other businesses;
- e-tailing: online retailing, usually B2C;
- business-to-business-to-consumer (B2B2C): e-commerce model in which a business provides some products or services to a client business that maintains its own customers;
- consumer-to-business (C2B): e-commerce model in which individuals use the Internet to sell products or services to organizations or individuals seek sellers to bid on products or services they need;
- consumer-to-consumer (C2C): e-commerce model in which consumers sell directly to other consumers;
- peer-to-peer (P2P): technology that enables networked peer computers to share data and processing with each other directly; can be used in C2C, B2B, and B2C e-commerce;
- mobile commerce (m-commerce): e-commerce transactions and activities conducted in a wireless environment;
- location-based commerce (l-commerce): m-commerce transactions targeted to individuals in specific locations, at specific times;
- intra business EC: e-commerce category that includes all internal organizational activities that involve the exchange of goods, services or information among various units and individuals in an organization;
- business-to-employees (B2E): e-commerce model in which an organization delivers services, information, or products to its individual employees;
- collaborative commerce (c-commerce): e-commerce model in which individuals or groups communicate or collaborate online;
- e-learning: the online delivery of information for purposes of training or education;

- exchange (electronic): a public electronic market with many buyers and sellers;
- exchange-to-exchange (E2E): e-commerce model in which electronic exchanges formally connect to one another for the purpose of exchanging information;
- E-government: e-commerce model in which a government entity buys or provides goods, services, or information to businesses or individual citizens (F.S. Parreiras, 2005: 12-25).

According to well-known specialists the trading partnerships that business-to-business electronic marketplaces are also known as „B2B e-markets".

There are several definitions that one must analyze in order to understand properly the problems related to business-to-business electronic marketplaces („B2B e-markets"):
  a) B2B e-markets represent electronic trading platforms that bring together businesses with the purpose of buying and selling (European Commission Staff Working Paper, 2002: 4-6).
  b) B2B e-marketplaces are regarded as „virtual online markets where buyers, suppliers and sellers find and exchange information, conduct trade, and collaborate with each other via an aggregation of information portals, trading exchanges and collaboration tools" (Prime Faraday Technology Watch, 2001: 9).

2. Benefits of E-business

An effective use of e-business can have many benefits. Examples of these benefits are:
- cost savings resulting from reduced paper transactions;
- shorter order cycle time and the subsequent inventory reduction, resulting from speedy transmission of purchase order related information;
- enhanced opportunities for the supplier/buyer partnership through the establishment of a web of business-to-business communication networks (T. Gulledge, R. Sommer, 1998: 12-21).
- E-business can enhance supply chain efficiency by providing real-time information regarding product availability, inventory level, shipment status, and production requirements.

- It has vast potential to facilitate collaborative planning among supply chain partners by sharing information on demand forecasts and production schedules that dictate supply chain activities.
- Furthermore, it can effectively link customer demand information to upstream supply chain functions (manufacturing, distribution and sourcing) and subsequently facilitate 'pull' (demand-driven) supply chain operations.

E-business brings benefits to the private and to the public sector. It offers advantages to organizations, consumers, but also to society as a whole.

Despite such potential benefits, not every firm is ready to embrace e-business as a purchasing tool (G. Lambros and S.Moschuris, 2001: 351-372). Some serious hurdles to the successful implementation of e-business include a host of security, legal and financial problems (M. Quayle, 2002: 151-159). In particular, the incoherence of the web and concerns about security and flexibility limit the confidence of business in internet based trading systems. Current e-business systems do not yet fully address these concerns, and most of them concentrate on bilateral relationships between sellers and buyers (R. Van Hoek, 2001: 21-28).

The rapid development of e-business as a mainstream reality has been such that it is difficult for legislators to catch up. The legal framework for trading on-line can therefore be a little unclear. Inevitably, the exponential rise in Internet usage and trading has not been met with the adoption of legal regulations over how to trade in the borderless World Wide Web.

The law and regulation of e-commerce is a rapidly developing area attempting to keep track of the growth of online business. The EU is to the forefront of ensuring that e-business is adequately regulated and that „e-customers" are provided with the protection enjoyed by consumers in the traditional markets.

Figure 1: Some benefits of E-business

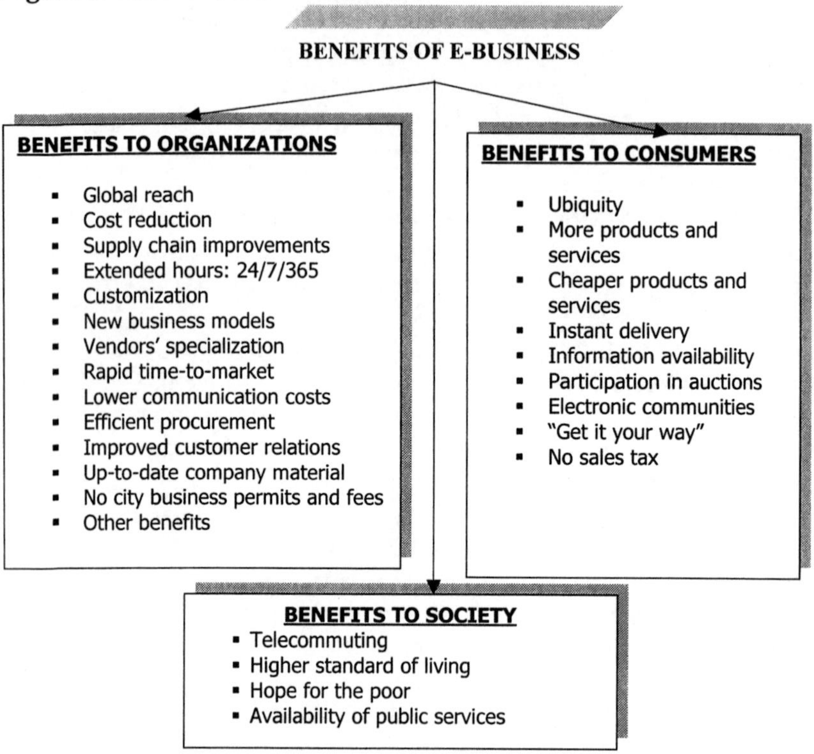

BENEFITS OF E-BUSINESS

BENEFITS TO ORGANIZATIONS
- Global reach
- Cost reduction
- Supply chain improvements
- Extended hours: 24/7/365
- Customization
- New business models
- Vendors' specialization
- Rapid time-to-market
- Lower communication costs
- Efficient procurement
- Improved customer relations
- Up-to-date company material
- No city business permits and fees
- Other benefits

BENEFITS TO CONSUMERS
- Ubiquity
- More products and services
- Cheaper products and services
- Instant delivery
- Information availability
- Participation in auctions
- Electronic communities
- "Get it your way"
- No sales tax

BENEFITS TO SOCIETY
- Telecommuting
- Higher standard of living
- Hope for the poor
- Availability of public services

The net can be both Europe-wide and international as well, so one has to think carefully about whom you want to advertise or sell to as well as the business conditions for that particular country. From a business perspective, economic opportunities and the penetration of the international market potential come with the growth and maturity of the Internet. Companies and individuals are still by nature reluctant to dive head first into reaping the rewards instead of choosing to weigh up the risk vs. cost analysis before implementation. The entrepreneurs that have made e-business work for them have understood the potential and applied themselves correctly to the sound principles of e-business management which involves researching basic contractual issues and putting into play basic business principles for doing business on-line.

From an individual (consumer's) perspective, there is still a reluctance to embrace on-line shopping because of perceived lack of security for conducting financial transactions, concerns about the reliability of online purchasing, privacy considerations in terms of personal information kept on them (spending practices, credit rating, etc.) and general lack of familiarity with the Internet environment, but this aspect is slowly improving.

3. E-business climate

E-businesses operate in a complex context of regulatory policies and institutional arrangements that set and enforce the rules of private action in a competitive marketplace. Where policies and practices favor e-business, returns on investment will be higher. Where competition is stifled or the rule of law is weak, investors rightly demand greater premiums for risk. Key elements include:
- The existence of effective competition among communication and information services providers;
- transparency and predictability of regulatory implementation, openness of government, rule of law, and general business risk (political stability, financial soundness);
- openness to financial and personal participation by foreign investors in ICT businesses;
- the ability of the financial system to support electronic business transactions.

The ratings show that much work is needed to promote a sound climate for the development of e-business, even in countries where the leadership has recognized the need to act. Although most countries are trying to open up markets to maximize competition and opportunity, many internal obstacles remain. Privatization, effective competition, and the independent regulation of telecommunications services are understood by most governments to be necessary for success.

The degree of regulation of Internet service providers ranges widely. Where governments attempt to curb market entry or control content, investors and entrepreneurs will display increasing reluctance as better opportunities emerge elsewhere. Electronic transactions remain generally exempt from special taxes, but must remain so for progress to continue. Similarly, enabling investment and participation from foreign firms interested in forming strong local partnerships is critical to success.

Predictability is of great value to business. Today's fast changing economic and technology environment creates great uncertainty, and increases the risk to investors.

4. The impact of ICT

Competing in mature markets requires not only optimized cost structures, maximal efficiency, and products or services of excellent quality, but also the ability to communicate effectively and indeed to cooperate with customers and with potential customers.

To radically improve the value proposition to client groups of increasing sophistication, customers are being integrated into planning, decision making, and production processes at an increasingly early stage. The flexibility offered by ICT applications permeating business operations is an essential precondition for this new relationship with customers. Particularly in enterprises serving large numbers of customers, complementary ICT systems such as CRM (customer relationship management) facilitate the comprehensive collection of data on marketing and sales activities, the analysis of this information, and their use for a broad range of strategic and operational decisions.

In service sectors such as tourism and telecommunications, ICT-based interaction with customers has become an indispensable element of marketing strategies, if not the most important channel of all. The impact on the competitive scenario in these industries has been substantial; the full transparency of prices and service depth has changed the balance of power between the players in the respective value systems. Though service sectors lead the way, ICT is already quite widely used in manufacturing sectors to improve service levels.

4.1. The influence on productivity

That ICT use in enterprises has an impact on their productivity is fully acknowledged in research and policy. Over the past 10-15 years the impact has been particularly strong on US enterprise. However, the impact in European enterprises has not been as great and this discrepancy continues to be a major concern in EU policy.

Maliranta and Rouvinen find strong evidence for productivity-enhancing impacts of ICT in *Finland*. After controlling for industry and time effects, the additional productivity of ICT equipped labor ranges from 8% to 18%, which corresponds to 5-6% elasticity of ICT capital. The effect was much higher in younger firms and in the ICT-producing sector, notably ICT producing services. "Manufacturing firms benefit in particular from ICT-induced efficiency in internal communication (...), while service firms benefit from efficiency in external (Internet) communication" (M. Maliranta, P. Rouvinen, 2006: 605-616).

Hempell studied the joint impact of ICT use and permanent technological innovation on productivity for *German and Dutch* service firms. He found evidence that such impact exists and is of the same magnitude in the two countries, while the direct impact of innovation on multi-factor productivity appears to be more robust for German companies. A general conclusion is that ICT is used more productively if it is complemented by innovation efforts in the firms concerned (T. Hempell, 2002: 32-45).

Gretton found for *Australia* that ICT and related effects raised Australia's annual multi-factor productivity (MFP) growth by around 0.2 percentage points in the 1990s. This is significant, even if it is a relatively small part of Australia's 1990s rate of MFP growth of 1.8% a year. The analysis found positive links between ICT use and productivity growth in all sectors that were examined (P. Gretton/J. Gali/D. Parham 2002).

4.2. The influence on innovation

Another important mechanism by which ICT impacts on competitiveness, which is closely related to productivity effects is the link between ICT and innovation. For a long time and for good reason the European Commission has placed great emphasis in policy actions on the critical role of innovation in ensuring European businesses stay competitive in the global economy. At the same time, competitive pressure provides powerful incentives for companies to engage continuously in innovation and R&D. Thus, innovation, competition, and competitiveness are closely intertwined.

In many cases, the implementation of e-business processes in a company will in itself constitute process innovation. In manufacturing sectors, e-business has triggered significant innovation inside the companies, notably in supply chain and delivery processes, such as automatic stock replenishing and improved logistics. In service sectors such as tourism, the innovative impact of ICT is more evident in the way that external transactions are accomplished. For example, if a company starts to sell its services online, this usually implies significant innovation in the service delivery process and in customer communication. (http://www.ebusiness-watch.org)

In some sectors, particularly in ICT manufacturing, consumer electronics and telecommunications, ICT are also highly relevant for product and service innovation.

As ever more companies strive to exploit the innovation potential of ICT, it becomes more difficult for the individual company to gain competitive advantage from this technology directly. In many fields of application where penetration rates are moderate or high, e-business has become a necessity in order to stay in business rather than a means to differentiate from competitors.

4.3. Disparities in ICT use for doing business

In international comparisons, EU enterprises are – on average – on a level with their counterparts in other advanced economies in their use of ICT. There are differences within the EU, however, particularly with regard to the average ICT maturity of smaller companies. In general, firms in Northern European countries are more advanced in linking their business processes internally and with business partners than companies in Southern European countries and from most of the new Member States.

The e-Business Index 2006, composed of 16 indicators, shows *Finland* as the e-business benchmark in a comparison of eight EU countries. Companies from *France*, the *Netherlands*, the *UK* and *Germany* are very similar in their use of ICT, particularly if emphasis is laid on the larger companies. Firms from the new Member States, although taking the lower ranks in this benchmarking exercise, are not far behind in their use of ICT. With the possible exception of the Nordic countries, the location of a company is by no means a reliable predictor of its level of e-business activity. This may be due to structural characteristics (The European e-Business Report 2006/07 edition: 15-40).

In *Italy*, for example, sectors dominated by small firms are much more prevalent than in other countries. Since large firms are more advanced in electronic business, aggregated data may point at a lower level of e-business activity in *Italy*. This reflects, at least to some extent, the structure of the economy rather than the overall e-maturity of firms. In contrast to *Italy*, the relative performance of *French* and *Dutch* companies is significantly better if the emphasis is on larger firms. These benchmarking results suggest a pronounced digital divide between small and large firms in these countries.

E-business activities of large companies are rapidly maturing. These companies have powerful ICT systems for linking business processes, understand their benefits and possess the necessary know-how to steadily improve these systems to their advantage.

Many smaller companies, by contrast, still struggle with the requirements of getting digitally connected with their suppliers and customers. If they cannot cope with requirements of the digital economy, they risk being eliminated from the value systems that tend to be orchestrated by large firms.

There are now over 19 million SMEs in Europe. In most EU Member States, they make up over 99 % of enterprises. SMEs generate a substantial share of GDP and are a key source of new jobs as well as a breeding ground for entrepreneurship and new business ideas. SMEs will also in particular benefit from the lowering of entry barriers to markets as a consequence of e-business. E-business is often described as the SMEs' gateway to global business and markets. Thus, the success of e-Europe is critically dependent on whether SMEs are fully engaged in this process.

Europe will only become a centre of E-business if European SMEs are fully committed to using the Internet as a leading-edge business tool (*The current and future barriers to SMe-volution*).

ICT implications for SMEs are ambivalent. On the one hand, ICT may offer increased economies of scale.

Large enterprises can afford powerful ICT systems at proportionally lower cost than SMEs have to meet for their comparatively simple infrastructure. The E-business Index 2006 confirms that the diffusion of ICT systems for internal and external process integration increases in a linear fashion according to firm size (The European e-Business Report 2006/07 edition: 15-40).

Table 1: Benchmark based on employment-weighted and on firm-weighted data

E-Business adoption as activity in firms		E-Business adoption as percentage of firms	
Benchmark based on employment-weighted data (indexed values: highest score = 100)		Benchmark based on firm-weighted data (indexed values: highest score = 100)	
Country	Percentage	Country	Percentage
FI	100	FI	100
FR	68	ES	93
NL	64	DE	89
ES	62	UK	88
UK	59	PL	83
DE	58	IT	77
PL	57	FR	75
HU	53	NL	72
CZ	48	CZ	68
IT	44	HU	56

Source: e-Business W@tch (2006)

E-business offers some opportunities for small firms, such as:
- facilitates cooperation: ICT usage facilitates cooperation in many ways (e.g. through project management tools, or online collaboration tools for design):
- new technologies;
- integrating: The value of any communication technology is proportional to the square of the number of users of the system. Large companies have recognized that they need to get their small business partners "on board" in order to reap the full benefits of e-business. Policy is also focusing on the integration of small firms in their "digital eco-systems";
- going international.

All companies – big corporations as well as SMEs – face various challenges when contemplating e-business implementation. These obstacles can be grouped into six main categories:
- Management and Strategy;
- Cost and Financing;
- Skills and Training;
- The Supply Chain;
- Technology Choices;
- Security & Reliability;

The decision to apply e-business technologies to a traditional business involves a huge number of choices at all levels of the organization – strategic, tactical or operational. In the current business environment one wrong choice could cause the company to close, but on the other hand the trend is generally towards the greater use of technology in business and one right choice could transform the company into an industry leader.

SMEs provide clear opportunities for economic development both locally and nationally. Developing SME e-business expertise is essential to sustaining (and in some cases, achieving) competitive advantage. SMEs appear to be aware of (even if they do not embrace) the basic elements of e-business. The challenge, perhaps, is getting them to realize the same elements are also prerequisites for developing an organization's competitive advantage. The future belongs to those who can use new technology to make themselves more efficient and develop better products and services. The results may not be instant. Nevertheless, SMEs ignore e-business at their peril.

References

The Emergence and Impact of the E-marketplace on SMEs Supply Chain Efficiencies, Prime Faraday Technology Watch, May 2001, pp. 9

European Commission Staff Working Paper on B2B Internet trading platforms: opportunities and barriers for SMEs - a first assessment, SEC, November 2002, pp. 4-6

The European e-Business Report 2006/07 edition, A portrait of e-business in 10 sectors of the EU economy, 5th Synthesis Report of the e-Business W@tch, pp. 15-40

Gretton P., Gali J. and Parham D. (2002), Uptake and Impacts of ICTs in the Australian Economy: Evidence from aggregate, sectoral and firm levels, Productivity Commission, Canberra

Gulledge T. and Sommer R. 1998: Electronic commerce resource an industry university partnership, in: ECRC Research Paper, Fairfax. USA, pp. 12-21

Hempell T. 2002: Does Experience Matter? Innovations and the Productivity of ICT in German Services, Discussion Paper 02-43. Center for European Economic Research (ZEW), pp. 32-45

Hoek R. van 2001: E-supply chains virtually non-existing, in: Supply Chain Management, Vol. 6, No. 1, pp. 21-28

Internet sources:
   ***www.ebusiness-watch.org
   ***www.epsilonium.com
   ***www.e-businessguide.gov.au
   ***www.e-bsn.org
   *** www.europa.eu.int/comm/enterprise/ict/policy/watch/index.htm

*** www.e-businessguide.gov.au
*** www.dcita.gov.au/smallbusinessbroadband
***http://europa.eu.int/comm/enterprise/consultations/sme_definition/consultation2/index_en.htm
*** http://europa.eu.int/information_society/topics/e-business/index_en.htm
*** http://www.usherproject.org.uk/support/index_scenarios.html

Lambros G. and Moschuris S. 2001: The influence of enterprise type on the purchasing decision process, in: International Journal of Operations and Production Management, Vol. 21, No. 3, pp. 351-372

Lundvall B.A. and Johnson B. 1994: The Learning Economy, in: Journal of Industry Studies, no. 1, pp. 23-42

Maliranta M. and Rouvinen P. 2006: Informational mobility and productivity: Finnish evidence, in: Economics of Innovation and New Technology, Taylor and Francis Journals, vol. 15 (6), pp. 605-616

Parreiras F. S. 2005: E-business: challenges and trends, NETIC, pp. 12-25

Quayle M. 2002: Purchasing in small firms, in: European Journal of Purchasing & Supply Management, Vol. 8, No. 3, pp. 151-159

Attachments:

ABSTRACTS (IN ALPHABETICAL ORDER)
EDITORS AND CONTRIBUTERS

ABSTRACTS

Liana Badea / Nicolae Nedelcu: *E-business – perspectives and challenges in global competition*

The explosion of digital connectivity, the significant improvements in communication and information technologies and the enforced global competition are revolutionizing the way business is performed and the way organizations compete. A new, complex and rapidly changing economic order has emerged based on disruptive innovation, discontinuities, abrupt and seditious change. These trends suggest that private and public organizations have to reinvent themselves through 'continuous non-linear innovation' in order to sustain themselves and achieve a strategic competitive advantage. After the Lisbon summit, E-business has gained new momentum in the EU and in other advanced economies of the world. The cost-saving potential of ICT has been broadly recognized by companies.

The aim of this paper is to show that in the emerging global economy, e-commerce and e-business have increasingly become a necessary component of business strategy and a strong catalyst for economic development. The integration of information and communications technology (ICT) in business has revolutionized relationships within organizations and those between and among organizations and individuals. Specifically, the use of ICT in business has enhanced productivity, encouraged greater customer participation and enabled mass customization, besides reducing costs.

Anastasia Bankova/Todor Yalamov: *Management, Knowledge, and Competitiveness of Organizations. A Study of Bulgarian Enterprises*

The paper presents a constructivist approach to the study of the relationship between knowledge economy policy and management, knowledge and competitiveness of Bulgarian small and medium sized enterprises. It considers the problematic areas in this relationship, as perceived by interviewed managers of enterprises, students' and authors' interpretations of those interviewed, benchmarked by findings of other researchers or other studies of authors by different methodologies. The paper concludes that system disfunctionalities exist in the national knowledge economy system. The paper calls for urgent steps to improve managerial and knowledge management practices at firm and policy levels and their interplay, based on standardization and prioritization.
Keywords: organizational learning, knowledge, knowledge map, competitiveness.

Diana Boyadzhieva: *Data Mining – Overview of the Technology and the Potential for Adoption in the Bulgarian Banking Industry*

Today, more than ever the stability of the financial institutions depends on their ability to quickly and effectively convert data into useful information, use it to make the respective well-founded business decisions and take respective adequate actions. The data mining (DM) technology could help the banks improve the existing models of business problems by finding additional information and patterns that were not known or discovered by some other form of analysis. This paper makes overview of the technology and presents some applications in the banking industry. The elaborated SWOT (Strengths, Weaknesses, Opportunities, and Threats) analysis of the banks' environment with respect to the DM application, given at the end of the paper, could be used as a benchmark when a bank evaluates its own environment and the appropriateness of the moment for adoption of the DM technology.

The overview of DM, followed by the examples for application in the banking industry is presented in a short but structured and easily comprehensible way, aiming to form a positive view towards the technology and its usage. The prepared SWOT analysis is done with respect to the DM adoption and gives unbiased assessment of the current prevailing environment in the Bulgarian banks. The general tendency found is that the current IT – related attempts of the banks do not include DM and are concentrated mainly on the integration and data warehousing projects.

Keywords: Data Mining, Business Intelligence, Banks.

George Chobanov: *Dynamic Equilibrium Stability of Two Markets*

The general equilibrium of a neoclassical economic system is considered as a tendency of its moving power. Going on, the dynamic equilibrium stability of two markets in connection with relativity of prices is investigated. In the case of saddle point stability the exact relationship of sticky prices is calculated.

Detelin S Elenkov: *Female Visionary-Transformational Leadership and Innovation: The Moderating Role of Multiple Intelligences and Ethical Leadership*

Using data from provided by 1,469 female executives residing in 21 countries, this study has investigated the moderating role of multiple (emotional, social, and cultural) intelligences and ethical leadership for the effects of female visionary-transformational leadership on innovation. Conclusions have been drawn for academic research and business practice.

Keywords: Female Leadership, Multiple Intelligences, Ethical Leadership, Innovation.

Ainhoa Herrarte / Felipe Sáez: *An evaluation of ALMP: the case of Spain*

In this paper we use non-experimental microdata to analyse the effects of several active labour market policies (ALMPs) carried out by the National Employment Institute (INEM) and the regional governments in Spain from 2001 to 2002. We compare the employment rates of the treatment group and the employment rates of a control group of non-participants selected by a random procedure from those unemployed registered in the employment offices who didn't participate in any program during the period of analysis. Our results differ depending on the group of beneficiaries: Participation in ALMP produced especially positive results for women and long-term jobseekers.

JEL Classification: J64, J68.
Keywords: active labour market policies, evaluation, labour market.

Anastasia Paris/Ioannis Patiniotis: *The Evolution of Gross Domestic Product of all Sectors of Greek Economy since 1963*

The paper looks at the Greek economy in relation to gross domestic product over the period 1963-2005. The six sectors considered are: Agriculture, Forestry, Fishing; Mining, Quarrying; Manufacturing; Electricity, Gas, Water; Construction; and Services. Furthermore, the contribution of eighteen manufacturing sectors to total manufacturing is looked at for the period mentioned above.

The forecast is studied for the years 2006-2010 for all sectors of the economy as well as the eighteen manufacturing industries. The purpose of this article is to look at the performance of Greece in relation to gross domestic product and the factors that affected its performance over the period 1963-2005.

JEL Classification: A11, C01, C53, C81, E23.

Guergana Stanoeva: *What Do Optimum Currency Area Criteria Tell Us about the Readiness of Central and East European Countries to Join the Eurozone?*

Optimum Currency Area (OCA) criteria are no official reference for the degree of preparation of candidates for the European Monetary Union (EMU). Nevertheless, their analysis provides a useful insight into the real convergence process towards the Eurozone. The study proposes an empirical evaluation of these criteria for the new Central and East European member states of the European Union as well as an econometric verification of their impact on nominal exchange rate volatility vis-à-vis the euro.

Keywords: Currency Areas, Countries in Transition, Exchange Rate Regimes.

Desislava Yordanova/ Maria-Antonia Tarrazon: *Determinants of Entrepreneurial Intentions Among Bulgarian University Students: An Exploratory Investigation*

Despite the importance and the potential role of entrepreneurship and the SME sector for economies in Central and Eastern Europe, little attention has been devoted to identifying which factors contribute to the entrepreneurial activity in the region. This study draws upon the Theory of Planned Behaviour (TPB) and previous empirical research to formulate and test hypotheses about the determinants of entrepreneurial intentions among Bulgarian university students. Our results indicate that the TPB is able to explain and accurately predict entrepreneurial intentions in our sample. In addition, a number of individual characteristics influence the probability of reporting strong entrepreneurial intentions. The study provides policy measures for enhancing entrepreneurial intentions and behaviour as well as directions for future research.

Keywords: entrepreneurial intentions, entrepreneurship education, role models, Bulgaria.

EDITORS and CONTRIBUTORS

Badea, Liana, Academy of Economic Studies, Faculty of Economics, Bucharest, (RO), *nutu_liana@yahoo.com*

Bankova, Anastasia, Prof. Dr., Sofia University "St. Kliment Ohridski", Faculty of Economics and Business Administration, head of the Department of Business Administration, Sofia (BG), *bankova@feb.uni-sofia.bg*

Boyadzhieva, Diana, Sofia University "St. Kliment Ohridski", Faculty of Economics and Business Administration, Sofia (BG), *dianaht@feb.uni-sofia.bg*

Chobanov, George, Prof. Dr., Sofia University "St. Kliment Ohridski", Dean of the Faculty of Economics and Business Administration and head of the Department of Industrial Economics and Management, Sofia (BG), *georgech@feb.uni-sofia.bg*

Elenkov, Detelin, Prof. Dr., University of Tennessee, Department of Management, Knoxville (USA), *delenkov@utk.edu*

Ganev, Georgy, Sofia University "St. Kliment Ohridski", of the Faculty of Economics and Business Administration, Sofia (BG), *cls@cls-sofia.org*

Gern, Jean-Pierre, Prof. (em.) Dr. , Université de Neuchâtel (CH), *jean-pierre.gern@unine.ch*

Herrarte, Ainhoa, Universidad Autónoma de Madrid, Dpto. de Análisis Económico: Teoría Económica e Historia Económica (E), *ainhoa.herrarte@uam.es*

Nedelcu, Nicolae, Anghel Saligny College, Rosiori de Vede (RO), *nedelcu_nae@yahoo.com*

Paris, Anastasia, Dr., European University, Centre for Management Studies, Athens (GR), *aparis@unipi.gr*

Patiniotis, Ioannis, European University, Centre for Management Studies, Athens (GR), *ipatiniotis@carras.gr*

Plöhn, Jürgen, PD Dr., Martin-Luther-University Halle-Wittenberg, Institute for Political Science and Japanology, Halle (D), *ploehn@hotmail.com*

Sáez, Felipe, Universidad Autónoma de Madrid, Dpto. de Análisis Económico: Teoría Económica e Historia Económica (E), *felipe.saez@uam.es*

Schellhaass, Horst, Prof. Dr., University of Cologne, Vicerector, Faculty for Economics and Social Sciences, Cologne (D), *schellhaass@uni-koeln.de*

Stanoeva, Guergana, Dr., Sofia University "St. Kliment Ohridski", Faculty of Economics and Business Administration, Department of Economics, Sofia (BG), *stanoeva@feb.uni-sofia.bg*

Tarrazon, Maria-Antonia, Dr., Autonomous University of Barcelona (E), *MariaAntonia.Tarrazon@uab.es*

Yalamov, Todor, M.A., M.Sc. , Sofia University"St. Kliment Ohridski", Faculty of Economics and Business Administration, Sofia (BG) *yalamov@feb.uni-sofia.bg*

Yordanova, Desislava: Sofia University"St. Kliment Ohridski", Faculty of Economics and Business Administration, Sofia (BG), *d_yordanova@abv.bg*

Sofia Conferences on Social and Economic Development in Europe

Editors: Prof. Dr. George Chobanov, PD Dr. Jürgen Plöhn,
Prof. Dr. Horst Schellhaass

Band 1   George Chobanov / Jürgen Plöhn / Horst Schellhaass (eds.): Towards a Knowledge-Based Society in Europe. 10th International Conference on Policies of Economic and Social Development, Sofia, October 5 to 7, 2007. 2009.

www.peterlang.de